PM Interview Questions

Over 160 Problems and Solutions for Product Management Interview Questions

RuHIT AHSAN

LEWIS C. LIN

With Teng Lu

ALSO BY LEWIS C. LIN

Case Interview Questions for Tech Companies: 155 Problems and Solutions for Real Interview Questions

Decode and Conquer: Answers to Product Management Interviews

Five Minutes to a Better Salary: Over 60 Brilliant Salary Negotiation Scripts for Getting More

Interview Math: Over 50 Problems and Solutions for Quant Case Interview Questions

Rise Above the Noise: How to Stand Out at the Marketing Interview

There are three types of people: winners, losers and winners that haven't learned how to win yet.
LES BROWN

Published by Impact Interview, 115 North 85th St., Suite 202, Seattle, WA 98103.

This book contains several fictitious examples; these examples involve names of real people, places and organizations. Any slights of people, places or organizations are unintentional.

The author and publisher have made every effort to ensure the accuracy and completeness of information contained in this book. However, we assume no responsibility for errors, inaccuracies, omissions or any inconsistency herein. This book is sold without warranty, either expressed or implied. Neither the authors, the publishers, distributors or other affiliates will be held liable for any damages caused either directly or indirectly by the instructions contained in this book.

This book uses trademarked names in an editorial fashion and to the benefit of the trademark owner, with no intention of infringement of the trademark. Hence we do not indicate every occurrence of a trademarked name.

Corporations, organizations and educational institutions: bulk quantity pricing is available. For information, contact lewis@impactinterview.com.

SECOND EDITION / Third Printing

Lin, Lewis C.
PM Interview Questions: Over 160 Problems and Solutions for Product Management Interview Questions / Lewis C. Lin.

Table of Contents

Chapter 1 Introduction

The product management (PM) interview is hard. Just consider the following questions, recently reported by Google, Facebook and Uber candidates:

Estimations	Estimate how much Gmail costs for Google per user, per year.
Product Design	What is the best decision tree for Facebook or LinkedIn's "People You May Know" feature?
Metrics	There was an 8% drop in hits to google.com. Larry Page walks into your office. He asks you to list what the reasons might be.
Go-to-market strategy	How would you start Uber operations in a city with no precedent?
Technical	Design a simple load balancer for google.com. What data structures would you use? Why? Define access/delete/add order of complexity for each data structure and explain your choices. Design an algorithm to add/delete nodes to/from the data structure. How would you pick which server to send a request? Why? Why not?

Why PM interviewers ask seemingly impossible questions

Hiring managers are getting increasingly risk-averse. They are afraid of making bad hires. Bad hires:

- Under-produce
- Affect team morale
- Devour excessive coaching resources
- Consume additional time and effort to identify replacements

As a result, it is no longer sufficient to *tell* the employer what you can do. Hiring managers ask that you *show* them what you can do. In the last few years, the "show me, not tell me" trend has accelerated. More employers are demanding that candidates now:

- Complete a take-home assignment, as part of the interview process
- Sign on as a temporary employee first, perhaps as a contractor or intern, before giving a full-time offer

Fortunately, not all employers have these requirements. However, there is a double-edged sword. In lieu of take-home assignments or temporary employment, interviewers ask interview questions that simulate work projects instead. We call interview questions, based on hypothetical work scenarios, case questions.

These questions cannot be reasonable

Candidates feel case questions are difficult and unfair, whereas interviews see them as sensible. Do keep in mind that every case question, asked in a PM interview, is typically part of a product manager's day-to-day responsibilities. Consider:

- *Estimations.* The PM provides a forecast to the supply chain manager, so that the supply team can buy an appropriate number of servers for a new cloud service.
- *Product Design.* The PM provides not only UX feedback but also product vision for the UX team, who executes on that vision and feedback.
- *Metrics.* The PM is the spokesperson for the product. They need to explain and investigate changes in business performance to executives.
- *Go-to-market strategy.* The PM is the quarterback of the launch team, which can include marketing, sales, operations, support and legal. The launch team expects the PM to bring leadership and detailed product knowledge.
- *Technical.* Engineers build the product; the PM provides the product vision, roadmap and prioritized backlog. Engineers are less likely to consent to a PM's vision, if the PM is not confident with technical details.

In the technology industry, many believe the product manager is the mini-CEO or general manager for a feature or product. As the mini-CEO, the product manager interacts with different functions from engineering to design to marketing. To interact, influence and lead effectively with these different groups, the product manager needs to speak their language. Speaking a functional language is easier when one has expert domain knowledge. That is what the PM interview is about: testing your domain knowledge. In real-time. Just like real life.

What this book is about and how it is organized

This book offers over 160 PM interview practice problems, with sample answers.

I have organized the questions by type. There are different question categories including product design, analytics and technical questions.

For the three most desirable companies, Google, Facebook and Amazon, I have created detailed preparation plans, which you will see later in the book.

Keep in mind that companies assess talent differently. Furthermore, their assessment methods may change over time. To use your preparation time wisely, research, either on the Internet or with a friend at your target employer, the kinds of questions a company is likely to ask.

How to use the book

By yourself

If you are using this book correctly, you should attempt the problems on your own and then compare *your* answer with the sample.

I never intended for you to tote this book on your next European holiday. In fact, I intentionally made it difficult to do so. There is no Kindle version; there is no audiobook. A book of this size is meant to sit squarely on a large table, accompanied with a notebook.

In fact, I wanted to leave blank pages in the book for you to show your work. So I've created blank pages for the first 10 questions. After that, I hope you get the idea: attempt the problems on your own. No cheating.

With others

You can also practice questions, in this book, with others.

Dedicated practice can lead to the perfect job. A reader completed an astonishing 102 mock interviews on my interview practice community: bit.ly/PMInterviewGroup, and it paid off. As a student from a top 400 US university, he beat the odds and got his dream job as a Google product manager. It is remarkable considering that his peers will be graduates from Stanford, MIT, and UC Berkeley.

Who should read this book

Over the years, readers of my first product management book, *Decode and Conquer: Answers to Product Management Interviews*, have inquired, "Where can I find a big bank of practice interview questions?" For all my readers who have supported me over the years, this book is that big bank of questions.

Sure, you can find plenty of questions on the Internet. But they don't have sample answers. This book has meticulously detailed answers. Lots of them.

Why I am confident you will get better

In 2015, I released a similar book called, *Interview Math: Over 50 Problems and Solutions for Quant Case Interview Questions. Interview Math* is targeted to aspiring management consultants applying at top-tier firms like McKinsey, Bain and Boston Consulting Group. It includes estimation, profitability, breakeven and pricing questions.

As readers made their way through every problem, they gained remarkable proficiency, including readers who believed they were not born to do math.

With *PM Interview Questions*, you will be empowered in the same way. You may be terrified of product design, metrics and technical interview questions now. And that's normal. We do not practice these interview questions every day. Nevertheless, I am positive that if you dedicate yourself, you will see a significant 10 to 15X improvement in your PM interview skills.

Have these books and frameworks within an arm's reach

Many of you have read my previous books. This book has brand new questions and sample answers.

If you have not read my previous books, you will want to get them so you can refer to the frameworks I recommend for solving each PM question. Here is a summary of books I would recommend:

- *Decode and Conquer* has explanations to PM-related frameworks including the CIRCLES Method, AARM and DIGS.

- *Interview Math* has great introductory material and provides more methods on how to tackle estimation, market sizing, ROI and lifetime value questions, especially if you find the harder analytical questions in this book too intimidating.
- *Case Interview Questions for Tech Companies* has even more practice questions and answers. In addition to PM questions, you will find non-PM case questions for the tech industry, including questions for marketing, operations, finance and business development roles. If you are looking for more PM practice problems or if you are considering non-PM roles, you will want to look at *Case Interview Questions for Tech Companies*.

How to get the most out of this book

Many of you will appreciate that this book has sample answers. However, do not get tempted into reading the answers as if you were reading a novel!

Instead, I recommend that you:

- Try solving the practice question(s) on your own
- Then compare your response with the sample answer

With consistent and deliberate practice, you will:

- Get comfortable answering questions that most candidates find difficult.
- Absorb the concepts more deeply.
- Create an efficient feedback-learning loop, deducing when and where your response underperformed or outperformed the sample answer.

Email me

I would love to hear your feedback, comments and even typos. Contact me at lewis@impactinterview.com.

Lewis C. Lin
September 2016

Chapter 2 Finding Practice Partners and Bonus Resources

To help further your learning, I have made it easy for you to find PM interview practice partners and provided several bonus materials, listed below:

Find PM Practice Partners

Practicing with others is incredibly beneficial. It will:

- Give you a fresh perspective
- Provide moral support
- Keep you accountable

To make it easy for you to connect with others who are preparing for the PM interview, I created a special Slack community for all of you. Enter the following in your Internet browser: bit.ly/PMInterviewGroup

Here is what people have said about the PM Practice partner community:

"Thanks for starting this community. It's pretty awesome." – A.P.

"Hey Lewis, you already know this, but you've built something amazing here. I've done a few practice interviews now and most folks have been welcoming and really helpful. You should be proud ☺ Congrats." – S.G.

"Hey Lewis, awesome group you got going here! A few of us loved your presentation at Berkeley Haas this past weekend and will be using your resources to get a few study groups together to work on cases. Looking forward to interacting with everyone here." – J.Z.

Interview Evaluation Sheets

I interviewed PM hiring managers and interviewers, and I asked them what they considered a strong response for design, estimation and behavioral questions.

I created these interview evaluation sheets, based off that research. The evaluation sheets will make it easier to provide feedback to your practice partner.

Interview Evaluation Sheet: Product Design

	Rating 1-5 1 = Not like the candidate at all 5 = Very much like the candidate	Interviewer's Explanation
Goals & Metrics Did the candidate define objectives before answering? Were the candidate's selections reasonable?		
Target Persona & Pain Points Did the candidate choose a target persona? Did the candidate explain the persona's pain points to the extent that demonstrated true consumer insight?		
Prioritization Did the candidate demonstrate ability to prioritize competing use cases or pain points convincingly?		
Creativity Did the candidate show creativity? Or were the ideas a replica of competitive products and features?		
Development Leadership When asked, did the candidate reasonably explain how to implement a proposed feature?		
Summary and Next Steps Did the candidate summarize their main argument at the end, including clear next steps?		

Interview Evaluation Sheet: Estimation

	Rating 1-5 1 = Not like the candidate at all 5 = Very much like the candidate	Interviewer's Explanation
Problem Solving Skills Did the candidate take an unfamiliar problem and develop a plan to solve it?		
Communication Skills Did the candidate communicate his or her action plan to the interviewer? Easy-to-follow? Or did the interviewer have to ask an excessive number of clarifying questions to unravel the candidate's thoughts?		
Comfort with Numbers Did the candidate confidently calculate numbers by hand? Or was the candidate hesitant? Did the candidate rely on using a calculator or computer to crunch numbers? Or did the candidate oversimplify calculations by needlessly rounding numbers?		
Judgment Did the candidate choose reasonable assumptions, backed by logical thinking? Or was the candidate sloppy in choosing assumptions, believing that reasonable assumptions do not matter?		

Interview Evaluation Sheet: Metrics

Downloadable copy for printing: bit.ly/InterviewEvalMetrics

	Rating 1-5 1 = Not like the candidate at all 5 = Very much like the candidate	Interviewer's Explanation
Understanding Metrics Did the candidate have an understanding of product metrics? Did the candidate provide a comprehensive and relevant list?		
Evaluating Metrics Did the candidate articulate which metrics are better than others, backed with sound logic and evidence?		
Diagnosing Metrics How was the candidate's diagnosis? Did the candidate provide an issue tree depicting drivers that affect that specific metric?		
Affecting Change on a Metric Did the candidate offer a plan on how to influence positively a metric, primarily through product changes but perhaps through other levers, including marketing and business development initiatives?		

Interview Evaluation Sheet: Behavioral

	Rating 1-5 1 = Not like the candidate at all 5 = Very much like the candidate	Interviewer's Explanation
Owner vs. Participant Did the candidate play a primary or marginal role?		
Good vs. Great Achievement Was the achievement impressive? Were the results largely due to the candidate's impact? Or would the results have occurred, even without the candidate's involvement?		
Communication Skills Is the candidate's story easy-to-follow and memorable? Was it a struggle to extract information from the candidate?		

Interview Evaluation Sheet: Other Question Types

Rating 1-5

1 = Not like the candidate at all

5 = Very much like the candidate

	Interviewer's Explanation
Communication Skills Did the candidate provide a response that is well organized and easy-to-follow? Or was it boring and disorganized?	
Thoughtful Insights Did the candidate provide thought-provoking insights? Did you feel smarter after talking to the candidate?	
Creativity Did the candidate show vision and imagination?	
Problem Solving Skills Did the candidate take an unfamiliar, unambiguous question, problem or situation and provide a plan as well as compelling leadership?	

PM Interview Cheat Sheet

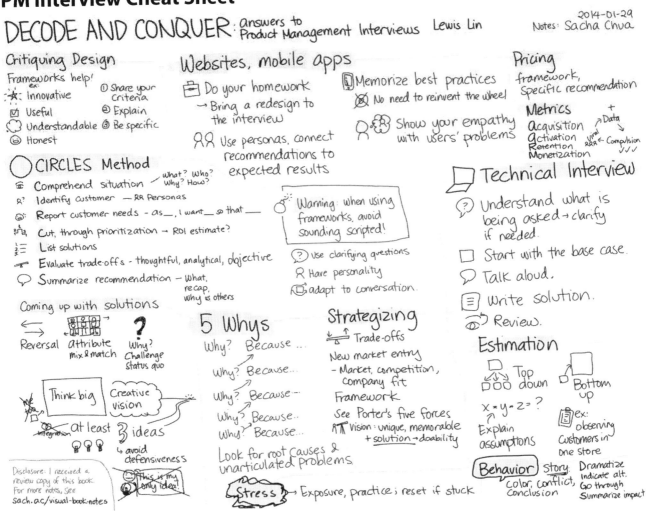

DECODE AND CONQUER: Answers to Product Management Interviews — Lewis Lin

Notes: Sacha Chua 2014-01-29

Critiquing Design

Frameworks help! ex:
- ☆ Innovative
- ☑ Useful
- Understandable
- Honest

① Share your criteria
② Explain
③ Be specific

⭕ CIRCLES Method
- Comprehend situation — What? Who? Why? How?
- Identify customer — RR Personas
- Report customer needs - as___, I want___ so that___
- Cut through prioritization → ROI estimate?
- List solutions
- Evaluate trade-offs - thoughtful, analytical, objective
- Summarize recommendation — What, recap, why vs others

Coming up with solutions
- Reversal
- Attribute mix & match
- ? Why? Challenge status quo

Think big Creative vision
Integration At least 3 ideas → avoid defensiveness

⚡ this is my only idea!

Disclosure: I received a review copy of this book. For more notes, see sach.ac/visual-book-notes

Websites, mobile apps
- 💼 Do your homework
  → Bring a redesign to the interview
- 🗣 Use personas, connect recommendations to expected results

Warning: when using frameworks, avoid sounding scripted!

- ? Use clarifying questions
- R Have personality
- Adapt to conversation.

5 Whys
- Why? Because...
- Why? Because...
- Why? Because...
- Why? Because...
- Why? Because...

Look for root causes & unarticulated problems.

Stress → Exposure, practice; reset if stuck

Strategizing
- ⚖ Trade-offs

New market entry
- Market, competition, company fit

Framework
See Porter's five forces
Vision: unique, memorable + solution → doability

Memorize best practices
- ⊗ No need to reinvent the wheel
- Show your empathy with users' problems

Pricing
framework, specific recommendation

Metrics
- Acquisition → Data
- Activation Viral ← Compulsion
- Retention RRR
- Monetization

💻 Technical Interview
- ? Understand what is being asked → clarify if needed.
- ☐ Start with the base case.
- 💬 Talk aloud.
- ☰ Write solution.
- 👁 Review.

Estimation
- Top down
- Bottom up
- $x * y * z = ?$ Explain assumptions
- ex: observing customers in one store

Behavior Story: Color, conflict, conclusion. Dramatize, Indicate alt. Go through Summarize impact

Screenshot / Lewis C. Lin

I created a PM Interview Cheat Sheet just for you: bit.ly/PMInterviewCheatSheet

It includes frameworks for product design, pricing, metrics, strategy and technical questions. If I could only bring one sheet of paper for an upcoming PM interview, I would bring this one.

Two-Week PM Interview Plan

Task Item	Topic	Resource	Deadline	Minutes to study	Minutes studied	% Complete
	Product Design Questions					
	Practice brainstorming					
	Define a list of 10 problems. Brainstorm 10 solutions to each problem without any time constraints.	Thinkertoys / SCAMPER brainstorming framework	5-Dec	40	15	38%
	Define a list of 10 problems. Brainstorm 10 solutions to each problem. This time, apply a 60-90 second time constraint.	Thinkertoys / SCAMPER brainstorming framework	4-Dec	20	10	50%
	Practice customer empathy	Thinkertoys / SCAMPER brainstorming framework	5-Dec	20	5	25%
	Define a list of customer problems. Practice "ranting" on why that problem is terrible		6-Dec	20	20	100%
	Lead the end-to-end product design discussion using CIRCLES Method™	Decode and Conquer	6-Dec	20	20	100%
	Practice 10 questions leading the end to end discussion		7-Dec	180	60	33%
	Build UX vocabulary by reviewing common design patterns for web and mobile	Web UI Design Patterns & Mobile UI Design Patterns	7-Dec	180	60	33%
	Practice wireframing	Guide to Wireframing	5-Dec	30	10	33%
	Metrics Questions		5-Dec	45	15	33%
	Pick 3-5 products					
	Brainstorm top metrics for each one of those products	Decode and Conquer, AARM Method™	10-Dec	180	45	25%
	Explain which metric is the most important, starting with a balanced pros and cons table	Decode and Conquer, Metrics Section	9-Dec	60	15	25%
	Discuss one potential feature for each product and explain why you should ship / no-ship	Decode and Conquer, Metrics Section	10-Dec	60	15	25%
	Estimation Questions		10-Dec	60	15	25%
	Read chapter 3: Assumptions					
	Complete the following exercise problems	Interview Math, Starting from Page 17	11-Dec	20	20	100%
	BMW Dealerships		11-Dec	20	20	100%
	Airports	Interview Math, Page 22	11-Dec	10	10	100%
	Read chapter 4: Estimation	Interview Math, Page 24	11-Dec	10	10	100%
	Complete the following exercise problems	Interview Math, Starting from Page 26	11-Dec	10	10	100%
	Chinese Diaper Market	Interview Math, Page 32	12-Dec	50	50	100%
	Women's Rain Boot Market	Interview Math, Page 34	12-Dec	10	10	100%
	TV Ads	Interview Math, Page 51	12-Dec	10	10	100%
	Subway's Sales	Interview Math, Page 56	12-Dec	10	10	100%
	Netflix Subscription Sales	Interview Math, Page 64	12-Dec	10	10	100%
	Lifetime Value Questions		12-Dec	10	10	100%
	Read chapter 8: Lifetime Value	Interview Math, Starting from Page 143				
	Complete the following exercise problems		13-Dec	90	45	50%
	Starbucks' Lifetime Value	Interview Math, Page 145				
	AT&T New iPhone Promotion	Interview Math, Page 147	13-Dec	15	5	33%
	New York Times Website	Interview Math, Page 157	13-Dec	90	45	50%
	Behavioral Questions		13-Dec	90	45	50%
	Read Winning the Behavioral Interview	Decode & Conquer, Page 193-202				
	Write down responses for Common Behavioral Interview Questions	Decode & Conquer, Page 193; Stories Sheet: http://bit.ly/1QJarRE	13-Dec	15	5	33%
	Minimum stories: 5		13-Dec	90	45	50%
	Include your written responses to "Tell me about yourself" and "Why do you want to work for this company?"		15-Dec	120	120	100%
	Verbally rehearse written responses		16-Dec	90	45	50%
	Technical					
	Read How to Approach a Technical Question	Decode & Conquer, Page 98	17-Dec	10	10	100%
	Review Big O notation	Wikipedia / http://bigocheatsheet.com / How to Ace the Software Engineering I	17-Dec	20	0	0%
	Review data structures: arrays	Wikipedia / How to Ace the Software Engineering Interview	17-Dec	20	0	0%
	Review data structures: linked lists	Wikipedia / How to Ace the Software Engineering Interview	17-Dec	20	0	0%
	Review data structures: stack & queues	Wikipedia / How to Ace the Software Engineering Interview	17-Dec	20	0	0%
	Review data structures: trees	Wikipedia / How to Ace the Software Engineering Interview	18-Dec	20	0	0%
	Review data structures: heap	Wikipedia / How to Ace the Software Engineering Interview	18-Dec	20	0	0%
	Review data structures: trie	Wikipedia / How to Ace the Software Engineering Interview	18-Dec	20	0	0%
	Review data structures: graphs	Wikipedia / How to Ace the Software Engineering Interview	18-Dec	20	0	0%

Screenshot / Lewis C. Lin

Download this spreadsheet to make your own customized interview preparation plan, filled with my suggestions: bit.ly/PMPrepPlan

Chapter 3 Study Guides for Coveted Tech Firms

The PM interview is already difficult as it is. There is no need to overwhelm you with another to-do: constructing your own preparation guide. Therefore, I have put together a sample preparation guide for the following companies:

- Google
- Amazon

I have also made suggestions on how to create a preparation guide for Facebook, Uber and LinkedIn roles.

Every candidate is unique; skills, experiences and timelines will differ. Tailor the suggested preparation guides to your situation.

30-Day Google PM Study Guide

Day 1. Getting familiar with Google's PM Interview

Tasks

- Read Google's official preparation note to its PM interview candidates: bit.ly/GOOGPMIntNote
- Search Google for Lewis' blog post and read: "How to Prepare for the Google Product Manager Interview"

Goal

Know the scope and nature of the Google PM interview.

Day 2. Getting familiar with the product design interview

Background Reading

- Read about the CIRCLES design method in *Decode and Conquer*.
- Review the product design examples from *Decode and Conquer* to see how CIRCLES is applied.

Exercises

Do the following pain point exercises in *PM Interview Questions*:

- Child's 1st Birthday Party
- Best Handyman
- Job Search Pain Points
- Finding Someone to Do Taxes

Do the following customer journey map exercises in *PM Interview Questions*:

- Expedia Journey
- AirBnB Journey

- Online Course Journey
- Job Search Journey
- Home Improvement Journey
- Customer Service Journey

Goals

- Learn about product design questions.
- Understand the product design framework, CIRCLES.
- Observe how others answer interview questions with CIRCLES.
- Practice two parts of the CIRCLES framework:
    a. Listing (brainstorming) solutions
    b. Reporting customer needs (customer journey map).

Day 3. Putting product design questions together with the CIRCLES method

Exercise

Do the following product design exercises in *PM Interview Questions:*

- Disney Experience with Your Phone
- Improving Google Hangouts

Goals

- Like a wine connoisseur, detect and deduce how your response differs from the sample. As you become more aware of the differences, your own responses will improve.
- For now, do not worry about response quality or speed. Getting started, by practicing, is half the battle.

Day 4 to 10. Putting product design questions together with the CIRCLES method

Exercise

Complete one example a day for the next seven days, choosing from the list of questions from *PM Interview Questions*, below.

1. Improving Google Play Store
2. Monetizing Google Maps
3. Mobile App Design for Nest
4. Favorite Product
5. Favorite Website
6. People You May Know
7. Car for the Blind
8. ATM for the Elderly

Goals

- Easily explain why CIRCLES leads to better interview responses.
- Understand when, how and why one should adapt CIRCLES.

Day 11-13. CIRCLES in Real-life

Exercise

Improve your product design skills further by applying the CIRCLES Method to real-life. For each one of the next three days:

1. Walk around the neighborhood.
2. As you walk, use the CIRCLES method to improve everyday items. Here are some design problems you can ponder:
   - How to improve sidewalks?
   - How can street lamps be more effective?
   - Build a product to solve the dog poop problem.
   - What new products can prevent flat tires in cars or bikes?
   - What innovation can make gardening less of a chore?
   - What innovative new product can make park gatherings be more social, with strangers?

Goal

Acculturating a product design mindset 24 hours a day, both at the interview and in your everyday life.

Day 14*. Find a practice partner for product design

Exercise

Sign up for the product management interview practice group on Slack: bit.ly/PMInterviewGroup

Post a request for a partner or partners in the #req-practice-ptr channel.

Take turns during your practice session. That is, Partner A (interviewer) gives a case to Partner B (interviewee). Then, swap roles.

Coordinate in advance which case each person will receive; to simulate the interview environment, the interviewee should do a case that they are not familiar with. The interviewer should take time to acquaint themselves with the question and the sample answer.

* Repeat the partner practice activity as often as you would like. The best candidates will have practiced at least 20 product design cases.

Goal

Master the product design interview. It is the number one reason why candidates fail the Google PM interview. If you have committed yourself to thoughtful practice, you should be an expert when it comes to tackling product design questions. Use the guidelines below to gauge your product design proficiency:

- A novice suggests the obvious or copies competitive features. An expert suggests novel and memorable ideas. An expert suggests ideas that make the interviewer go, "Hmm, I wish I thought of that; maybe I should build a company based off of that idea."
- A novice mentions shallow user insights. The novice does not take interest in users or their motivations. The novice is deficient in user empathy. The expert is a lifelong learner of human psychology and behavior. An expert continually asks questions about what people do and why they do it. As a result, an expert easily points out insights that are urgent, relevant and surprising.
- A novice follows the CIRCLES method step-by-step, like a home cook trying to make a sophisticated soufflé for the first time. The novice is afraid of making mistakes and clings tightly to a prescribed framework. The novice is so busy trying to recall the different steps of the CIRCLES framework that the novice's responses sound robotic and textbook. The expert understands that a framework is a checklist, not a recipe. The expert understands that CIRCLES is there to prevent errors of omission. CIRCLES is there to help ensure that the listener's experience is complete, satisfying and possibly even entertaining.

Day 15. Getting familiar with the metrics interview

Background Reading

- Read about the AARM framework in *Decode and Conquer*.
- Read metrics examples in *Decode and Conquer* to get familiar with metrics questions in an interview setting.

Exercises

Do the following metrics brainstorming exercises in *PM Interview Questions*:

- Metrics for eCommerce
- Metrics for Two-sided marketplaces
- Metrics for SaaS
- Metrics for Mobile Apps
- Metrics for Publishers
- Metrics for User-Generated Website
- Metrics for Support Tickets

Do the following metrics prioritization exercises in *PM Interview Questions*:

- Most Important Metric: Two-Sided Marketplace
- Most Important Metric: Mobile App
- Most Important Metric: eCommerce

Goal

Get more familiarity in coming up with and identifying good metrics.

Day 16. Diagnosing metrics problems

Exercises

Complete the following examples in this book, on your own or with a partner:

- Shopping Cart Conversions
- Mobile App Ratings
- Reddit Posts

Goals

Gain proficiency in brainstorming a complete and exhaustive list of issues when troubleshooting a metric.

Day 17 and 18. Putting the metrics problem together

Exercises

Complete one example a day for the next seven days, both on your own and with your practice partner, from this book.

- Your Favorite Google Product
- Drop in Hits
- Declining Users
- Slow Download on Kindle
- Pinterest Metrics
- Go-to-Market and Success
- Metrics for Uber Pick-up

Goals

Build proficiency in identifying, prioritizing and diagnosing metrics issues.

Day 19. Getting familiar with the estimation interview

Tasks

- Read about estimation questions in *Interview Math*.
- Read the following estimation examples in *Interview Math* to get familiar.
  - Women's Rain Boot Market
  - Smartphone Case Market
  - Subway's Sales

o   Netflix Subscription Sales

Goals

1. Learn about estimation questions.
2. Learn how to setup estimation questions using issue trees.
3. Learn how to make assumptions.
4. Try the following estimation questions:
    a. Cars in Seattle
    b. How Many Google Apps Users
    c. Revenue from YouTube Red

Day 20. Practice estimation questions

Tasks

Complete one example a day, from this book, for the next seven days.

1. Planes in the Air
2. Gmail Ads Revenue
3. Google Buses
4. Gmail Costs
5. Driverless Car Purchases in 2020
6. Storing Google Maps
7. Facebook's Ad Revenue

Goals

Master estimation questions. Not only is response quality important, but also you should complete most estimation questions in about 10 to 15 minutes.

Day 22. Learn more about strategy questions

Tasks

Read the following chapters in *Decode and Conquer*.

- Strategizing: Tradeoffs
- Strategizing: New Market Entry
- Strategizing: CEO-Level Issues

Goals

- Learn about common strategy question types.
- Figure out how to approach strategy questions using frameworks.
- See how to apply frameworks to common strategy questions.

Day 23. Practice strategy questions

Tasks

Practice the following strategy questions, in this book, either on your own or with your practice partner:

1. Google's TV Cable Service
2. iPhone Exclusive Partnership

Goals

Provide a response that is thoughtful, logical and addresses the company's objectives. For more examples of thoughtful strategy responses, refer to the popular blog, stratechery.com.

Day 24. Learn more about pricing questions

Tasks

Read the "Pricing" chapter in *Rise Above the Noise*.

Goals

- Learn about pricing questions, including the difference between pricing new vs. existing products.
- Figure out how to approach pricing questions using frameworks.
- See how to apply pricing frameworks to popular questions.

Day 25. Practice pricing questions

Tasks

Practice the following pricing questions, either on your own or with your practice partner:

- Pricing New Products
  - Google Driverless Car Pricing
  - Google and Teleportation
- Pricing Existing Products
  - AWS Price Reduction
  - Kindle Pricing at Target

Goals

1. Google's Strategy
2. Google vs. Microsoft
3. Google Moonshot Projects
4. Google Maps in Mongolia
5. Google Store

Day 26. Traditional and Behavioral Questions

Tasks

- Read the "Winning the Behavioral Interview" chapter in *Decode and Conquer*.
- Draft and polish your answers for the following questions:
    - Tell me about yourself.
    - Why Google?
    - Influencing your team
- Practice and get feedback from your practice partner

Goals

While Google has an affinity for case questions, you should spend some time preparing for traditional and behavioral questions. Google interviewers usually ask traditional icebreaker questions like "Tell me about yourself" and "Why Google?" However, behavioral interview questions like "Tell me a time when you influenced a team" is a newer occurrence. Google's HR department, since 2013, has asked its PM interviewers to ask more behavioral interview questions.

Day 27. Getting Familiar with Technical Interview Questions

Tasks

Review the technical topics suggested in: bit.ly/PMPrepPlan

Goals

Gain familiarity with technical concepts and questions. At Google, technical interview questions are reserved for on-site interviews, usually for candidates who have succeeded in other parts of the interview such as product design, analytics and strategy questions.

Day 28. First Try at Technical Interview Questions

Tasks

Attempt the following technical interview questions:

- 100-Story Building and Two Eggs
- Reducing Bandwidth Consumption

Goals

Try some technical interview questions, with a focus on calming your nerves and approaching questions with open curiosity. The "100-Story Building and Two Eggs" question is an example of an algorithm question. "Reducing Bandwidth Consumption" is an example of a technical architecture question.

Day 29-30*. Second Try at Technical Interview Questions

Tasks

Attempt the following technical interview questions from *PM Interview Questions*:

- Load Balancer for google.com
- Dictionary for Scrabble
- Google Search Services
- Bayesian vs. AI

* Repeat the technical interview practice activity, as necessary.

Goals

Build confidence tackling technical interview questions.

How to Modify the Google PM Prep Guide for Facebook, Uber and LinkedIn

Unlike Google, most companies do not ask difficult technical interview questions at the PM interview. At most, these companies may ask you to explain a technical concept such as:

- What happens when you type facebook.com into a Google Chrome browser?
- Tell me a time when you had to assess a technical tradeoff.

At most hiring companies, PM candidates will not be asked whiteboard coding or technical architecture questions. Thus, to modify the Google PM prep guide for Facebook, Uber and LinkedIn, simply do the following:

- Cut out technical interview prep
- Read Lewis' overviews of Facebook, Uber and LinkedIn PM interview processes on Quora.
  - What should I expect in a Product Manager interview at Facebook and how should I prepare? qr.ae/N8tV5
  - What should I expect in a product manager (PM or APM) interview at Uber, and how should I prepare? qr.ae/TXWCbT
  - What kind of questions should I expect in a product manager interview at LinkedIn? qr.ae/TXWAox
- Instead of Google-centric practice questions, swap in Facebook, Uber and LinkedIn examples, as appropriate.

36-Day Amazon PM Study Guide

Day 1. Getting familiar with Amazon's PM Interview

Tasks

Search Google and read Lewis' Amazon PM interview process overview: "How to Prepare for the Amazon Product Manager Interview"

Goal

Get to know the scope and nature of the Amazon PM interview.

Day 2. Traditional and Behavioral Questions

Tasks

- Read the "Winning the Behavioral Interview" chapter in *Decode and Conquer*.
- Review Amazon's Leadership Principles: www.amazon.jobs/principles
- Draft and polish your answers for the following questions:
    - Tell me about yourself.
    - Why Amazon?
- Practice and get feedback from your practice partner

Goals

Of all the tech companies, Amazon is the most devoted to its corporate values, called the Amazon Leadership Principles. This devotion manifests itself heavily in their interview process. At least half of your interview questions will be behavioral in nature, focused on their 14 Leadership Principles.

Internalize Amazon's values deeply as you will have a lot of work ahead of you when preparing your behavioral interview responses.

Day 3-7. Drafting Responses to Behavioral Questions

Task

Using the DIGS method, prepare behavioral interview responses for each Amazon Leadership Principle below. I have provided this template for you to draft your responses: bit.ly/AMZNInterviewStories, to make it easier for you.

AMAZON PRINCIPLE	SUGGESTED QUESTION	SAMPLE ANSWER*
Customer Obsession	Walk us through a time when you helped a customer through a difficult process and what that looked like.	Helping a Customer
Ownership	Give me an example of when you took a risk and failed.	Risk and Failure
Invent and Simplify	Tell me a time when you created an innovative product.	Creating an Innovative Product
Are Right, A Lot	Tell me about a time when you observed two business opportunities to improve ROI, and how did you determine they were connected?	Connected ROI
Learn and Be Curious	How do you find the time to stay inspired, acquire new knowledge, and innovate in your work?	Learning Outside of Work
Hire and Develop The Best	Tell me about a time when you had to deal with a poor performer on your team.	N/A
Insist on the Highest Standards	Tell me a time when you could have stopped working on something but you persisted.	N/A
Think Big	Tell me a time when you proposed a new business.	See chapter *Strategy: New Market Entry* for inspiration
Bias for Action	Describe how you would handle a busy situation where three people are waiting for help from you.	Handling a Busy Situation
Frugality	Tell me a time when you came up with a clever way to save money for the company.	N/A
Earn Trust	Tell me a time when you earned the trust of a group.	Earning the Trust of a Group
Dive Deep	Tell me about a time when you had to dive deep into data and the results you achieved.	Diving Deep into Data
Have Backbone; Disagree and Commit	Tell me about the most difficult interaction you had at work.	Most Difficult Interaction
Deliver Results	Tell me a time when you overcame an obstacle and delivered the results.	Overcoming an Obstacle

*Refer to the table of contents for the appropriate section in this book

Source / *PM Interview Questions* and Amazon.com website

Goals

Complete drafts for each Amazon Leadership Principle.

Day 8. Get Feedback to Your Behavioral Responses

Task

Find a practice partner and get feedback on your responses. You can either present your stories in outline form or a more formal mock interview setting.

Goal

Have answers that are:

- Easy-to-understand and follow
- Thoughtful
- Indicate your role in the story, especially whether you were an owner vs. a participant
- Have an impressive, not merely good, achievement

Day 9 and 10. Get familiar lifetime value questions

Background Reading

- Read the *Lifetime Value* chapter in *Interview Math*.
- Follow the lifetime value (LTV) example in *Interview Math*: Starbucks' Lifetime Value.

Exercises

Do the following exercises:

- In *PM Interview Questions*
    - Apple iPhone LTV
    - Kindle Pricing Error
- In *Interview Math*
    - AT&T New iPhone Promotion
    - American Express I
    - American Express II
    - Crest Toothpaste
    - New York Times Website

Goal

- Internalize the LTV framework.
- Gain mastery in applying LTV, in detail, to a variety of challenging questions.

Day 11 and 12. Get familiar pricing questions

Background Reading

Get familiar with the two categories of pricing questions, new and existing products, by reading the Pricing chapter in *Rise Above the Noise.*

Exercises

Do the following exercises:

- Existing Product Pricing in *Interview Math*
  - Google Nexus Phone
  - Star Wars 7 Ticket Price
  - Starbucks Coffee Latte
- New Product Pricing in *PM Interview Questions*
  - Google Driverless Car Pricing
  - Google and Teleportation
  - Pricing UberX

Goals

- Know the difference between existing and new product pricing questions.
- Know which framework to use for each one.
- Gain proficiency in answering both types of questions

Day 13 to 36. Follow Day 2 to 25 from the Google PM prep guide.

Substitute exercises with Amazon-specific ones from *PM Interview Questions*. It is unlikely that Amazon PM interviews will include coding or technical interview questions, so you can disregard technical interview prep, if you are short on time.

Chapter 4 Abbreviations, Terms and Concepts

Abbreviations

This book will deal with large numbers in the thousands, millions and billions. To save space, I will use the following abbreviations:

- K = thousands
- M = millions
- B = billions

For instance, 10K refers to 10,000. 10M is equivalent to 10,000,000, and 10B is equivalent to 10,000,000,000.

I will also use these shorthand abbreviations:

- Q = quantity
- P = price
- R = revenue
- C = cost

Terms and Concepts

AARM metrics™

An analytical framework that defines the metrics for a product.

- **A**cquisition: Tracking customer signups for a service. The bar for signing up for a service has gotten lower and lower, thanks to the popularity of free signup and pay later "freemium" models. The typical metric to track here is lazy registrations.
- **A**ctivation: Getting users that have completed a lazy registration to register fully. For a social networking site like Google+, this may include uploading a photo or completing their profile page.
- **R**etention: Getting users to use the service often and behave in a way that helps the user or business. Key metrics include adding more information to their profile page, checking the news feed frequently or inviting friends to try the service.
- **M**onetization: Collecting revenue from users. It could include the number of people who are paying for the service or the average revenue per user (ARPU).

Before and After Analysis

A way to interview answers to consider the before and after impact of a change.

Big Picture Framework

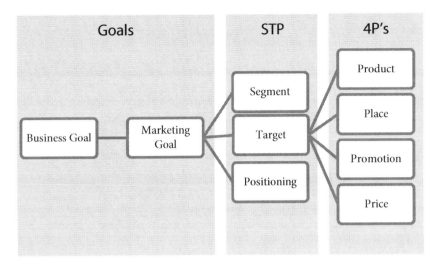

A comprehensive model that provides an effective way to answer interview questions about marketing plans and campaigns. There are three parts to the framework: Goals, STP (segmentation, targeting, and positioning) and the 4P's (product, place, promotion, and price).

- Goals: State the overall business objective and intermediate marketing objectives that contribute to it.
- Segmentation: Group buyers by attributes to identify customers that would benefit from the product.
- Targeting: Choose segments that would appreciate and seek out the product's benefits.
- Positioning: Create a product image for customer segments through the 4P's.
- Product: Develop new product ideas using the CIRCLES Method.
- Place: Choose the distribution channel that best meets the business goal(s).
- Promotion: Match promotional tactics with your strategies.
- Price: Use breakeven analysis for existing products, and the pricing meter for new products.

CIRCLES Method™

A guideline that provides complete and thoughtful responses to product design questions.

- **Comprehend the Situation:** Avoid miscommunication by asking clarifying questions (5W's and H) and/or stating assumptions.
- **Identify the Customer:** List potential customer personas, and choose one to focus on.
- **Report the Customer's Needs:** Provide a user story that conveys their goals, desires, and potential benefits. *As a <role>, I want <goal/desire> so that <benefit>.*
- **Cut, Through Prioritization:** Showcase your ability to prioritize, assess tradeoffs, and make decisions. Create a prioritization matrix that estimates valuable metrics (revenue, customer satisfaction, etc.)
- **List Solutions:** Brainstorm at least three BIG ideas that exploit future trends in technology and customer behavior. Use the following frameworks for inspiration: 1) Reverse the situation to uncover new possibilities. 2) Mix and match product attributes to get new combinations. 3) Challenge the status quo.
- **Evaluate Tradeoffs:** Define your tradeoff criteria and analyze the solution through a pro and cons list.

- **S**ummarize Your Recommendation: Specify which product or feature you would recommend, recap its benefits to the user and/or company, and explain why you preferred this solution compared to others.

Critical Path Dependency

A strategic relationship between a preceding and succeeding task in a sequence of activities that affects the project end date. Predecessor tasks must be finished before the start of successor tasks.

DIGS Method™

To get a job offer, I believe that candidates have to do just two things: be likable and show credibility that they can do the job. DIGS Method™ is a behavioral interview framework that promotes credibility and likability in your response.

- **D**ramatize the situation: Provide context and details that emphasizes the importance of your job, project or product.
- **I**ndicate the alternatives: Be thoughtful and analytical by listing three different approaches to a problem.
- **G**o through what you did: Convince the listener that you were the driving force.
- **S**ummarize your impact: Provide numbers and qualitative statements that validate your impact.

5Es Framework

An acronym and checklist to help brainstorm different stages of the customer experience. The 5Es framework helps you build a customer journey map effortlessly. Here are the 5Es:

- **E**ntice. What event triggers a user to enter into the UX funnel?
- **E**nter. What are the first few steps in the UX funnel?
- **E**ngage. What task(s) is the user trying to accomplish?
- **E**xit. How does the user complete the task?
- **E**xtend. What follow-up actions occur after the user completes the task?

Increase your effectiveness in answering product design questions by building a customer journey map. Customer journey maps help you uncover product improvement opportunities easily.

Five Ws and H

A checklist of questions to get the complete facts on a situation. For example, when understanding a new product, here is what listeners want to know:

- **W**hat is it?
- **W**ho is it for?
- **W**hen is it ready?
- **W**here will it be available?
- **W**hy should I get it?
- **H**ow does it work?

Five Whys

A technique to determine cause of a particular situation. It involves asking "Why?" in succession.

Issue Trees

A problem-solving diagram that breaks down a 'Why' or 'How' question into identifiable root causes or potential solutions, respectively.

Marketing funnel

An analytical model that tracks the customer journey towards a purchase of a product or service. There are four general steps, indicated by the AITP acronym:

- **A**wareness: Bring recognition to a product brand.
- **I**nterest: Stir fascination with a product (what it does, how it works, and what benefit it delivers.)
- **T**rial: Compel a prospective user to try the product.
- **P**urchase: Get the customer to buy into the product.

MOB

A marketing framework that evaluates the effectiveness of a product advertisement or commercial.

- **M**emorable: Does the ad grab your attention? Is it worthy of future discussion with your friends, acquaintances and social media?
- **O**h, Product: Is this product and brand promoted clearly and definitively?
- **B**enefit: Does the ad explain and provide evidence for the product's benefit? Is there a clear reason why the consumer should choose this product over a competitor's?

Rule of Three

A communication principle that suggests that responses that are bundled in threes are more effective and satisfying.

Pro and Con Analysis

A communication principle that a particular point of view is more readily accepted if the speaker provides a balanced view, in other words both the advantages and disadvantages.

Porter's Five Forces

A model proposed by Harvard business school professor, Michael Porter, on the competitive forces affecting a product or service. Here are the key components of Porter's Five Forces:

- Threat of new entrants
- Threat of substitutes
- Bargaining power of buyers
- Bargaining power of suppliers
- Industry rivalry

Razor-and-Razorblade Strategy

A popular business strategy where a business sells the platform, such as a razor, at cost or less. Then the business sells complementary products, such as razorblades, at a substantial profit, offsetting the reduced profit from selling the platform.

Root Cause Analysis Tree

A hierarchical diagram that identifies the root causes of a problem and provides potential corrective actions to benefit the outcome or prevent recurrence.

SCAMPER

A creative thinking framework used to develop innovative ideas for a topic, product or service.

- **S**ubstitute: What components of the topic can be substituted?
- **C**ombine: What ideas, products or services can be added to the original topic?
- **A**djust: How can the topic be altered to be more flexible and adaptable?
- **M**odify: What components can be enhanced, reduced or changed?
- **P**ut to other uses: How can the topic, product or service be used in different scenarios or situations?
- **E**liminate: What ideas or components can be removed?
- **R**everse, Rearrange: What new approaches can be formed from the original topic?

SWOT Analysis

A structured planning method to evaluate the strategic elements of a business, industry or product to find its competitive advantage.

- **S**trengths: Attributes that provide an advantage over other competitors.
- **W**eaknesses: Attributes that provide a disadvantage relative to other competitors.
- **O**pportunities: Elements that can be utilized to maximize advantages or trends.
- **T**hreats: Elements in the environment that can be an obstacle or risk to your business or product.

Chapter 5 Frequently Asked Questions

I have read the questions in *PM Interview Questions*. I find it unrealistic to know about every single product mentioned. Every sample answer seems as if the candidate just "happened" to be extremely well versed in that particular subject.

You are not the only one to feel that way. You may not know:

- How corporate taxes work
- What the YouTube API includes
- What celiac disease might be

Nevertheless, what seems unreasonable without a job description can be reasonable with it. For instance, a recent MBA graduate applying for a corporate finance role should know how corporate taxes work. A seasoned product manager applying for the YouTube API team should not be surprised when they are asked about the details of the publicly available YouTube API.

That being said, there is an important reminder that goes for all interviewing situations: the interviewer has the power to ask whatever they want. They might ask a question that requires you to be knowledgeable about celiac disease, even when you have no clue or if it is irrelevant to the role.

You will have to know how to react when you are in that uncomfortable position. It may feel unfair. However, be honest and be courageous. Do not dodge the question.

The workplace is filled with scenarios, where you feel awkward, due to your limited knowledge. The interviewer may justify the use of such questions to detect your poise and grace under pressure.

How am I supposed to react when interviewers ask me something I have no idea about?

The interview is not a police interrogation. In other words, you, the candidate, have the power to ask questions.

In one of the answer examples in *Decode and Conquer*, the interviewer asks the candidate, "You are the CEO of Yellow Cab taxi service. How would you respond to Uber?" It is hard to fathom that candidates have not used Uber, especially those that are passionate about tech. However, in the sample answer, the candidate handles the situation gracefully by asking, "I apologize. I have never used the Uber service. Can you tell me more about it?" And the interviewer accedes, giving the candidate the information he needs to do well.

If the interviewer is being difficult and refuses to give you the context and knowledge to be successful, you need to have the self-awareness and courage to persist, despite the interviewer's resistance. Your success is at stake. Give yourself a fair chance to give the best answer possible.

How do I know when I have done enough preparation?

Do not worry about over-preparation. There is no such thing. I have spent nearly 20 years as a PM, and I still do not know it all. Every single minute you spend investing in your PM abilities is an investment in your career - whether you intend to be a PM for only a decade or for several more.

Do note that when interviewers say a candidate is over-prepared, what they really mean is that a candidate comes across as robotic or is memorizing their responses. Neither is good, but it is not a symptom of over preparation. Instead, being robotic or memorizing responses is a symptom of the wrong type of preparation. So don't be a robot. And no memorizing. Chemistry and rapport, with the interviewer, counts.

How do I prepare for company X?

I have provided preparation plans for the most coveted PM roles at Google, Facebook and Amazon. If you have a PM interview with another company, you can construct your own preparation plan by leveraging the following resources:

- **Job Description**. The job description, especially the job responsibilities section, offers clues on what categories of questions the interviewer will likely ask.
- **Glassdoor.com reviews**. Candidates share interview questions they have received.
- **Internal employees**. Find a friend (or make a new one) at your target company or group. Ask them what kind of questions they are likely to ask. Sebastian Sabouné, a product manager at Hive and one of our reviewers, remarked, "As an interviewer, I love having people interested in my product. So if you come prepared with ANY question about it, it will leave a good impression."

Then, based on what you have researched as probable questions, modify the bit.ly/PMPrepPlan template to create your preparation plan.

What should I do if I have less than X days to prepare?

I am a firm believer that "success comes when preparation meets opportunity."

However, life happens, and we do not always have enough time to prepare. It is impossible for me to come up with a plan for every candidate's time constraints; I am sure someone will want a 15-minute study guide!

Instead, I have created a table on how to best allocate your preparation time, based on the most sought-after firms. With the time you have available, allocate your preparation time based on my recommendations below.

	Product Design	Metrics	Estimation	Pricing / LTV	Strategy	Traditional	Behavioral*	Technical
Google	50%	20%	19%	3%	5%	1%	2%	0%**
Facebook	50%	20%	10%	10%	7%	1%	2%	0%
Uber	50%	20%	10%	3%	14%	1%	2%	0%
Amazon	20%	10%	7%	15%	7%	1%	40%	0%
Microsoft	30%	5%	15%	5%	10%	5%	30%	0%

Include hypothetical questions as part of your behavioral preparation

** *Only prepare for technical questions if you have an on-site final round interview. It is unlikely technical questions will appear in earlier rounds. If you do have an on-site interview, spend almost as much time with technical preparation as you would product design.*

Chapter 6 Analytics: Estimation

Gmail Costs

Estimate how much Gmail costs for Google per user, per year.

Show your work below. Make any assumptions as necessary. Answer on the next page.

Answer

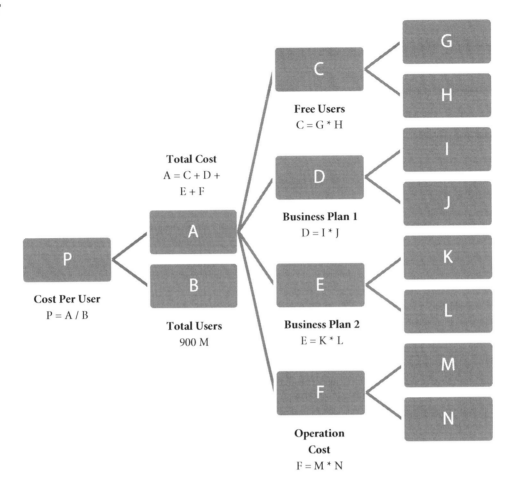

Assumptions

- Global users
- Monthly storage and bandwidth costs per user is roughly $0.05, based on Amazon Web Services data.
- Assume 900 million active users.
- Assume users are split into three tiers: free users, business users on 15GB plan, and business users on the unlimited plan with a 75%, 20%, and 5% share respectively.
- Assume free and 15GB plan business users use roughly 7.5GB on average whereas unlimited plan business users use roughly 100GB.
- Only operational costs are employee salary, not including anything else.
- Around 15,000 employees in Google. Gmail team is probably ~200 people (out of 15,000 total Google employees. Average annual salary is about $100,000.

Legend & Mini-Calculations

Free Users, Marginal Cost

G: # Free Users = Total Gmail Users * % Free Users = 900M * 75% = 675M

H: Marginal Cost per Free User = $.05 / GB / month * 7.5 GB * 12 months = $4.50 per Year

Business Users, 15GB Plan, Marginal Cost

44

I: # 15GB Biz Users = Total Gmail Users * % 15GB Biz Users = 900M * 20% = 180M

J: Marginal Cost per 15GB Biz User = $.05 / GB / month * 7.5 GB * 12 months = $4.50 per Year

Business Users, Unlimited Plan, Marginal Cost

K: # Unlimited Biz Users = Total Gmail Users * % Unlimited Biz Users = 900M * 5% = 45M

L: Marginal Cost per Unlimited Biz User = $.05 / GB / month * 100 GB * 12 months = $60 per Year

M: Total Number of Gmail Employees (200)

N: Employee Average Annual Salary ($100,000)

Calculations

C = 675M * $4.50 = $3.0375B

D = 180M * $4.50 = $810M

E = 45M * $60 = $2.7B

F = 200 * $100,000 = $20M

A = $3.0375B + $810M + $2.7B + $20M = $6.5675B

Answer

P = $6.5675B / 900 M = ~$7.30

Revenue from YouTube Red

Estimate how much revenue Google is making from YouTube Red, a no ads premium subscription service.

Show your work below. Make any assumptions as necessary. Answer on the next page.

How much revenue 1 month?

1 year ~ 12 months

How many YouTube users are there & what % like YouTube red?

1 B & 10%.

How much does YouTube Red cost?

$10 /mo

1 B x .1 =   .1 x 10 = 1 x 12 = 12 x 8mo

100,000,000 x 10 = 1,

Total revenue : $12 billion

Answer

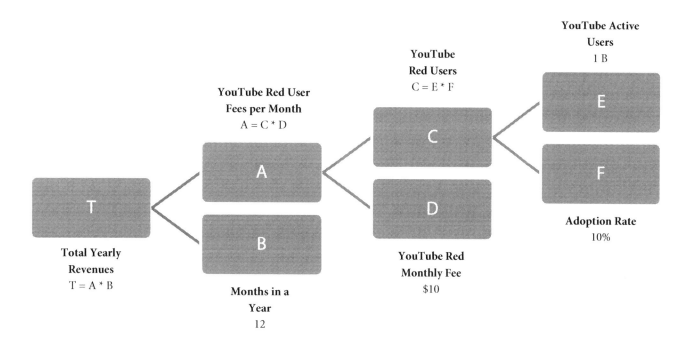

Clarifications

- Assuming that we are looking for annual revenue calculation.
- Assuming a global audience even though today YouTube Red is only available in Australia, New Zealand, and the United States.

Calculations

C = 1B * 10% = $100M

A = 100M * $10 = $1B

Answer

T = $1B * 12 = $12B

Storing Google Maps

How much storage space do you need to store all the info from Google Maps?

Show your work below. Make any assumptions as necessary. Answer on the next page.

Answer

Assumptions

- Google Maps only. Does not include Google Street View or Google Earth.
- There are three types of data being stored:
  - Picture data including logos and location pictures.
    - Each location uses four pictures, which is about 2 MB in size.
    - 25% of locations have a company logo, which takes 100 KB of storage.
  - Location data such as street names.
    - Location data takes 1000 bytes.
  - Street data such as street names.
    - Street data takes 250 bytes
- Each major city has 1,000 streets and 50,000 locations.
- Each minor city has 250 streets and 12,500 locations.
- There are around 2,000 major cities in the world, and probably 50,000 minor cities.

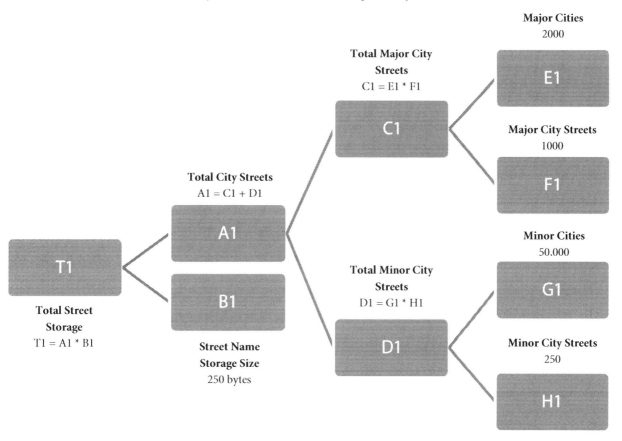

Calculations

D1 = 50,000 * 250 = 12.5M

C1= 2,000 * 1,000 = 2M

A1 = 12.5M + 2M = 14.5M

Sub-Answer T1

T1 = 14.5M * 250 = 3.625GB

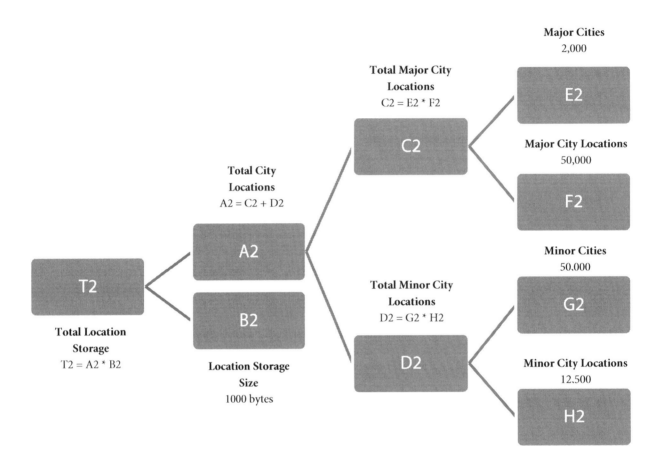

Calculations

D2 = 50,000 * 12,500 = 625M

C2 = 2,000 * 50,000 = 100M

A2 = 625M + 100M = 725M

Sub-Answer T2

T2 = 725M * 1000 = 725 GB

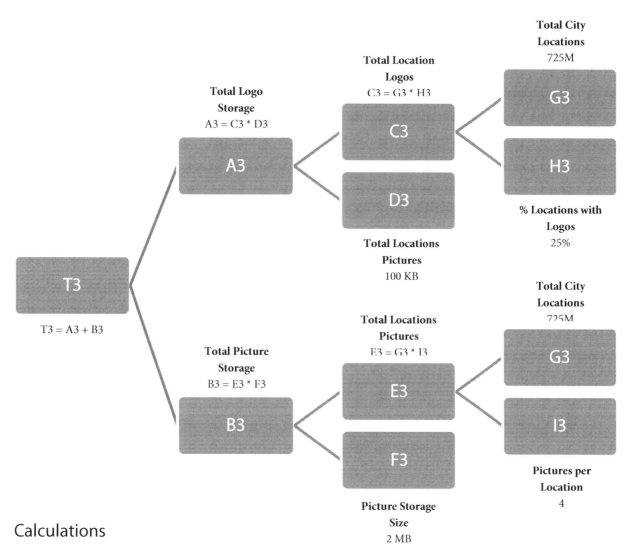

Calculations

E3 = 725M * 4 = 2.9B

C3 = 725M * 25% = 181.25M

B3 = 2.9B * 2 MB = 5.8B MB

A3 = 181.25M * 100 = 18.125B KB

Sub-Answer T3

T3 = 5.8B megabytes + 18.125 kilobytes = ~5.82 petabytes

Total Answer

T = T1 + T2 + T3 = 3.625 GB + 725 GB + 5.82 petabytes = ~5.82 petabytes

How Many Google Apps Users

Assume that Google makes $7 billion per year from Google Apps for Work. How many paying Google Apps users are there?

Show your work below. Make any assumptions as necessary. Answer on the next page.

Answer

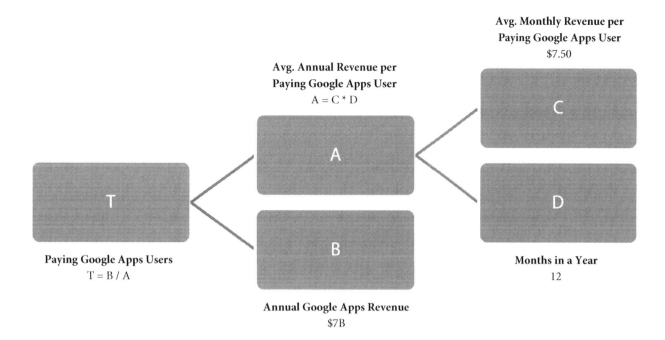

Avg. Monthly Revenue per Paying Google Apps User
$7.50

Avg. Annual Revenue per Paying Google Apps User
A = C * D

C

A

D

T

B

Paying Google Apps Users
T = B / A

Annual Google Apps Revenue
$7B

Months in a Year
12

Assumptions

Google has two paid versions of Google Apps for Work: a $5 and a $10 per month user. Let us assume that the paid customer mix is 50-50, which gives us average revenue of $7.50 per monthly user.

Calculations

A= $7.50 * 12 = $90

Answer

T = $7B / $90 = 77,777,778 users

Google Buses

How many buses does Google need to transport employees between their Mountain View headquarters and the employees' Bay Area residences?

Show your work below. Make any assumptions as necessary. Answer on the next page.

Answer

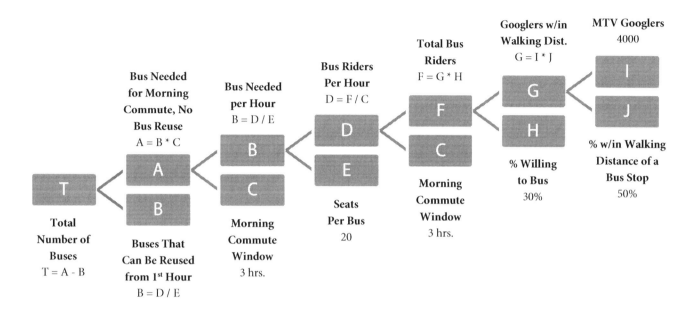

Total Number of Buses
T = A - B

Buses That Can Be Reused from 1st Hour
B = D / E

Bus Needed for Morning Commute, No Bus Reuse
A = B * C

Bus Needed per Hour
B = D / E

Morning Commute Window
3 hrs.

Bus Riders Per Hour
D = F / C

Seats Per Bus
20

Total Bus Riders
F = G * H

Morning Commute Window
3 hrs.

Googlers w/in Walking Dist.
G = I * J

% Willing to Bus
30%

MTV Googlers
4000

% w/in Walking Distance of a Bus Stop
50%

Assumptions

- Assume the morning commute window is three hrs. (6-9 am)
- Assume the buses used for the morning commute can be used for the evening commute
- Assume the buses used for the 1st hour of the commute can be used the 3rd hour of the commute because it takes about 1 hr. to travel back

Calculations

G = 4000 * 50% = 2000

F = 2000 * 30% = 600

D = 600 / 3 = 200

B = 200 / 20 = 10

A = 10 * 3 = 30

Answer

T = 30 - 20 = 10

Gmail Ads Revenue

How much revenue did Gmail make from ads last year?

Show your work below. Make any assumptions as necessary. Answer on the next page.

Answer

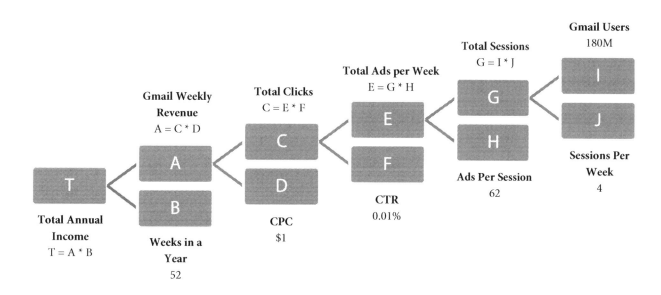

Assumptions

- 900 million active users in Gmail annually. 20% of the users are probably from the US, making it 180 million yearly active users.
- People probably open Gmail 4 times a week, and an average of 30 emails per day. That is 2 ads per email + 2 ads looking at the inbox = 30 * 2 + 2 = 62.

Calculations

G = 180M * 4 = 720M
E = 720M * 62 = 44.640B
C = 44.640B * 0.01% = 44.64M
A = 44.64M * $1 = $44.64M

Answer

T = $44.64M * 52 = ~$2.3B

Potential Users in Ireland

How many Dropbox users could there potentially be in Ireland?

Show your work below. Make any assumptions as necessary. Answer on the next page.

How many people are there in Ireland?

5 million users

How what percentage of them use computers?

80%

What percentage of these users need to either store files or store data / pictures?

80%

$5 \times .8 = 4 \times .8 = 3.2$

3.2 million potential users in Ireland

Answer

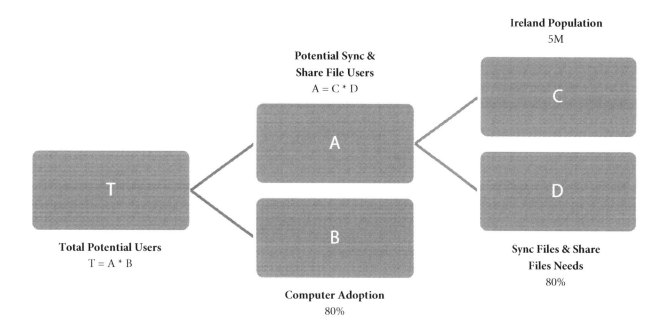

Total Potential Users
T = A * B

**Potential Sync &
Share File Users**
A = C * D

Computer Adoption
80%

Ireland Population
5M

**Sync Files & Share
Files Needs**
80%

A = 5M * 80% = 4M

Answer
T = 4M * 80% = 3.2M

Dropbox in Paris

Dropbox is now installed on Samsung smartphones. Estimate how many new users Dropbox acquired last month in Paris.

Show your work below. Make any assumptions as necessary. Answer on the next page.

Answer

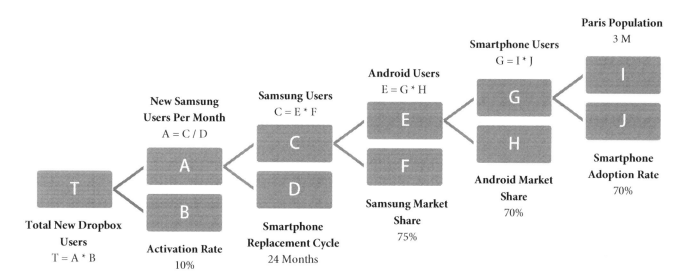

Clarifications

Dropbox will only show up on Samsung devices sold by stores recently.

Calculations

G = 3M * 70% = 2.1M

E = 2.1M * 70% = 1.47M

C = 1.47M * 75% = 1.1M

A = 1.1M / 24 = ~46K

Answer

T = 46K * 10% = ~4,600

Amazon Echo Partnership

A travel startup wants Amazon to auto-install their personal travel agent bot on all Amazon Echoes.

What is the value of the partnership to the travel startup?

Show your work below. Make any assumptions as necessary. Answer on the next page.

Answer

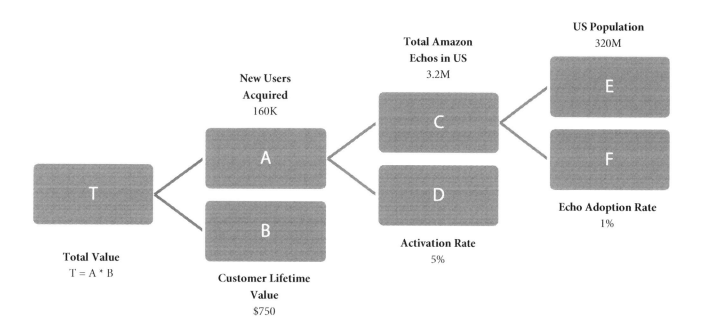

Assumptions

United States only

Industry press reports 3M Amazon Echo devices

Customer lifetime value = $750 for a travel industry customer according to Roomstorm

Calculations

C = 320M * 1% = 3.2M

A = 3.2M * 5% = 160K

Answer

T = A * B = 160k * $750 = $120M

Facebook's Ad Revenue

Estimate Facebook's ad revenue.

Show your work below. Make any assumptions as necessary. Answer on the next page.

Answer

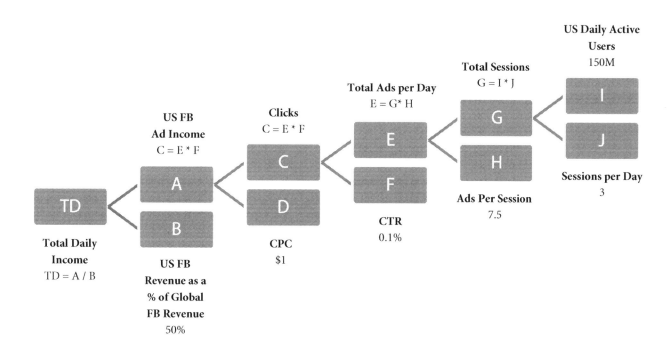

Assumptions

- Assume global ad revenue.
- Assume revenue based on ads only.
- Assume both mobile and web usage.
- Assume that Facebook shows 3 ads that rotate 2.5 times per session. That gives us 7.5 ads per session (H).

Calculations

G = 150M * 3 = 450M

E = 450M * 7.5 = 3.375B

C = 3.375B * 0.1% = 3.375M

A = 3.375M * $1 = $3.375M

TD = $3.375M / 50% = $6.75M

Answer

T = $6.75M * 365 days per year = ~$2.46B

Monthly Reviews on Yelp

Estimate how many reviews users write, each month, on Yelp.com.

Show your work in your own notebook. Make any assumptions as necessary. Answer on the next page.

This is the last time I will prompt you to show your work. Keep up the good practice. And no peeking at the answer; sample answers are reserved for finishers!

Answer

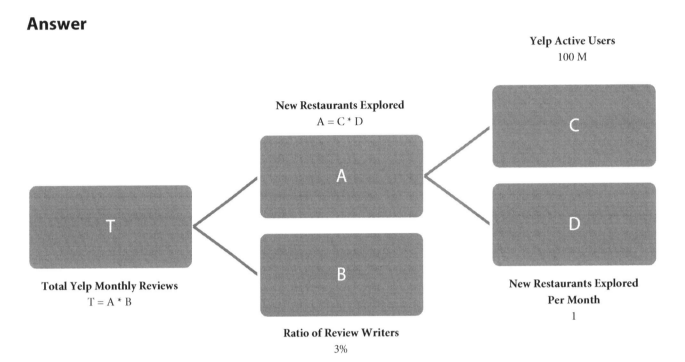

Yelp Active Users
100 M

New Restaurants Explored
A = C * D

Total Yelp Monthly Reviews
T = A * B

Ratio of Review Writers
3%

New Restaurants Explored Per Month
1

Calculations

A = 100M * 1 = 100M

Answer

T = 100M * 3% = 3M

Kinect Sports 2

How would you forecast the sales volume of the new Xbox game, Kinect Sports 2?

Answer

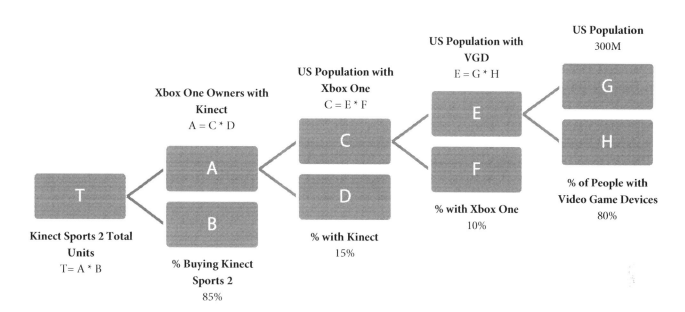

Calculations

E = 300M * 80% = 240M

C = 240M * 10% = 24M

A = 24M * 15% = 3.6M

Answer

T = 3.6M * 85% = 3.06M

Apple and Lyft Partnership

Apple and Lyft are considering a partnership where Lyft is pre-installed on new Apple iPhones in the United States.

How many users will Lyft gain from the partnership in NYC?

Answer

Assumptions

- Estimate for a single year
- The pre-install will occur on all Apple iPhones

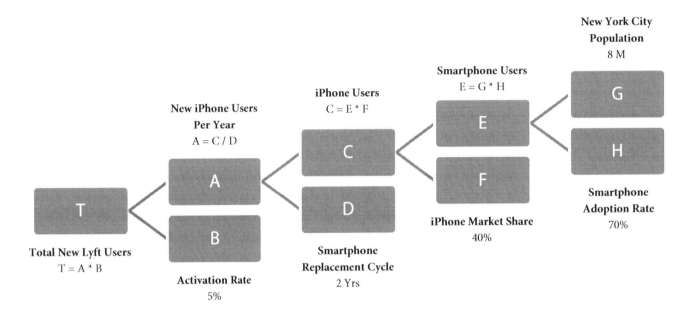

Calculations

E = 8M * 70% = 5.6M

C = 5.6M * 40% = 2.24M

A = 2.24M / 2 = 1.12M

Answer

T = 1.12M * 5% = 56,000

NYC Uber Driver

How much does an Uber driver in New York City make in a day?

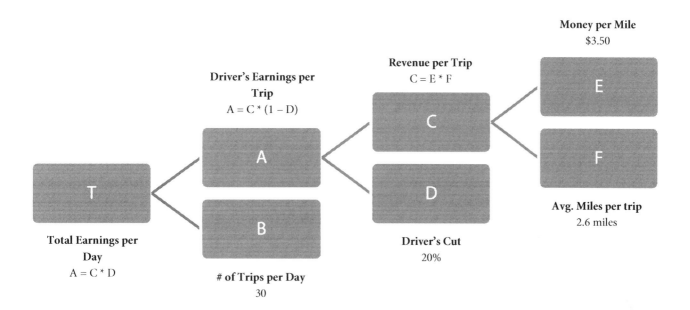

Money per Mile
$3.50

Revenue per Trip
C = E * F

Driver's Earnings per Trip
A = C * (1 – D)

E

F

C

Avg. Miles per trip
2.6 miles

D

A

T

B

Total Earnings per Day
A = C * D

# of Trips per Day
30

Driver's Cut
20%

Calculations

C = $3.50 * 2.6 miles = $9.10

A = $9.10 * (1 – 20%) = $7.28

Answer

T = $7.28 * 30 = $218.40 per Day

Uber Drivers

Uber is planning to open a new market. How many Uber drivers do we need?

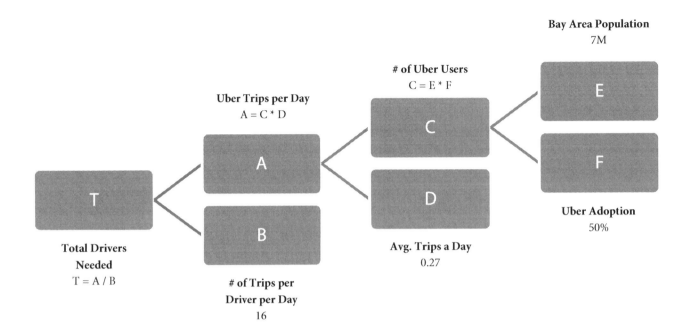

Answer

Assumptions

- **Average Trips a Day**. Assume that there are three types of Uber users: heavy, moderate and casual. 20% are heavy, 40% are moderate, and 40% are casual. Heavy users use Uber once a day. Moderates use Uber once a week. Casuals use Uber once a month. The weighted average number of trips, based on these assumptions is 0.27 trips per day.
- **# of Trips per Driver per Day**. Assume that an Uber driver works 8 hours a day, doing approximately 2 trips per hour.

Calculations

C = 7M * 50% = 3.5M
A = 3.5M * 0.27 = 945K

Answer

T = 945K / 16 = 59K drivers

Cab Ads for the Burrito Shop

You own a burrito shop and you want to advertise in a fleet of 100 cabs in San Francisco. Only the passenger(s) will see the ad. How much are you willing to pay per month?

Answer

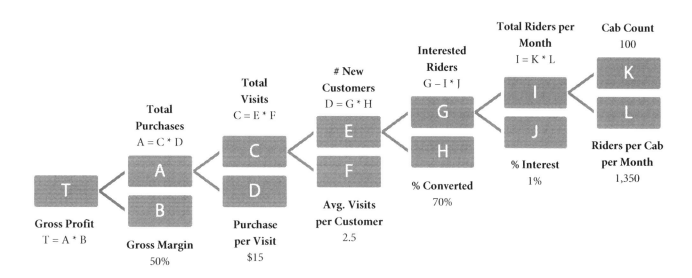

Assumptions

- **Cab rides per month.** Assume 30 trips a day, 30 days in a month and 1.5 riders per trip.
- **Avg. Visits per Customer.** Some new customers will return more than once.
- **Purchase per Visit.** Burrito is roughly $10, but some customers might buy a drink or appetizers. Other customers might buy food for others in their party such as a family member.

Calculations

$I = 100 * 1,350 = 135,000 = 135,000 * 1\% = 1,350$

$E = 1,350 * 70\% = 945$

$C = 945 * 1.5 = {\sim}1,418$

$A = 1,418 * \$15 = \$21,270$

Answer

$T = \$21,270 * 50\% = {\sim}\$10,635$

The gross profit is the breakeven amount for the adverting campaign, so the owner should pay no more than this amount for the ad.

Cars in Seattle

How many cars are in Seattle?

Things to Consider

- Answer this question in less than 5 minutes. Most interviewers consider this a simple estimation question.
- Scope the problem correctly by clarifying with the interviewer whether it is okay to focus on consumer only versus consumer + enterprise.
- Most interviewers will not give you assumptions. If you are stuck, build upon assumptions you know. For example, you might not know Seattle's population, but you do know San Francisco's is 837K. Seattle feels to be 75% the size of SF. After doing the math, you assume that Seattle's population is 628K. (Seattle's actual population is 650k.)

Common Mistakes

- Not having a game plan and trying to figure it out as you go along.
- Communicating poorly, making it hard for the interviewer to understand your thinking.
- Getting scared of doing math and unnecessarily rounding up or down. For instance, you should be comfortable multiplying and dividing numbers such as 500 / 3.

Answer

Clarifications

- Consumer only, not business.
- Not counting cars at car dealerships and junkyards.

Assumptions

- Seattle population is around 650k.
- 2.5 people per household.
- 1.5 cars per family.

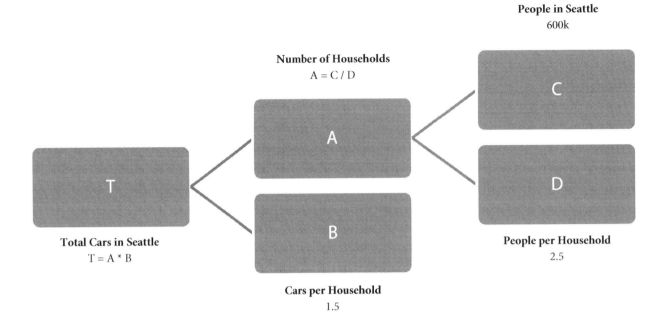

People in Seattle
600k

Number of Households
A = C / D

C

A

D

Total Cars in Seattle
T = A * B

B

People per Household
2.5

Cars per Household
1.5

Calculations

A= 600K * 2.5 = 1.5M

Answer

T = 1.5M * 1.5 = 2.25M

Driverless Car Purchases 2020

Estimate the number of driverless cars purchased in 2020.

Answer

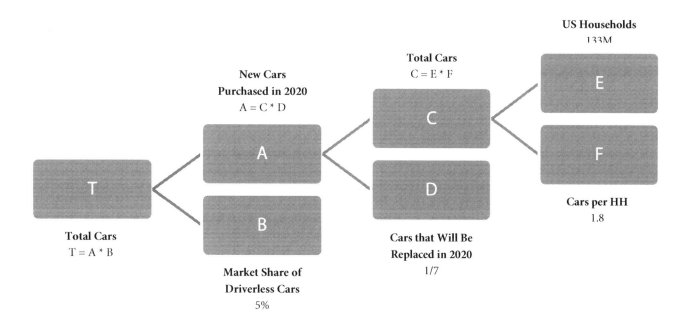

Calculations

$C = 133M * 1.8 = 239.4M$

$A = 239.4M * 1/7 = 34.2M$

Answer

$T = 34.2M * 5\% = 1.71M$

College Campus Bandwidth

Estimate Internet bandwidth required for a college campus.

Answer

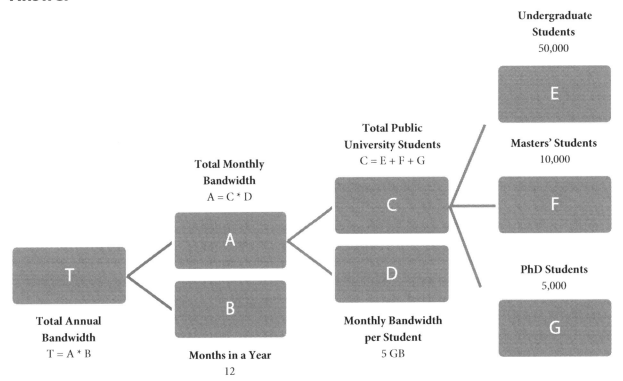

Assumptions

- US only.
- Public.
- Students only, no staff. Students include undergraduate and graduate students.
- Annual.

Calculations

C = 50,000 + 10,000 + 5,000 = 65,000

A = 65,000 * 5 GB = 325,000 GB

Answer

T = 325,000 GB * 12 = 3.9 petabytes

Planes in the Air

How many airplanes are in US airspace at 9 am PT time zone?

Answer

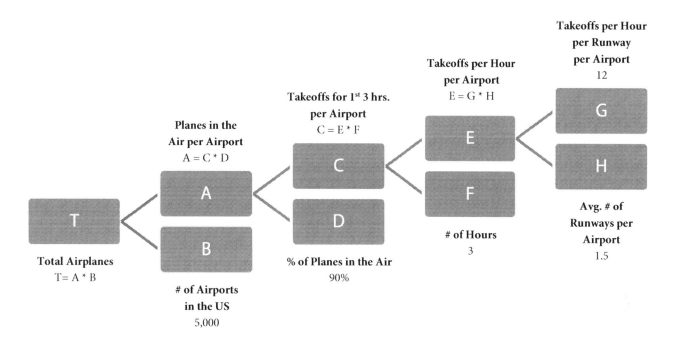

Assumptions

- Assume the first flight leaves at 6 am. So between 6-9am there are three hours of takeoffs.
- 90% of flights that begin between 6-9am are still in the air. The other 10% may have landed, especially if the flights have a shorter duration.
- There are approximately 5,000 airports in the United States with paved runways.
- Do not include non-US flights in US airspace.

Calculations

E = 12 * 1.5 = 18
C = 18 * 3 = 54
A = 54 * 90% = 48.6

Answer

T = 48.6 * 5000 = 243,000

Chapter 7 Analytics: Data Science

Tying Strings

You have a bag of N strings, and at random, you pull out an end of a string. You pull out another end and tie the two ends together. You take another two string ends and tie them together. You repeat this until there are no loose ends left to pull out of the bag. What is the expected number of loops?

Things to Consider

- Understand what is being asked.
- Work through the simple base case.

Common Mistakes

- Not talking aloud, missing a chance to get tips from the interviewer.

Answer

CANDIDATE: To get some momentum, let's work through some simple base cases.

Analysis: Number of Open Ends

N = 1 string

- Number of open ends = 2
- After tying together, number of open ends = 0

N = 2 strings

- Number of open ends = 4
- After tying together, number of open ends = 2

N = 3 strings

- Number of open ends = 6
- After tying together, number of open ends = 4

Takeaway #1: For any N, anytime we tie an open end, we reduce the number of open ends by 2.

Analysis: Number of Loops

N = 1 string

- Number of open ends = 2
- Probability of closing the loop by grabbing the other end of the same string = 1

N = 2 strings

- Number of open ends = 4
- Probability of closing the loop by grabbing the other end of the same string = 1/3

N = 3 strings

- Number of open ends = 6
- Probability of closing the loop by grabbing the other end of the same string = 1/5

Takeaway #2: There are 2N string ends. Probability of closing the loop at the first attempt is $1/(2N-1)$.

Takeaway #3: The question prompt asks us for the expected number of loops, if we keep repeating. Therefore, we sum the probabilities to get the expected number of loops. Expressed in equation format:

Expected number of loops = $1/(2N-1) + \ldots + 1/5 + 1/3 + 1$

University Acceptance Rate

A university's overall acceptance rate is higher for men than women, but each department's acceptance rate for women is higher than men. How is this the case?

Things to Consider

- Work through a simple example.
- Explain in words why the phenomenon occurs.

Common Mistakes

- Being rattled.
- Not working out an example.
- Poorly explaining why the phenomenon occurs.

Answer

This example illustrates this phenomenon.

	Male Applicants	Males Accepted	Female Applicants	Females Accepted
CS	90 (90%)	72 (80%)	10 (1%)	9 (90%)
Business	10 (10%)	4 (40%)	1000 (99%)	500 (50%)
Total	100	76 (76%)	1010	509 (~50%)

It's called Simpson's paradox. That is, a trend that appears in groups of data (this case, higher female acceptance) disappears when the groups combine. In this example, Simpson's paradox occurs because a higher percentage of females applied to the more competitive business department than males.

Ladder of N Steps

You have a ladder of N rungs (aka steps). You can go up the ladder by taking either one or two steps at a time, in any combination. How many different routes are there (aka combinations of one or two steps) to make it up the ladder?

Things to Consider

- Start with working out simple base cases.
- Identify the common pattern for different ladders of length N.
- Specify a formula for the N case.
- Recursion may help.

Common Mistakes

- Being stressed out.

Answer

CANDIDATE: Let us work out all the basic N (rungs) first to see if we can spot a pattern:

- N = 1: 1 way
- N = 2: 2 ways: 1+1, 2
- N = 3: 3 ways: 1+1+1, 1+2, 2+1
- N = 4: 5 ways: 1+1+1+1, 2+1+1, 2+2, 1+2+1, 1+1+2. We can also think of this is going to N = 1, then picking the 3 ways of N = 3 and going to N = 2, and picking the 2 ways of N = 2. 3 + 2 = 5.
- N = 5: 8 ways. Pick N = 1, then picking N = 4 (5 ways) and N = 2 and picking N = 3 (3 ways). 5 + 3 = 8.
- …

We can then express this in this formula: Ways(N) = Ways(N-1) + Ways(N-2). This is a classic recursion algorithm.

Counting Handshakes

If in a room, there are 10 persons and if each person has to shake hands with all other. How many total handshakes will be there?

Things to Consider

- Take a moment to work through a simple base case to increase comprehension.
  - E.g. How many handshakes are there if there are two people?
  - In addition, how many handshakes if it's 3? 4?
- Check with the interviewer if he or she wants you to write the generalized solution for N number of people.

Common Mistakes

- Blurting the first answer that comes to mind.

Answer

CANDIDATE: Hmm, if there are 10 people, each person needs to shake hand with 9 other people. This means 90 handshakes. But, since when you are handshaking someone, they are also handshaking you as well, so we don't want to count that twice. So realistically, it should be 10 * 9 / 2 which should be 45.

INTERVIEWER: Hmm, I am not convinced that is the correct answer. How can you prove it?

CANDIDATE: Okay, let's do this incrementally. Let say we have N people.

N = 1: 0, no handshakes since it's just one person.

N = 2: 1, they handshake with each other and we are done.

N = 3: 3 = 1 + 2. So let say we originally had 2 people. They shook hands once and that was that. Then a new person joins, and he shakes hands with both of the people.

N = 4: 6 = 1 + 2 + 3. Let's build on the previous case. Now there is a 4th person coming, and he needs to shake hands with the 3 original people.

We now see a pattern. Whenever we have a newcomer, he needs to shake hands with everyone else that were already here. The formula then becomes: 1 + 2 + 3 + … + (N-1).

If we plug in 10, we have 1 + 2 + 3 + 4 + 5 + 6 + 7 + 8 + 9 = 45.

Weighing 27 Balls

There are 27 balls. One ball that is heavier than others are. How many attempts do you need to make to find which ball it is using a seesaw?

Things to Consider

- Ask for a moment to collect your thoughts if the prompt overwhelms you.
- Ask clarifying questions if you do not understand the situation.

Common Mistakes

- Being stressed and giving up.

Answer

CANDIDATE: 3.

First I check 9 balls vs. 9 other balls. We have two cases here:

- The ball is in one of the 9 balls we checked.
- The ball is in the 9 balls we didn't check.

Either way, we checked once already, and this problem is now reduced to 9 balls. We then check 3 balls vs. 3 other balls. And like the last step, we have two cases here:

- The ball is in one of the 3 balls we checked.
- The ball is in the 3 balls we didn't check.

Now it's two checks, and we have 3 balls left. We then check 1 ball vs. 1 other ball and have another two cases here:

- The ball is in the two balls we are checking.
- The ball is the ball we didn't check.

That totals to 3 steps.

Chapter 8 Analytics: Pricing New Products

Google Driverless Car Pricing

How much should Google charge for a driverless car?

Things to Consider

- When pricing new products, evaluate these price points:
  - **Customer Value**. Also known as customer's willingness to pay, customer value refers to the utility a customer gets out of a product or service? For example, a haircut might cost a bride $400. However, to look good in her wedding photos, which she plans to look at for the rest of her life, is priceless. In other words, the bride's willingness to pay, in this scenario, may be much, much larger than $400.
  - **Competitors' Prices**. A company must consider competitors' prices, especially if the competitors' offer substitute goods.
  - **Cost of Goods Sold**. What does it cost to make the particular product?
- If the goal is to maximize profits, then consider pricing the product *above* the competitor's prices. It'll allow you to extract more gross margin. It is also possible to maximize profits by pricing below competitor's prices. Doing so sacrifices margin, but you may overcome decreased margin with increased sales volume.
- If the goal is to gain market share, consider pricing *below* competitor's prices. Gaining market share is a reasonable objective for winner-take-all markets.

Common Mistakes

- Proposing a pricing strategy without substantial explanation.
- Incorrectly using a price elasticity framework to solve a new pricing question.

Answer

CANDIDATE: Are we talking about a one-time payment or a down payment with a pricing plan?

INTERVIEWER: A one-time payment.

CANDIDATE: Can I ask some clarifying questions?

INTERVIEWER: Go ahead.

CANDIDATE: Are we pricing just one car or several models?

INTERVIEWER: Just one car.

CANDIDATE: Are we working with anyone in manufacturing our cars or are we doing everything ourselves?

INTERVIEWER: That's up to you.

CANDIDATE: What about the demographic? Are we going for luxury cars or regular cars?

INTERVIEWER: There will be no more information given. Why don't you determine all of this and give me why you think you are going for this way?

CANDIDATE: Okay. Can you give me some time to brainstorm?

Candidate takes one minute.

CANDIDATE: I need to first talk about some ideas I had. I think it's better if Google manufactures and sells the car itself. Tesla did it and they did fine. I think it would really help Google's branding. It would also be bad to depend on someone else to manufacture it. We already had this problem with Android and the market is now fragmented. I don't think we want to repeat it.

As for our demographic, I would like to go for luxury cars. The reason is because the driverless car is still a new concept to the public. Even with safety reports and everything, many people will be unconvinced. Buying a car is a huge thing for the middle class, but not for the rich. It would also be good to market because it's a brand new thing and judging from the positive response Tesla got, it would work. In addition, if the rich people are okay with getting driverless cars and nothing bad happened, when we eventually launch for our regular car models we would have an easier time.

INTERVIEWER: Okay. What about the price?

CANDIDATE: Okay. I am thinking around the price of Tesla. I think a Tesla is around $50,000 as a base. I think getting it up to $70,000 is not uncommon. I am thinking $50,000 as a base. With enough add-ons, it could exceed $100,000. Add-ons could be things like better paint, stereo, better wheels and rims, etc.

I think it is a good price, because it is not too expensive but it is out of the range of regular cars. The good thing about Tesla is that they offer free repairs and the fuel is free. The bad thing is that you can only repair in Tesla stores and refuel at their stations, which is limiting them to several locations. For us, we do not have the problem with fueling, and with targeting the rich oil prices is not really an issue.

Repairs are going to be a big problem for us. For the car itself, it's easy. It might be hard for every regular car shop to fix regular car problems with Google cars, but people who buy luxury cars don't go to those. High-end shops are typically more skilled so I don't think they have a problem. It's the hardware tied with the technology that concerns me. It would be too much for repair shops, so Google pretty much needs to offer it.

Just to be safe, I would offer a lifetime service for hardware repair related to driverless technology. I would also offer a one-year warranty on regular problems. After that, I think it's plenty time for other repair shops to pick up the skill of repairing regular car problems with Google cars.

Google and Teleportation

Let's say Google created a teleporting device: which market segments would you go after? How would you price it?

Things to Consider

- For market segments, develop your criteria first. Potential criteria can include customer need, willingness and ability to pay, and market size.
- For pricing, consider customer value, competitive pricing, and cost of goods sold.
- Do not forgot to include substitutes, such as airplane flights, as a potential competitor for your pricing analysis.

Common Mistakes

- Not considering substitute products.
- Having poor rationale for target segments.

Answer

CANDIDATE: Can I ask some clarifying questions?

INTERVIEWER: Go ahead.

CANDIDATE: Is there a delay when traveling through time?

INTERVIEWER: It's instant.

CANDIDATE: Is there a cost attached to this? Does it cost more based on distance? Does it cost more based on weight or size of objects?

INTERVIEWER: Nope, each trip costs a constant of $1 million.

CANDIDATE: Is there a limit to the size or weight?

INTERVIEWER: Yes, you can't teleport anything bigger than an average person.

CANDIDATE: Can it teleport anything? Even life forms?

INTERVIEWER: It cannot teleport life forms.

CANDIDATE: How does it teleport? Like can it just teleport any object anywhere, or do you need another one on the other side?

INTERVIEWER: You need another one on the other side.

CANDIDATE: How many of these devices do we have? Does it have a cooldown? I want to understand our supply.

INTERVIEWER: We only have one, and we will not be getting any other any time soon. It has a cooldown of 5 minutes.

CANDIDATE: All right, can I get some time to brainstorm?

Candidate takes one minute.

CANDIDATE: Here are a few lucrative markets.

- **Military.** Send supplies or top-secret objects back and forth between military bases. It's safer than traveling in these cases.
- **Luxury Gifts.** For those who are really trying to impress their friends. It's for the sake of being able to afford this on a whim.
- **Government Exchange.** Exchanging top-secret documents or objects? This is a 100% guarantee, safe way.

I would price this at around $2 million. The profit margin is 50% because it's unlikely this machine will be used that often. The government and military spends millions of dollars all the time on security and safety, so it wouldn't be that farfetched. Obviously, I could price it higher, but I think currying favor from the government and military will be worth more in the long run for Google.

Pricing UberX

How would you go about pricing UberX or any other new Uber product?

Things to Consider

- Consider customer value, competitive pricing and cost of goods sold.
- Acknowledge that in real life that you may do a pricing survey to gauge the appropriate price.
- As a follow-up question, interviewer may ask you to estimate potential revenue for this newly priced service.

Common Mistakes

- Forgetting to consider substitutes, such as walking or riding the subway, as competition too.

Answer

CANDIDATE: In real life, I would run a pricing survey with prospects. However, I imagine you want my gut instinct on how I would price it, correct?

INTERVIEWER: That's correct. Nevertheless, your pricing survey suggestion is noted.

CANDIDATE. Great, there are multiple variables we need to think about to price UberX. Here are my top 4:

- **Driver's Payment**. It needs to make up two things: gas and time. Remember that minimum wage is about $10 per hour in California.
- **User's Payment**. The user can't pay that much, otherwise they'll use some other service instead. It needs to be more expensive than say, Caltrain or other public transportation (which averages out to be about $10 per hour) but less expensive than competitors like Yellow Cab, which is about $100 for an hour trip.
- **Our Own Cut.** We need to make profit on each trip. I am thinking around 30% fee right now, but that can change.
- **Bonus Rates.** Maybe there are not enough cars around this hour, so we need to increase the rates the customers must pay in order to attract more drivers. This could double or even triple during holidays.

I am going to make some assumptions. Last time I drove from Sunnyvale to San Francisco, it took about an hour with light traffic. That's about 40 miles. Gas is around $2 per gallon. A regular car has about 30 mpg. So really, each mile averages to be around $0.67. Now gas prices can go up, so we need to consider this. I would say we should just up the price to be around $2 per mile as a lower bound.

Most trips probably take about 10 miles. If you combine that with the car coming in and the time it takes to communicate, it should be around 30 minutes per trip. Therefore, we are talking 20 miles and 2 trips per hour. Also, remember that you will not get a passenger every time you are done, so to be safe it should be about 1 trip per hour.

So imagine if we did $2 per mile and there is only one trip per hour. That ends up costing the customer around $20. If we take a 30% cut, that's $14 for the driver and $6 for us. This is the bare minimum, which is more expensive than the Caltrain and it is higher than the minimum wage.

If it's rush hour or holidays, it could go up to $40 per trip or even $60. This number seems good.

Finally, we need to add in a price for starting an Uber ride, otherwise people will try to do really short trips which is bad for profit. I say around $5 is good enough. Therefore, it's about $25 for a 10-mile ride.

To conclude, I would price it as $2 per mile with $5 as the starting point.

Chapter 9 Analytics: Pricing Existing Products

Kindle Pricing at Target, Qualitative Version

Target asked Amazon to give a 20% price discount on the Kindle. Should Amazon grant this pricing request?

Things to Consider

- The interviewer may want a qualitative or quantitative discussion. If it is not clear, ask for clarification.
- If it is a qualitative discussion, a pro and con analysis would suffice.
- If it is a quantitative discussion, treat is as a price elasticity question.

Common Mistakes

- Not acknowledging that granting a price discount for Target may require granting a similar discount to all retailers.

Answer

CANDIDATE: Is this a permanent discount or something for sales?

INTERVIEWER: Let us say it is permanent.

CANDIDATE: This is the price Target is buying from Amazon, correct? And not the final price to the customers?

INTERVIEWER: Yes.

CANDIDATE: What is the price Amazon is selling it to Target? I am trying to gauge the profit margin for a Kindle sold on Amazon vs. Target. I imagine selling Amazon will net us more profit. The question is, how much more?

INTERVIEWER: Let say Amazon is making 20% more when selling through the Amazon.com channel vs. the Target channel.

CANDIDATE: Is there any reason why Target is asking for this discount?

INTERVIEWER: Target representatives believe that customers are trying the Kindle in their stores, only to purchase them online on Amazon.com.

CANDIDATE: Okay, it's the classic showrooming problem. Are we selling the Kindle for the same price on both Amazon and Target channels?

INTERVIEWER: It's cheaper when purchasing through Amazon.com.

CANDIDATE: Is Target selling any other Amazon products? I am trying to gauge if Target is promoting a series of Amazon products. There are two factors. First, we don't want to upset Target if Target is carrying lots of

Amazon products. Second, we want to gauge the benefit of having Target promote Amazon products to customers.

INTERVIEWER: Target does carry multiple Amazon products, aside from Kindle.

CANDIDATE: May I ask for the historical Kindle sales data from both Amazon and Target channels?

INTERVIEWER: I can't reveal these unfortunately. Can you wrap up your answer, based on what you know so far?

CANDIDATE: I think I can. Give me a second to wrap up my thoughts.

Candidate takes 20 seconds.

I recommend that we give the discount. There are several reasons why:

- **Showrooming benefit**. Trying out the Kindle is an important part of the purchase process. Since Amazon.com doesn't have physical stores, Target's showrooms provide an incredible benefit.
- **Razor-and-razorblade model**. Amazon wants to establish Kindles as a media consumption device. Since they can generate profit from future media purchases such as books and movies, it's more important to sacrifice short-term profits to gain device market share.
- **Minimize channel conflict**. Amazon should strive to keep price parity across all channels. Not only does it upset its retail partners, but it may also upset customers who purchase Kindles on Target, only to find that they could buy it for less on Amazon.com. This could lead to customer dissatisfaction and more customer complaints.
- **Domino effect**. Losing Target as a retail partner can lead other retail partners to remove Kindle from their shelves.

The downside of giving a discount is that it affects Amazon's overall profit, unless there's an increase that offsets units sold. Also conceding on a price discount may lead other retail partners to demand a similar discount.

Kindle Pricing at Target, Quantitative Version

Target asked Amazon to give a 20% price discount on the Kindle. Should Amazon grant this pricing request?

Things to Consider

- The interviewer may want a qualitative or quantitative discussion. If it's not clear, ask for clarification.
- If it's a qualitative discussion, a pro and con analysis would suffice.
- If it's a quantitative discussion, treat is as a price elasticity question.

Common Mistakes

- Not acknowledging that granting a price discount for Target may require granting a similar discount to all retailers.

Answer

$79

Assumptions

- Assume 3MM Kindles sold last year
- Target's channel share was 5%
- Amazon.com's channel share was 80%

Profitability via Target Retail Channel

Profitability via Target Retail Channel	Old	New
Price	$60	$48
COGS	$30	$30
Unit Margin ($)	$30	$18
Volume	150,000	350,000
Subtotal: Gross Profit via Target	$4,500,000	$6,300,000

Profitability via Target Retail Channel	Old	New
Price	$60	$48
COGS	$30	$30
Unit Margin ($)	$30	$18
Volume	150,000	350,000
Subtotal: Gross Profit via Target	$4,500,000	$6,300,000

Total Profitability	$122,100,000	$122,675,000

AWS Price Reduction

AWS has a Fortune 500 Company that is asking for a price reduction. What factors internal, external, financial and nonfinancial would you consider in the price reduction request?

Things to Consider

- Treat this negotiation request and utilize a negotiation checklist. Here's a sample:
    - Value to Fortune 500 Company (aka maximum price)
    - AWS Cost (aka minimum price)
    - Market alternatives (aka competitor's price)
    - Switching costs
    - Intangible value (aka using the Fortune 500 company as a customer reference)

Common Mistakes

- Not accurately assessing the Fortune 500 company's leverage (e.g. forgetting that there's switching cost)
- Over propensity to please the customer
- Over propensity to stick with hardball negotiation tactics

Answer

CANDIDATE: First, I would start by asking how much money we're making from this company. Once I have this number, I would want to know if this is average for a Fortune 500 Company. After that, I would want to know how many Fortune 500 companies AWS is working with as well as how much percentage this profit accounts for annually for AWS.

The reason is I am trying to gauge how important this customer is. Let's say this customer is very important. We then need to think about why they are asking for a price reduction. Are they not doing well financially? If that's not the case, are they asking because they are considering a competitor like Microsoft Azure or IBM's SoftLayer?

I would also consider their growth. This is more for small companies though. If they are a startup, they could be a company with a lot of potential. I want to help them out in hopes that some day when their companies grow I can be a valued partner.

Obviously, if this number is below our profit margin, as in, we are making a loss of profit, then that's something I don't really want to consider.

INTERVIEWER: Okay, is that it?

CANDIDATE: I would also think about other companies. It depends on if this will get out. I don't want to start a precedent where a bunch of companies come knocking asking for a price reduction too. Even if I get a NDA, word might get out.

I also need to consider the company. It depends on my position in this. Do I even have the authority to do this? If this is my client, and I am offering it, it could be a bad precedent in every manager trying to lower the price to get more clients. There are also office politics to consider. If I am a senior executive and I am allowing this, but not allowing it for other clients. Even if the numbers make sense, it could feel like I am playing favorites.

Finally, I would consider this client itself. Besides its financial standing, does the client have influence? Could this client refer other customers? If so, I'd have to consider the potential profit from these referrals.

Chapter 10 Analytics: ROI

Kindle Pricing Error

Assume an Amazon's Kindle normally retails for $199. However, a pricing error occurred and Amazon's website states that the retail price was $19. Before Amazon corrected the error, Amazon sold 300,000 units. The price was fixed on the website to the originally $199. Amazon has not shipped or invoiced any of the $19 units. What would you recommend, as the finance person on this team?

Things to Consider

- What is the financial cost of fulfilling the mispriced Kindles?
- What is the PR impact?

Common Mistakes

- Not factoring in shipping costs.
- Not factoring in benefit from subsequent Kindle-related purchases such as books, movies and music.

Answer

CANDIDATE: How much does the Kindle cost?

INTERVIEWER: Around $170.

CANDIDATE: Has something similar like this happened on Amazon before? What is our usual policy?

INTERVIEWER: Let's assume none of this has happened before, and we don't have a policy for this (we do).

CANDIDATE: Let me calculate how much loss we would suffer before I talk about other reasons. What are the shipping distributions? How many people have Prime? How many are doing 2-5 days? How many people are doing super saver shipping?

INTERVIEWER: I don't have data on that.

CANDIDATE: Okay. I know Prime is about 50% of the users, so they probably have two-day shipping which should cost us around $25. Are we around holiday seasons?

INTERVIEWER: We are not, why do you ask?

CANDIDATE: If it's closer to holiday, many customers would want fast shipping. Since it's not, then I would say 45% of the users are probably using the cheapest shipping. Did this item qualify for super saver shipping? Usually it requires $35 and a $199 would qualify, but it's technically $19 right now.

INTERVIEWER: It does not qualify because of the price tag.

CANDIDATE: Okay, then I would say around 45% would be using 5-8-day shipping which would cost around $5 for us. The remaining 5% is probably using 3-5 days, which would cost $10. Of these, we should be making $5 profit and $8 profit, respectively.

Let's calculate the loss on the sale first:

$$Sale\ Loss = Units\ Sold * (Actual\ Cost - Error\ Price)$$

$$Sale\ Loss = 300,000 * (\$170 - \$19)$$

$$Sale\ Loss = \sim\$45\ million$$

Let's calculate the shipping loss:

$$Shipping\ Loss = Units\ Sold * (\%\ Prime * Prime\ Shipping\ Cost - \%\ Super\ Saver * Super\ Saver\ Profit - \%\ Other * Other\ Profit)$$

$$Shipping\ Loss = 300,000 * (0.5 * \$25 - 0.45 * \$5 - 0.05 * \$8)$$

$$Shipping\ Loss = \sim\$3\ million$$

Adding them together:

$$Total\ Loss = Sale\ Loss + Shipping\ Loss$$

$$Total\ Loss = \$45\ million + \$3\ million$$

$$Total\ Loss = \$48\ million$$

Therefore, it'll cost us around $48 million if we let this order go through. That is a lot. Now let's think about what happens if we cancel this order.

- **Customer Satisfaction**: It would make 300,000 customers very unhappy.
- **Branding**: This will hurt our brand.
- **PR**: This will definitely blow up on the Internet, and many people will know. The fact that the Kindle is on sale for $19 was probably trending which caused 300,000 sales.
- **Labor**: Customer service is going to be very busy getting complaints from these users. In addition, fulfillment will have to cancel all 300,000 orders, leading to missed revenue.

What are some positive sides to this?

- Kindle uses the razor-and-razorblade model, so it's not as if we make a lot of profit from Kindle sales anyway. Profits come from the digital purchases after the Kindle sale.
- More Kindle users increases word-of-mouth marketing and engagement between users.
- We can put a positive spin on this in terms of PR.
- Kindles probably trended on the Internet as a result. The extra PR buzz may have led to more Kindle sales.

I would also venture a guess that Amazon makes around 3-5-million-dollar profit a month, so by letting this sale go, we are losing a whole year of profit.

In the end, I think I would cancel this order. The loss is excessively high. The blowback will be severe, but it is just too much money at hand.

Apple iPhone LTV

Calculate the lifetime value of an Apple iPhone customer.

Things to Consider

Use the following lifetime value equation:

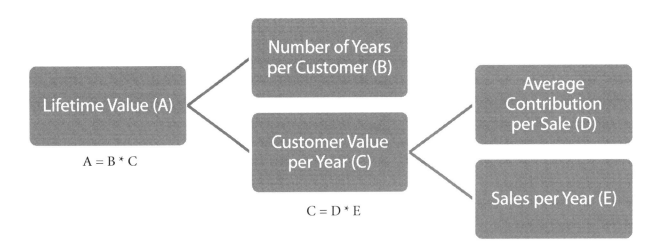

Common Mistakes

- Not knowing the customer lifetime value equation.
- Not factoring in both one-time and recurring revenue.
- Muddled, disorganized calculations.

Answer

Assumptions
- iPhone is replaced once every 3 years.
- The average iPhone costs $687.
- iPhone's gross margin is 69%.
- 75% of new users stay with the iPhone for their next purchase (aka customer retention rate).
- Average iPhone customer loyalty is 12 years.
- Typical iPhone user buys $5 of digital goods a month. This is primarily apps, but can also include books, music and movies.
- Apple's revenue share is 30% for the digital goods.

Calculations
LTV from phone sales

LTV = Contribution per Sale * Transactions per Year * Number of Years Customer

LTV = ($687 * 69%) * (Once every Three Years) * (12 Years)

LTV = $474.03 * 1/3 * 12 = $1,896.12

LTV from digital goods

LTV = Contribution per Sale * Transactions per Year * Number of Years Customer

LTV = ($5 * 30%) * (12 Transactions per Year) * (12 Years)

LTV = $1.50 * 12 * 12 = $216

Total LTV

Total LTV = Phone LTV + Digital Goods LTV = $1,896.12 + $216 = $2,112.12

Chapter 11 Product Design: Customer Journey Map Exercises

Expedia Journey

Develop the customer journey map for Expedia.

Things to Consider

5Es Framework

Common Mistakes

Not adapting frameworks into new situations, making the application of a framework feel forced.

Answer

Research and Planning	Shopping	Book	Pre-Travel	Travel	Post-Travel
• Talk to friends • Search the Internet • Browse destination photos	• Lookup airplane schedules • Lookup airplane prices • Try alternative air routings • Compare prices	• Buy online • Check if flight can be purchased with loyalty points	• Print ticket or load ticket onto mobile device	• Contact customer service for assistance	• Complain about experience on social media

AirBnB Journey

Develop the customer journey map for an AirBnB traveler.

Things to Consider

- Do most consumers book flights first or book hotels first?
- Do travelers book instantly or not?

Common Mistakes

- Forget about traditional alternatives like hotels

Answer

Entice	Enter	Engage	Exit	Extend
• Encourage traveler to go on a trip • Browse potential destinations • Plan trip • Purchase airplane tickets	• Browse AirBnB choices	• Compare AirBnB with alternatives • Ask AirBnB host questions • Purchase AirBnB travel • Depart for trip • Check-in at AirBnB room • Enjoy trip	• Post trip feedback survey	• Receive notifications to book future trips

Job Search Journey

Draw the journey map for an Indeed.com job seeker who just graduated from college.

Things to Consider

Use the 5Es framework

Common Mistakes

Accidentally drawing the journey map for an employer when the interviewer is asking for the candidate-side journey map.

Answer

Entice	Enter	Engage	Exit	Extend
• Graduated from school • Prepare resumes & cover letters	• Browse job postings on Indeed.com	• Fill out applications on Indeed.com	• Wait for interview invites • Do interview • Wait for results for the phone interview • Get invited to an in-person interview • Wait for results of the in-person interview • Get job offer • Accept or decline	• Resign from current job • (Optional) Take a vacation • (Optional) Prepare for relocation • (Optional) Get ready for new job

5 E'S:

ENTICE

ENTER

ENGAGE

EXIT

EXTEND

Online Course Journey

Develop the customer journey map for an online course.

Answer

Entice	Enter	Engage	Exit	Extend
• Hear about the event via marketing material • Make decision to attend	• Book class	• Introduce yourself to others • Listen to lectures • Do homework • Take quizzes and tests	• Post class survey	• Save and archive class slides, notes and materials • Keep in touch with classmates and teachers • Consider taking next course in the sequence

Home Improvement Journey

Develop the customer journey map for a home improvement project.

Answer

Entice	Enter	Engage	Exit	Extend
• Figure out what needs to be worked on.	• Identify a list of potential contractors.	• Get estimates and vet contractors. • Narrow down to a shortlist of potential contractors considering quality, cost, availability and completion date. • Select a contractor and make necessary deposits. • Kickoff project. • Monitor project. • (Optional) Make milestone payments. • Do a final walkthrough as project is completed. • Request necessary changes. • End project by completing final payment.	• Provide feedback or write a review. • Recommend to others.	• Receive a coupon for future work. • Ask client for a testimonial.

Customer Service Journey

Develop the customer journey map for a customer service encounter for a billing issue.

Answer

Entice	Enter	Engage	Exit	Extend
• Receive billing statement.	• Open & read billing statement.	• See a charge that's not familiar. • Call customer service. • Talk to customer service agent. • Get angry.	• End call. • Complain on Facebook and Twitter.	• Customer receives automated email asking customer to rate their customer service experience.

Chapter 12 Product Design: Pain Point Exercises

Child's 1st Birthday Party

Rant about organizing a child's 1st birthday party.

Answer

CANDIDATE:

1. Don't know whom to invite.
2. Have to invite parents who have to ask their kids.
3. Have to invite both parents and kids.
4. Don't know who is coming to the party so I can order the right amount of food.
5. Don't know where to hold the party.
6. Don't know what day and time to hold the party.
7. Children will probably cry at the party.
8. Have to think of parking with so many cars.
9. Have to make sure things, like clowns, arrive in time.
10. Have to make food both for the child and the adults. They don't eat or drink the same things.
11. Some attendees have food allergies.
12. It will be messy everywhere.
13. There will be children of all ages. For example, babies will require lots of diaper changes.
14. I will have to think of a gift for the child.
15. Parents will stay and chat about the child. It gets tiresome.
16. It is pointless to hold a party when the child is too young to remember it.
17. It is a lot of work to beg attendees to share photos from the event.

Best Handyman

Rant about finding the best home repairperson.

Answer

CANDIDATE:

1. Hard to find good reviews on home repair people.
2. Other reviewers have different tastes from mine.
3. They live in a different style of home than me. Is their review even applicable?
4. Have to call them to give them directions to my house, and they definitely will not find it.
5. They probably cannot find parking here.
6. Have to set up a time when I am home, and they are never available when I am out of work.
7. Can't do anything or feel comfortable while they are working. Will take a few hours.
8. Don't trust them in my house alone.
9. Don't trust them in another room even though I am in the house.
10. They walk around with shoes on. Sure, they clean my carpet after, but I don't want them to walk around with shoes on in the first place.
11. Have to offer a tip even if they do a bad job.
12. Will probably have to pay in cash. I don't have cash on me.
13. They may be charging me more because I don't know how much time it takes to complete tasks.
14. Have to clean my house a bit since they might judge me.
15. Maybe they think I am crazy with some of the stuff I have, and I have to hide them.
16. I don't like it when other people come in my house or my personal room.
17. Have to offer them water, which means I need to go buy plastic cups.
18. They are using my bathrooms. I don't like it when other people use my bathrooms.
19. They are doing work while I am away, and they don't pick up the phone or return my texts when I need to reach them.
20. They might waste time on-site, which will annoy me because I have urgent deadlines.
21. They don't do everything as promised in the contract.

Job Search Pain Points

Rant about searching for a job.

Answer

CANDIDATE:

1. Don't know how to make my resume better.
2. Don't have time to make my resume better.
3. Don't know the right layout to make my resume more effective.
4. Don't know how to write a resume to get past applicant tracking systems.
5. Can't seem to network effectively with hiring managers to get a job interview.
6. Don't know who to network with.
7. Can't seem to interview well.
8. Get tongue-twisted when given an interview question.
9. Don't know the status of my application.
10. Can't stand all the waiting and uncertainty of the job search process.
11. Discovering new jobs and applying is time consuming.

Finding Someone to Do Taxes

Rant about finding someone to help you prepare your taxes.

Answer

CANDIDATE:

1. Have to do taxes early; otherwise, I might not get it done in time.
2. Have to sit there and answer questions about what is this and what is that.
3. Knows all of my financial transactions. I like to keep my finances private.
4. Do not remember every income or expense that is tax-deductible or needs to be reported.
5. Do not trust them with my financial information.
6. Will try to sell me other services.
7. I will have a lot of questions. They will be impatient about answering them.
8. Making me do all the work even though I am paying them to do this.
9. Don't know if they'll even save as much as if I do it.
10. Will remember me and remind me to come again around the same time next year. What if I think they didn't do a good job? I'll have to think of some excuse to refuse them.
11. Costs a lot to get tax preparation help.

Chapter 13 Product Design: Brainstorm Exercises

Validating the Newsfeed

Imagine you are the Facebook newsfeed PM. In your research, you have found that users crave validation. That is, when Facebook users write a new post or perhaps share a photo or video, they want someone to click Facebook's "like" button. They feel empty when their friends do not "like" it.

Brainstorm at least 10 solutions that solve this problem.

Answer

CANDIDATE: Here are my ideas:

1. Put new posts at the top of friends' news feeds, increasing the likelihood the Facebook user will get likes
2. Create a marketplace where users can purchase likes
3. Feature that user's posts in a "content just like this" recommendation widget, increasing the likelihood the Facebook user will get likes.
4. Similar to the previous idea, create a "users who like that content, also likes this" feature that will increase potential likes.
5. Provide feedback on the user's posts, predicting the likelihood the post will get likes and offer concrete suggestions on how to improve their posts such as:
6. Use a more positive or negative tone
7. Use vivid language
8. Tap into reader's emotions
9. Minimize typos and grammatical mistakes
10. Create simulated Facebook users (aka bots) that like user's content when the content is worthy of a Facebook like
11. Using a facial recognition feature, have a Facebook bot user apply a like when there's a smile in the photo
12. Create a liking contest among friends. All contest participants can see posts and like the content. This will artificially create events to like Facebook content.
13. Create a search box that allows you to search for posts based on criteria.
14. Create a "show me a random post" feature. This self-explanatory feature increases the chance that someone will like a user's post.
15. Create a chart that tracks the most liked content for the entire system or subset. By highlighting posts, it increases the chance that others will like that user's posts.
16. Post stickers or badges on the user's content based on some criteria. For example, a post could get a flame icon if the post has a lot of views. This will generate extra attention, which will increase the likelihood of getting likes.
17. Automatically tag groups of people in photos. This will lead to more likes because the auto-tagged users will receive a notification, which increases the likelihood they will like the photo.

Internet Car

Google is thinking of creating an Internet-enabled car.

Brainstorm at least 10 interesting use cases.

Answer

CANDIDATE: Here are a couple of ideas:

1. Automatic payment for tolls based on your Google Wallet.
2. Google Maps GPS built in. GPS and tracking.
3. Roam as a mobile Wi-Fi hotspot.
4. Communicate with other Internet-enabled cars to avoid collisions.
5. Panic button to ask for help and send messages to selected contacts via email and Hangouts.
6. Livestream your journey on YouTube.
7. Built-in calling or video calling via Google Voice.
8. Compare gas prices via Google Shopping.
9. Stream music through Google Music and YouTube Music.
10. Stream audiobooks through Google and YouTube.
11. Surf the Internet using your voice.
12. Allow the car to sell itself when it gets obsolete.
13. Allow the car to rent itself out to other drivers when it is not in use.
14. If the car is self-driving, it could deliver food and packages on its own.
15. Google search anything.
16. Voice your schedules via Google Calendar.
17. Voice your ideas via Google Docs.
18. Monitor the environment as a CCTV solution, similar to the 1.85 million CCTV cameras monitoring the UK.

Voice-User Interface for Job Search

Apple's Siri and Amazon's Echo have made voice-user interfaces incredibly popular.

Brainstorm 10 solutions that solve the job search problem using voice-user interfaces.

Answer

CANDIDATE: Here are my ideas, five for candidate-side and five for employer-side, for a total of 10.

Candidate-Side

1. Fill out job applications by voice
2. Schedule interview appointments using voice
3. Browse new job openings by voice
4. Indicate job preferences using voice
5. Eliminate paper resumes and replace with a voice-based resume

Employer-side

6. Accept and reject resumes by voice
7. Delete resume review by voice
8. Request candidates by voice
9. Read a resume to the employer
10. Playback a recorded interview by voice

Mood API

Brainstorm some app ideas using a mood API.

A mood API is an API that has sensors that can learn about your mood.

Answer

CANDIDATE: I can think of a few app ideas and features:

1. Posts everyone's mood via a social network's news feed. Users can compare moods. Users can also receive alerts about others' moods.
2. Reveals the audience's mood at a conference or a meeting.
3. Shows happy pictures when your mood is sad or calming pictures when your mood is angry.
4. Plays music based on your mood.
5. Plays TV shows or movies based on your mood.
6. Shows you games that is appropriate for your mood.
7. Shows you things you can buy to counteract or enhance your mood.
8. Shows you places to go to counteract or enhance your mood.
9. Calls a therapist when you are feeling depressed.
10. Calls 911 when you are feeling scared or threatened.
11. Automatically connects someone depending on your mood. If you are happy, it connects you with someone who is sad to help him get happy.
12. Suppress or alert when you are attempting to a social media post when you are in an angry or otherwise negative mood
13. Highlight everyone's mood around you.
14. Calls your contact depending on your mood.
15. Monitor your moods in real-time to provide more self-awareness.

Relatable Review

Imagine you are the TripAdvisor reviews PM. Some users are unsure of whether they should believe reviews they read because they are concerned an author has different hotel preferences than they do. For example, one TripAdvisor review author may like luxury hotels, but the reader may like staying at hostels.

Brainstorm 10 solutions that solve this problem.

Answer

CANDIDATE: I have a few ideas:

1. Provide a number that represents how similar you and other users are.
2. Show the detail of the trip (budget, length, etc.) during a review.
3. Provide a summary page of all the hotels this reviewer has ever stayed in. If he usually prefers one type of hotel, then you would know.
4. Similar to the last idea, except you are showing it based on the hotel. Show the summary of all reviewers into one nice, simple summary page. You can then tell what kind of hotels people who reviewed this hotel typically like.
5. A filter where you can sort people who specifically tend to stay in similar hotels vs. people who like other types of hotels.
6. Show reviews from users who tend to stay in hotels you've liked before.
7. Filter a reviewer's helpful votes based on voters' preference of hotels.
8. Show alternative (and outstanding) hotels in the area and compare them with this hotel. You can filter them by type of hotels. You can see how your preferred type of hotels are doing compared to this one.
9. Allow a filter where they are only seeing reviews with pictures. This way it provides more information on a review and the user can judge it for themselves.
10. Compare all nearby hotels in the area, and show a nice summary of average rating and top reviews based on hotel types. Now the user has an easier time choosing.

Image Search for Recruiting

Smartphone cameras have made it easier to search by image.

Brainstorm 10 solutions that use image search when recruiting.

Answer

CANDIDATE: Here are my ideas:

1. Identify similar candidates by selecting from a picture of known talent.
2. Identify similar candidates by selecting 10-second video snippets of candidates a recruiter likes.
3. Identify candidates by selecting logos of desired skills.
4. Identify candidates by selecting logos of desired former companies.
5. Identify candidates by selecting logos of desired universities where candidates graduated.
6. Shortlist candidates based on candidates that show good body language during the video interview.
7. Take a picture of a meeting in a conference room, provide data on which candidates are desirable, similar to Yelp's augmented reality feature, Yelp Monocle.
8. Take a picture of a conference; provide data on which attendees are desirable recruiting targets.
9. Take a picture of employees in a competitor's parking lot and identify desirable candidates.
10. Take a picture of someone's portfolio such as a developer's GitHub account or a designer's Dribbble account and recommend other candidates who have similar work quality.

Restaurant Hours

We want to get the hours restaurants are open and closed.

Brainstorm 10 creative ways to make this happen.

Answer

CANDIDATE: I have a few ideas:

1. Have the users fill it in.
2. Have the restaurant owners fill it in.
3. Determine closing hours based on satellite images to see if there are lights still on in the restaurant.
4. Determine closing hours based on satellite images to see if there are any cars still in the restaurant parking lots.
5. Google street view cars can drive around that time and see.
6. Crawl Yelp for opening and closing hour data.
7. Crawl restaurant websites to find opening and closing hour data.
8. Check third party websites like Eat24 for opening and closing times.
9. Create a software program that automatically dials the business and requests the data.
10. Determine hours based on check-in data from FourSquare, Facebook or some other check-in service.
11. Determine hours based on Android or iOS GPS data near the restaurant.
12. Hire people to take photos of hours open and closed signs at the restaurant and upload.
13. Scan publicly available photos such as Google StreetView and Instagram for open hours.

Better Phone Batteries

If scientists said that phone batteries could not get any better, what would you do to make a better phone battery?

Answer

CANDIDATE: I have a few ideas related to improved phone battery technology:

1. Bigger batteries.
2. Reduce size for phone components to allow a bigger space for batteries.
3. Add solar panels to the phone, which can charge the battery.
4. Charge the battery based on kinetic movement.
5. Charge the battery based on warmth.
6. Wireless charging.
7. Swappable batteries.
8. Make it lightweight.
9. Use other types of batteries, like nuclear.

I also have some ideas related to using existing phone battery technology more effectively:

10. Use software that manages power consumption more effectively. For example, the phone could go into low-power mode when the user shouldn't be using the phone such as watching a movie in a movie theater or driving a car.
11. Create chargers that power batteries faster.
12. Create a product that allows a user to charge disposable phone batteries, just like an Energizer AA battery.
13. A service that allows you to clone another phone, so that when one phone's battery runs out you can pick up where you left off with the backup phone, thanks to the cloning software.

Traffic Cones

What is a traffic cone good for other than regular traffic control?

Answer

CANDIDATE: I have a few ideas:

1. Nice hat for one.
2. Good for decorations.
3. Tape the bottom and use them as holders.
4. Use as a goal for throwing tennis balls.
5. Making a pyramid.
6. Stack enough of them and you can use them as support columns.
7. Tear them apart and use them as floor mats.
8. Use them as stable bowling pins.
9. Use them to make a course. You can use them to help student drivers practice, or you can use it as a racing course.
10. Use it to amplify sound.
11. Use them as fountains.

Chapter 14 Product Design: Putting it Together

People You May Know

What is the best decision tree for Facebook or LinkedIn's "People You May Know" feature?

Things to Consider

- What are real-life signals for identifying friends?
- What data does Facebook have available?
- Did you come up with clever ways to suggest friends to Facebook users?

Common Mistakes

- Answering too casually.
- Not drawing the solution on a whiteboard.
- Using all seven steps of the CIRCLES Method especially when it is clear that this is strictly about implementation.

Answer

CANDIDATE: Hmm, I can't think of a tree right off the top of my head. I would like to do a brainstorm exercise first to think of all the things we can read that may be able to find a new friend for a user.

INTERVIEWER: Go ahead.

CANDIDATE: So let me assume A is the user, B is the possible new friend, and C is a mutual friend of A and B:

- Does A and B have a mutual friend C?
- Does B have the same interests as A? We want to prioritize this based on how well liked these interests are by A and B. We can rank these based on related pages or posts.
- Does B attend the same events as A?
- Does B like the same pages as A?
- Does B attend the same school as A?
- Does B work in the same place as A?
- Does B already know A via email or other contacts (e.g. LinkedIn)?
- Does B have the same major as A?
- Does B live close to A?
- Has B ever lived anywhere that A has?

I think this is a good base to work off.

INTERVIEWER: Could you organize this into a tree?

CANDIDATE: Sure:

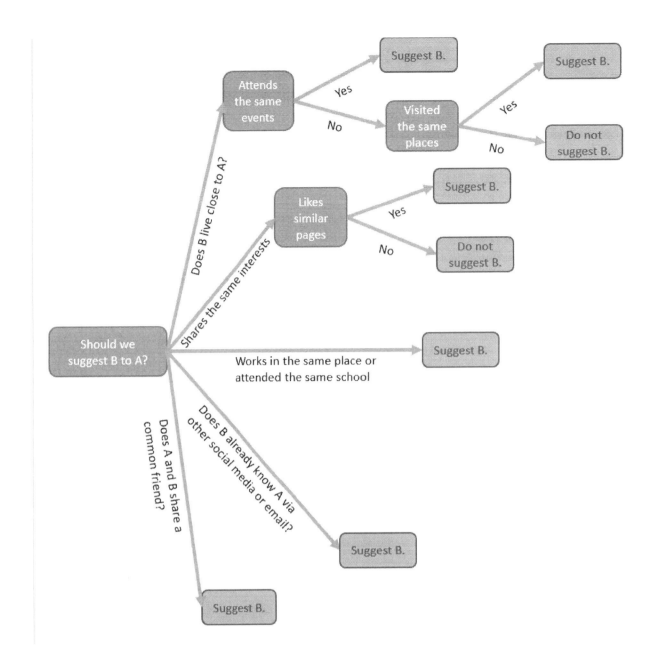

INTERVIEWER: I feel like there is some stuff missing from your tree. What if A and B went to the same school but don't know each other? I mean, there are many people who attended to the same school. How would you know which one to suggest first?

CANDIDATE: You bring up a good point. I was thinking of that as I did this. I don't think a tree is a good idea for this system. If it were up to me, I would do a point value system, where every checkbox, such as "does A and B attend the same school" would award certain points. Then we suggest people who meet a minimum amount of points, and suggest people who have the highest points first.

INTERVIEWER: Okay. Which do you think are worth the most points?

CANDIDATE: Knowing a common friend, knowing through other social media or email, and liking the same pages.

Design In-Game Store Menus

Pitch designs for in-game store menu.

Things to Consider

- This question tests a candidate's UI wire framing skills.
- It is better to have multiple recommendations to increase a candidate's chances of having a winning design. It also protects the respondent from being defensive about their only solution.

Common Mistakes

- Fear of wire framing.
- Having detailed and visually stunning designs but not having insightful commentary that explains critical design choices.
- Drawing out UI interfaces that are unconventional. For instance, a photo capture mobile UI with the capture button on the top, not bottom.

Answer

CANDIDATE: Can I get some time to brainstorm?

Candidate takes one minute.

CANDIDATE: I have three ideas in mind:

Candidate draws the following on the whiteboard.

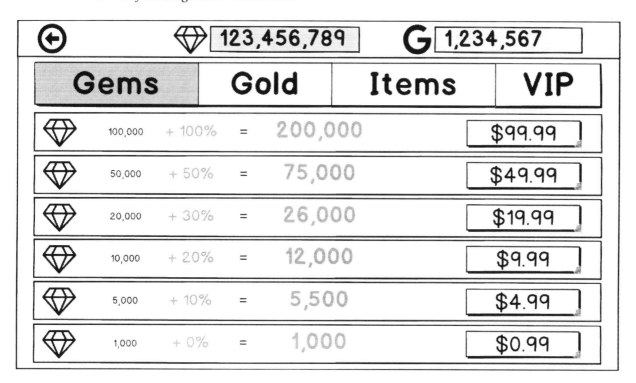

CANDIDATE: This idea puts all purchases in one screen. The focus is on the bonus percentage and the final currency. Since spending money to buy hard currency is the most important, it's on the first tab. Another currency is in the second tab. Items you can buy are on the third tab. VIP, being a huge factor in most games, will also show up as one of the tabs.

The purchases rank from highest to lowest to encourage players to buy the highest amount. The player's currency totals for gems and gold are shown at the top. When the user purchases more gems or gold, the user gets the satisfaction of seeing their totals go up.

In the upper left, there is a back button. I intentionally omitted a close 'X' button on the right; the reasoning is that I wanted to avoid unintended clicks, especially on a critical monetization page.

CANDIDATE: The second design option is vertical instead of horizontal. The design is familiar, but there are two differences.

First, I can't fit all 6 purchases here, so the screen will be scrollable. I also added space for scrolling, animated ads. Ads are annoying, but monetization is critical, even with free users.

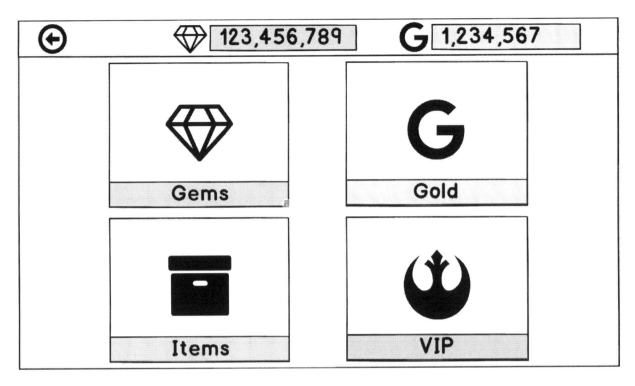

CANDIDATE: The Metro design style inspired the third and final design option. We start with four big buttons: gems, gold, items, and VIP; they correspond to the same categories as the two previous designs. After pressing an option, you'll see the items listed in this manner:

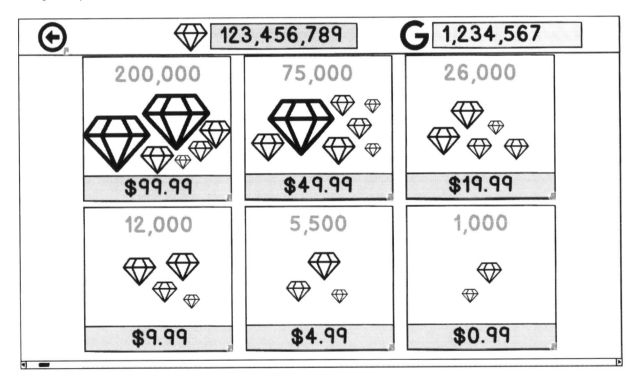

This design is more visually pleasing. However, the drawback is that is requires an additional click from the user.

One more thing I wanted to call out with this design: the button background color is consistent with the currency: green for gems (shown) and yellow for gold. This will help players more quickly recognize the purchase they are considering.

Amazon Home & Lighting

Let us assume you are on the Home and Lighting team, how would you go about improving our category page?

Things to Consider

- Use the CIRCLES Method
- Give memorable names to your feature and product ideas.
- If you are not familiar with Amazon's Home and Lighting category page, either ask the interviewer or share your best guess before proceeding. It puts you and the interviewer on the same page. It also gives the interviewer a chance to correct any misunderstandings.

Common Mistakes

- Not thinking creatively or big enough.
- Answering too casually. The interviewer is looking for a detailed and thoughtful response.
- Spending too much time asking for context. It comes across as not wanting to answer the question.

Answer

CANDIDATE: Could I ask some clarifying questions?

INTERVIEWER: Sure.

CANDIDATE: Are there specific metrics we are targeting? Maybe engagement or retention? Revenue?

INTERVIEWER: What would you recommend?

CANDIDATE: I would target revenue. Anything that boosts direct revenue should be something we pursue.

INTERVIEWER: Okay. What's next?

CANDIDATE: Give me time to brainstorm some ideas.

Candidate takes some time.

CANDIDATE: I have a few solutions in mind.

Candidate writes the following ideas on the whiteboard.

- *Recommendations*
- *Virtual Setup*
- *Try and See*

The Recommendations feature shows what types of lighting is good for your home. For example, if you were purchasing a particular light, the page would show you other lighting recommendations that complement your choice. It's similar to Amazon's "Other people also purchased this" except this would be more geared toward visual matching.

Try and See is a unique feature just for this category. Customers can buy these lights and try them on for a few days. If they don't like it, they can ship back the products to us and purchase something else for free. Again, as I mentioned above, people want to know if the lights look good in their home. If we can give them a guarantee that they can return and choose something else if it doesn't fit, it would most likely make the purchase easier.

The Virtual Setup feature allows you to visualize what lights would look like in your home or office. When using this feature, the user would create a virtual room model by uploading a 3-D model of a room, using a specially designed Amazon camera. Then the user can try different lights. We may even allow the user to adjust the windows in the room, the color of the wall and furniture, and the natural lighting and shadows, based on the time of day. I'm excited about this feature because people want to see how lighting pairs with their current home; compared to buying, trying, and returning a product, this saves the user time and hassle while saving us the cost of processing returns.

Notice how I am focusing on helping the users decide and pick based on what looks good. Amazon has a natural disadvantage here compared to stores like Home Depot. I can go to Home Depot and look at what my light actually looks like. As an Internet retailer, Amazon has a harder time depicting this. All of my solutions alleviate or fix this problem.

INTERVIEWER: Your solutions are thoughtful. If you could only pick one, which one would you recommend?

CANDIDATE: I would probably pick Recommendations. It's the easiest and least costly to do.

Virtual Setup is the best solution. However, it would require a lot of engineering effort; it would also require assistance from our manufacturers and vendors. Virtual Setup will be far from self-explanatory; it would require significant on boarding and support resources.

Try and See is a nice alternative, but shipping could be costly down the road. I could also see some users abusing it to try on lights and then purchasing them at a local store.

INTERVIEWER: Okay, now that we've figured out what to do, how do you convince engineering managers to support your idea? Keep in mind engineers are a limited resource at Amazon.

CANDIDATE: I would first:

- Put together my argument
    - Research supporting data points
    - Document this in a short proposal

One data point would be, "How many users return purchased lights because they did not look right?" I would cross-reference this data with "How many lights in average do customers consider before making a purchase?" This would reveal choosy customers that frequently return lights because the lights do not match. I would also check whether these customers purchase lights even after a return. If they do not, then they may have lost faith with Amazon's purchasing experience.

I would then poke around to see how much revenue stores like Home Depot and Lowe's make on an annual basis and compare that with Amazon. I have an inkling that it would be a lot more. I would try to convince engineering managers that this is lost revenue because we don't offer nearly the same experience as local stores do. If we replicated these experiences by implementing the Recommendations feature, we could gain a bigger piece of the pie.

Adding to Amazon Prime

We are considering adding a new feature to Amazon Prime, while continuing to price it at $99/year. What should the additional feature be?

Also, include a light analysis of the feature you have chosen. For instance, estimate the revenues from additional subscriptions and costs that would come along with the additional feature; give justification for your assumptions.

Things to Consider

- Start by exploring needs for existing and / or prospective Amazon Prime customers.
- Brainstorm several ideas, not just one.
- Justify your reasoning.

Common Mistakes

- Believing that Amazon Prime is perfect, as-is.
- Not wanting to suggest new ideas and fearing that they will be perceived as dumb.
- Afraid of doing the calculations and talking about benefits from a qualitative, not quantitative, perspective.

Answer

CANDIDATE: Can I get some time to brainstorm this?

Candidate takes a minute.

CANDIDATE: First, I would like to understand why users purchase Amazon Prime. Here are a few reasons I can think of:

Candidate writes the following on whiteboard.

- *They enjoy getting items quickly. Paying an attractively priced flat-fee for two-day shipping on all products feels like a good value.*
- *They like watching the included Amazon Prime videos, music and books.*

From here, we can design our new features. The point of adding new features is to acquire new Amazon Prime members and generate more revenue.

I propose these three ideas:

- **Better Selection of Kindle Books for Amazon Prime customers.** Amazon Prime offers its user the Kindle Owners' Lending Library. However, reviews indicate that the selection is dismal. I'd recommend that Amazon expand its selection. Amazon started as a bookstore; many of its loyal customers are avid readers. A better selection may attract new Prime users. Getting some exclusive books or magazines would be great.

- **Purchasing Points.** Add gamification to the system. That is, any Prime users that purchased enough items in the current quarter would get next quarter's Prime membership for free. The idea is to keep the Prime users spending. If the spend requirements drove sufficient incremental revenue, this benefit could pay for itself.
- **Exclusives.** I like how Amazon allows Prime customers to pre-order games, a benefit non-Prime customers do not have. I recommend that we expand these benefits further, which I will call Exclusives. Sometimes, Exclusives will allow Prime members to purchase new products early. Other times, Prime members will get exclusive discounts instead. We might be able to get vendors to subsidize the cost, who may consider this an opportunity to get more awareness for their products. Who wouldn't want to be on the front of the Prime Exclusives page?

INTERVIEWER: Hmm, interesting. Which feature would you recommend?

CANDIDATE: I recommend Exclusives. This doesn't require a lot of technical effort on our part. However, it will require work from our business team. Creating the Exclusives program and Prime Exclusives pages is knowledge we have internally; I'd recommend leveraging knowledge from the Amazon App Store team. And as I mentioned earlier, vendor partnerships might lead to unique exclusives as well discount subsidies.

INTERVIEWER: How much additional revenue do you think this will make? And what will it cost?

CANDIDATE: Are we talking about annually?

INTERVIEWER: Yes, annually.

CANDIDATE: Okay, can you give me some time to brainstorm?

Candidate takes a minute.

CANDIDATE: For revenue, I feel like there are two parts:

- **Incremental signups**. How many more people will sign up for Amazon Prime?
- **Incremental revenue**. How many more sales would we get from featuring products?

For cost, I believe there's just one part:

- **Discount subsidies**. How much does it cost? This number could change if we can get manufactures to subsidize.

Let's calculate incremental signups and the corresponding revenue first:

I feel 3% of Amazon customers would be compelled to sign up for the program. My reasoning is 2% of my friends are coupon clippers, but my friends have higher income than the average person does. So let's adjust the 2% upward to 3%.

From there, let's assume that the Amazon Prime annual membership is $100 to make the math easy. Last time I checked, Amazon Prime had about 50 million users. Jumping into the calculations:

$$New\ Prime\ Membership\ Revenue = Current\ Members * Incremental\ Signups * Prime\ Price$$

$$New\ Prime\ Membership\ Revenue = 50\ million * 3\% * \$100$$

$$New\ Prime\ Membership\ Revenue = 50\ million * \$3$$

$$New\ Prime\ Membership\ Revenue = \$150\ million$$

CANDIDATE: Next, let's calculate incremental revenue:

I have read that Amazon Prime users purchase about $1,100 worth of products each year. I'm guessing that Prime users purchase often to maximize their shipping benefits, so if I were to guess, they make roughly two purchase transactions per month as a Prime user. If I do some quick math:

$$Amazon\ Prime\ Customer\ Annual\ Spend = \$1,100$$

$$Purchases\ per\ year = 12\ months\ per\ year * 2\ purchases\ per\ month = 24$$

$$Prime\ Customer\ Monthly\ Spend = \frac{\$1,100\ annual\ spend}{24\ transactions\ per\ year} = \$45.83 \cong \$50$$

Therefore, the average transaction would be around $50.

Next, "What are the incremental sales from featuring products?" As a proxy, I'm thinking of the featured app feature on Google Play or Apple's App Store. Let's assume these two app stores a similar DAU as Prime every day. I know from anecdotal experience that getting something to feature on the App Store would get you about 50K organic installs a day; Google Play would be around 100K installs, so the total number of new installs each day would be 150K. The conversion would be a lot less in Amazon Prime since it's a purchase not a free install. So let's call the conversion 70% of what we'd expect across those two platforms. So let's say the new purchases is 150K * 70% = 105K.

Let's say the average Amazon item costs $50, and we're going to do a 20% discount on the feature products, making it $40. Jumping into the calculations:

$$New\ Purchasing\ Revenue = New\ Purchases * Item\ Price * Days\ in\ a\ Year$$

$$New\ Purchasing\ Revenue = 105,000 * \$40 * 365$$

$$New\ Purchasing\ Revenue \sim 1.5\ billion$$

CANDIDATE: Finally, we want to calculate the initial cost of subsidizing the items. We can the numbers we used in the previous formula. I would say this would probably only last 3 months before we can get manufacturers and vendors on board and have them subsidize their own products. We can calculate this with the following formula:

$$Subsidy\ Cost = New\ Buyers * Item\ Price * Days\ in\ 3\ Months$$

$$Subsidy\ Cost = 105,000 * \$40 * 90$$

$$Subsidy\ Cost = \$378\ million$$

CANDIDATE: Please keep in mind that this is potential cost. Meaning we are making less profit when people buy things. I know Amazon has a low profit margin, but it should definitely be higher than 20%, which is the price cut we made, so I don't think there is actually any cost.

Now we can talk about the cost of shipping the items. We can also use numbers from the earlier formula. First, let's think about the average shipping cost. Two-day shipping should be around $12.

$$Additional\ Shipping\ Cost = New\ Buyers * Shipping\ Cost * Days\ in\ a\ Year$$

$$Additional\ Shipping\ Cost = 105,000 * \$12 * 365$$

$$Additional\ Shipping\ Cost = \$459.9\ million$$

CANDIDATE: To conclude, the additional revenue would be 1.5 billion, and the cost will be around 837.9 million.

Recommendation Algorithm for Amazon Instant Video

Amazon Instant Video wants to come up with a recommendation algorithm. Pretend the product does not already have one.

1. What are the considerations and data points that go into it?
2. Broadly, how would you go about implementing it?
3. What data points would you use to evaluate success?

Things to Consider

- Part 1 is asking for the features or variables that would predict whether a recommended video would be suitable.
- Part 2 is about execution. Do you know what to do launch the feature?
- Part 3 is about identifying relevant success metrics.

Common Mistakes

- Incorrectly focusing on the UX, not algorithm, design.
- Proposing a rule-based, not artificial intelligence-based (aka neural network) system.
- Not brainstorming enough features (aka prediction variables) for the AI-based system.

Answer

CANDIDATE: Can I take some time to brainstorm?

Candidate takes one minute.

CANDIDATE: I can think of four things that we want to consider when doing this.

- **Similar Genre**. If someone is really into *Game of Thrones*, we want to show videos that are fantasy and/or intended for the more mature audience. It makes sense they would like something similar.
- **Similar Length.** If someone loves watching TV series with 30-minute episodes, they probably want to see more of the same. Showing them a movie or a TV series with 60-minute episodes would not do as well.
- **What Others Are Watching.** Similar to "People who purchased this also purchased" feature on Amazon. If you watched *Game of Thrones*, you probably would like similar shows that other *Game of Thrones* fans watch.
- **Demography.** Therefore, if someone is a stay-at-home mom, we want to recommend them videos that other stay-at-home moms watch. This is especially important when you throw kids into the mix. We want to make sure our suggestions are kid-friendly depending on the user.

INTERVIEWER: How would you go about implementing this?

CANDIDATE: Well, to start, I would actually validate my theory first by pulling up some data. Once that is verified, I would work on specific user segments first. It's probably easier to start with just movies because they are short-term. Movie watchers would be more inclined to watch another movie vs. TV watchers who just finished a series jumping on to another series. I would pick a genre that has numerous films, say, comedy, and try this first. I would slowly add other genres and video types once this has shown success and continue to tweak my algorithm based on user data.

INTERVIEWER: What data points would you use to evaluate its success?

CANDIDATE: An obvious one to check would be how many people are actually jumping on to watch the recommended videos through clicking the recommendations. I would also check to see if we are seeing data that are more similar across users now since we are suggesting based on what other users are watching. Finally, I would also look at if users were watching recommended videos vs. unrelated videos.

Changing Amazon Prime

What factors would you consider in making changes to Amazon Prime?

Things to Consider

- Think broadly about the Amazon Prime's definition. It is not just free two-day shipping or videos. It is a membership club, with the purpose of driving customer loyalty.
- Consider other membership clubs such as Costco.

Common Mistakes

- Erroneously focusing on a secondary metric such as increasing share of wallet of existing customers when Amazon's true goal is to increase Prime signups.
- Thinking small by suggesting underwhelming adjacent features. For example, triggered by Amazon's video offering, many candidates suggest that Prime should offer free Audible books.

Answer

CANDIDATE: This is an interesting question. Here are the factors I would be considering:

- Prices for Amazon of the free super saver shipping.
- Prices for Amazon of the two-day shipping.
- Number of users using Prime.
- Number of users not using Prime.
- Number of packages Prime users buy vs. non-Prime users. This determines shipping cost for us.
- Average spending per package for Prime users vs. non-Prime users.
- Prime vs. non-Prime users purchase frequency per month. This helps us calculate yearly revenue.
- Average profit margin per purchase for Prime users vs. non-Prime users.
- Current annual fee for Amazon Prime.
- Typical purchases for Prime vs. non-Prime users.
- Any other perks for Prime.

Once I know these, I can understand how the pricing structure works and exactly how much profit we are making. I'll also know the breakdown of the non-Prime users vs. Prime users. I'll also know what both sets of users buy. Here are a few things I would do:

- If we can make more by changing the price, we should probably do it.
- If we can add Prime features or rewards for certain users (e.g., let say games are a huge part of non-Prime users), we can try that to see if we can get more Prime users from that sector.
- If free super saver shipping is costing us too much money, we can see if we can up the requirement for that.

INTERVIEWER: That's a thorough way of looking at it. Do you think there are any benefits to Prime besides additional revenue?

CANDIDATE: Of course, there are a few:

- People tend to buy more because they think they'll lose money if they don't. This has retention and engagement benefits as well.
- People feel a sense of exclusivity with Prime.
- People talk to other people about Prime, increasing our word-of-mouth marketing.

Improving Facebook Login

What would you do to improve the Facebook login?

Things to Consider

- What are some of the flaws of the Facebook login?
- What is the purpose of the Facebook login feature?

Common Mistakes

- Assuming there is no room for improvement for Facebook login.
- Suggesting half-hearted ideas like make the button more visible or colorful.

Answer

CANDIDATE: Do you mean in terms of user experience?

INTERVIEWER: It's up to you.

CANDIDATE: Do you mean mobile or browser? I am assuming you mean logging onto the Facebook and not using Facebook account to login somewhere else.

INTERVIEWER: Yes, I do mean the Facebook website and app. Why don't we try mobile?

CANDIDATE: Okay. I would say there is really only one thing we are trying to improve here: activation. Once a user has already downloaded the app, we already got the acquisition. We are also really improving just one stage here: activation. Now there are two scenarios:

- **User does not have a Facebook account**. We need to work on the sign up process.
- **User does have a Facebook account**. He just needs to log in for the first time on his phone. He'll never log in again unless he logs out, and most people probably won't do that.

I am going to work on both of these separately. Let's start on the use case where they already have a Facebook account. This one is pretty well thought out already, but it's missing an essential function. In most cases, a user's browser on his phone will be synced to his browser on the computer. Why don't we let the user be able to log in through the browser the first time for authentication purposes? This way they don't even need to input a password. They can just log in with just one click.

Now, for the new user, I have a few ideas:

- **Sign Up Using Apple or Google ID**. Let the user sign in with these. Now, I don't mean we tie Facebook to them, I mean we use your email on these accounts to sign up Facebook for you. This saves you the trouble of typing in your email address. You still need to input your password though. Please note that I am not saying we are tying your Facebook account to these accounts.
- **Auto Fill Information**, including your real name, birthday and gender. This information is probably tied to your phone. Getting permission will be a challenge; I'm not sure if Apple and Google would be comfortable with apps getting this info. If they do, it would make the process faster and easier.

- **Existing Account**. I noticed Facebook doesn't check if your account already exists until the last step. This is actually frustrating, because you just wasted a minute. It should check as soon as the user enters an email.

INTERVIEWER: Which one would you recommend?

CANDIDATE: I think all of them are good, but the existing account one is the "lowest hanging fruit" so to speak. It's easy to do technically. The other two may have a lot of problems just figuring out if they are doable.

INTERVIEWER: It's interesting you specifically mentioned not tying the Facebook account to Apple ID or Google ID. Why are you so adamantly against it? Plenty of websites allow Facebook or Google log in. Wouldn't offering the same service make it more convenient for the user?

CANDIDATE: See, the strength of Facebook is the user base, among other things. We have the most users out of pretty much every other service. Apps and websites want to use Facebook login to make it easier for other people. We don't need to do that, because we have enough incentives for new users to join. In addition, Google and Apple are competitors. If we allow this, we are giving up our advantage. Moreover, even if we agree to this, they'll never let Facebook be a way to login on their website, so no, I don't think we should offer the same service.

Instagram UX

Instagram currently supports 3 to 15 second videos. We are considering supporting videos of unlimited length. How would you modify the UX to accommodate this?

Things to Consider

- Ponder how user behavior changes when interacting with a 3-second vs. a 15-second video. 12 seconds does not feel like much, but user needs can change dramatically.

Common Mistakes

- Freezing up
- Unstructured, stream-of-consciousness discussion.
- Assuming user engagement is identical for 3 and 15 second videos.

Answer

CANDIDATE: Are we considering the web or mobile interface?

INTERVIEWER: Let's go with the web interface.

CANDIDATE: My understanding is that Instagram videos doesn't currently have video controls. You can only play or pause with a tap of the finger like this:

Candidate draws on the whiteboard.

Screenshot / @kimkardashian, processed by pho.to

INTERVIEWER: That's correct.

CANDIDATE: When I think of user needs, here's some new information and controls that the user would need:

Information

- Length
- Popularity, including likes and comments
- Time remaining

Controls

- Play and pause, as before
- Fast forward and rewind

As far as I know, Instagram doesn't give viewers the option to choose different video playing resolutions, like YouTube. Therefore, that's a control we don't have to worry about. I believe simplicity is the best UX.

INTERVIEWER: Agreed. Your recommendations seem reasonable. Can you draw what the UX looks like on the whiteboard?

CANDIDATE: You mean now?

INTERVIEWER: Yes.

CANDIDATE: Okay, I'll give it a shot.

Candidate draws on the whiteboard.

CANDIDATE: The bottom right screenshot depicts the neutral state. It gives the user an indication of how long the clip is, along with its popularity.

The bottom left shows what happens the mouse cursor hovers over the image. A play control appears in the dominant center position, making it clear that's the desired call-to-action.

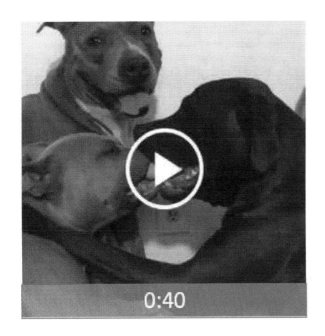 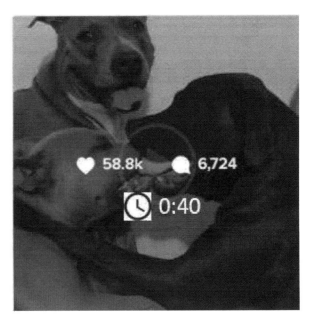

Screenshot / *PM Interview Questions* and Instagram

The following rendering shows what the UX looks like when it's playing but paused.

Screenshot / *PM Interview Questions* and Instagram

Finally, this last diagram shows what the UX looks like when the video is playing.

You can see I wanted to keep the control familiar without adding excessive functionality. By reducing barriers, I feel we will maximize engagement.

INTERVIEWER: That's a good tradeoff. Thanks for the whiteboard renderings.

Bing's Salesperson Use Case

A Bing.com salesperson has a 30-minute sales meeting with a prospective client. Build a feature that will help this salesperson be prepared for the meeting.

Things to Consider

- Use the CIRCLES Method.
- Empathize deeply with the salesperson's pain points.

Common Mistakes

- Not factoring in the 30-minute constraint.
- Automatically assuming that this is about improving Bing.com vs. just helping the salesperson in general, perhaps outside of building a Bing.com feature.

Answer

CANDIDATE: Just to clarify, you mean we are developing a feature for Bing that will prepare a salesperson for a pitch with a general manager in 30 minutes, is that correct?

INTERVIEWER: Yes.

CANDIDATE: Okay. Do we have any restrictions?

INTERVIEWER: Well, engineers are swamped at Bing, so it can't be something that'll take a very long time or incur a lot of cost. You'll also need to convince the managers that your ideas are worth their time.

CANDIDATE: Okay, can I brainstorm for a bit?

Candidate takes one minute.

CANDIDATE: I have a few solutions in my mind:

- **Company Business Model**. A search will bring up what the company's business model is. It'll talk in-depth about how the company makes money, what kind of growth it has seen, and other specific information.
- **Employee History**. A search will bring up all of the employees' history (past jobs and all that). This will give a broad overview of the company culture and view point, and the salesperson can specifically focus on the general manager.
- **Investor History**. A search will bring up investment information. This way, the salesperson can know what investors have funded the company, what kind of industry they are in and how to appeal to the business.

All of these are centered on information. The more the salesperson learns of the company, the higher his success. We want to know what makes this company or this general manager click. If we can bring value to what they hold dear, and do so at their perspective, it's easier to win over a deal. Since we only have 30 minutes, it's unrealistic to present a lot of information, so I've thought of three ideas that we can approach.

Personally, I like the employee history quite a bit.

INTERVIEWER: Oh? Why is that?

CANDIDATE: I feel like getting at the heart of what the company believes in will resonate more will the general manager than what the company sells and what investors do.

INTERVIEWER: Can you dive deeper into this idea?

CANDIDATE: Sure. I am thinking of placing the employees on a hierarchical structure. This way, the salesperson knows who is in charge of what, and especially who has the final say in the deal. This may not be the general manager. You can tell a lot from a company based on its hierarchical structure. If the upper management isn't that abundant, you know the company probably has everyone taking a lot of responsibility.

The salesperson will also see the history of all the employees. For example, if numerous employees came from startups, you know the company probably encourages wearing many hats, and the culture is a bit on the casual side and less on the business side. You'll also know they pride themselves on innovation, and they are looking for increase their revenue or market, more so than public companies, because they are looking for their next round of funding.

Finally, it's important to know about the history of the person, in this case the general manager, you are proposing the deal to. Their past work experience tells a lot about their ethics, views on the company culture, and what they find valuable.

Slack App Builder

Slack started an $80 million investment fund for app builders. What app would you build and why?

Things to Consider

- Think about what people are trying to achieve inside Slack.
- It's not just about the process. Creative ideas count. So brainstorm big ideas.
- Use frameworks such as SCAMPER to facilitate brainstorming.

Common Mistakes

- Focusing too much on what to build (e.g. build a bot) without describing why it needs to be built.
- Suggesting ideas that a candidate doesn't know is in the application already such as custom emoji.

Answer

CANDIDATE: Let's see think about Slack's untapped markets. This could be an underserved geography or customer segment. I would like to focus on an underserved geography.

INTERVIEWER: Okay.

CANDIDATE: I am thinking of markets in Asia, such as China, Japan, and Korea. I want to focus on China, since it's a market I know best, and it is possibly the largest market of the three, especially in terms of population.

INTERVIEWER: Go ahead.

CANDIDATE: Let's first think about Slack. Slack is a communication tool for work, and there are integrations with instant messenger apps like Google Hangouts. The business growth spawned from individual customers really liking it, and then because of their word of mouth, it spread to businesses. So I am thinking of doing the same thing.

China mostly uses QQ on the desktop and WeChat on mobile. They also use these tools for work. Since WeChat is mostly mobile, QQ becomes the de facto tool. The problem is that QQ is also used for personal purposes as well, so if we decide to approach the same way, we'll have to fight QQ.

I am actually thinking of avoiding a head-on collision, and target the business market straight away. Chinese companies don't use the management tools we are adjusted to here, so we'll have to integrate with Chinese specific tools to appeal to the market. I am thinking of doing an app like this. Specifically, I am thinking of doing something similar to Balsamiq. I know a lot of PMs use Photoshop or PowerPoint to draw wireframes, and they are definitely not as good at that task as Balsamiq.

INTERVIEWER: Why should Slack not just integrate with QQ and WeChat?

CANDIDATE: Because Tencent, the company who owns both, would never allow it. Uber tried doing the same thing and Tencent has banned them from using WeChat Pay. It's only natural Slack would not be able to do the same as well.

INTERVIEWER: What's stopping an existing management tool, like Balsamiq, from going to China themselves?

CANDIDATE: Because China uses different tools than the West, it's unlikely Balsamiq will find much success. Also, it's hard to appeal to a market that is so different than the West without acculturation. The companies that are slotted for success will have to be based in China and have Chinese-minded PMs to bring about a successful product.

INTERVIEWER: How do you guarantee that your app will work?

CANDIDATE: It's an untapped market right now. It's true that most Chinese companies have gotten along fine without such a tool, but when a better tool comes along, they'll certainly reconsider. Of course, I cannot say it will work 100%, but it is an opportunity.

Geographical Tweet

You are a PM for Twitter. You are launching a feature that tracks the geographical position of every tweet. Go!

Things to Consider

- Be prepared for follow-up questions revolving around privacy issues.
- A/B testing can help resolve uncertainty around whether to launch a feature, especially if the feature involves sensitive issues, like privacy.

Common Mistakes

- Not attempting the question after declaring the question does not make sense.
- Insulting the interviewer after declaring the question does not make sense.

Answer

CANDIDATE: I am not exactly clear on this question. Do you want me to implement this feature? Or do you want me to find creative ways to use this feature?

INTERVIEWER: How would you launch this feature? Tell me the entire process.

CANDIDATE: Okay. This is a sensitive issue. Sure, it is a feature that several services already have, like Facebook. However, it is also a privacy issue. We need to make sure it is something the users are aware of whenever they tweet. Facebook does this by having you select "share location" whenever you post anything.

We need to make sure this is right below the tweet box. It shouldn't be selected by default either, because people might accidentally share their locations when they don't mean to.

It'll also be something we need to be aware of in terms of PR. We need to frame it as an extra convenient feature for the users. People will put a spin on it anyway, so we need to make sure the ones we are working with are wording it nicely. Something along the lines of, "Let your friends know what and where you are up to" has a nice ring to it.

Also, we need to make an announcement on our blog, and the first time the user uses it we need to highlight this feature. "If you want your friends to know where you are right now, why not try this feature?"

Ideally, I would test this on a small subset of users first and gauge their reaction. We may find that having it off by default is not necessary, or that this feature isn't that unpopular with users despite it being touchy with privacy issues.

That's how I would launch this feature. Is there any particular part that you want me to expand on?

INTERVIEWER: You mentioned having this feature be off by default. Wouldn't that cause the adoption rate to be low? Since most people don't even bother looking.

CANDIDATE: Yes, I did think about that. It's definitely going to cause our adoption rate to go down, but I think it is better to be safe than sorry. What we can do is have an option called, "Always Share Location" in the user's profile setting. We can point the user to turn this on the first time they try the new feature. If someone is enamored with this feature, the user will turn it on. This is similar to asking users to allow push notifications on a mobile app.

INTERVIEWER: Let's say you launched this feature, and everyone is criticizing you for privacy problems. What would you do?

CANDIDATE: It depends on Twitter's stance on location sharing. Let's assume Twitter is against sharing location info unless the user allows it, then we need to make sure this point is heard. We'll say this is our stance, and this feature is optional. If you don't feel comfortable, Twitter is not forcing you to share your location. In fact, we want users to use this function cautiously.

INTERVIEWER: What you are saying is the ideal state. What if Twitter hasn't made a stance yet concerning location sharing?

CANDIDATE: That could happen. In that case, I would focus more on asking the users to use this cautiously. Twitter added this as an optional feature. If you don't want to use it for whatever reason, don't. If you have any feedback concerning this issue, reach out to us. We can also try to reach out to the users ourselves, such as doing an AMA on Reddit or posting a video on YouTube to explain.

Improve Facebook for the Web

Redesign the Facebook Newsfeed for the Web.

Things to Consider

- Use the CIRCLES design framework.
- Do not confuse Facebook's Newsfeed and Timeline feature.

Common Mistakes

- Suggesting copycat improvements.
- Considering only superficial problems such as removing ads.
- Considering only superficial needs such as "User needs the ability to share photos."

Answer

CANDIDATE: All right, can I get some time to brainstorm?

Candidate takes one minute.

CANDIDATE: Many different people use Facebook. I think we should first start by thinking about the users. Here are some users I am thinking of:

- **Updaters**. These people love updating about their lives. It could be through shares, updates, pictures or videos.
- **Socializers**. These people just want to socialize. They are looking for comments and to comment. They want to see the whole comment thread.
- **Regulars**. These people aren't hardcore Facebook users. They go on Facebook occasionally to catch up on what's going on.
- **Influencers**. These people post a lot for a purpose. They are looking to promote something.

I feel like we can see problems with the current newsfeed by looking at the needs of these groups. I can think of a few:

- Updaters sometime want to post things in a more real-time manner. There are innumerable newsfeed items makes it difficult to do that, as new posts would pop up on the feed.
- The way the newsfeed comments work is actually inconvenient. It's hard to find where a thread starts and there are so many threads.
- If you have numerous friends or subscribe to many pages, you could get a torrent of updates, especially if you don't check Facebook that often. Sometimes I am only interested in a certain page and I can't filter. I have to click on that page to see all their news.
- Influencers pretty much have the same problem as the Updaters.

I feel like the biggest problem is really that there is a lot of content on the newsfeed and it makes it hard to find stuff you are interested about. Sure, a lot of what contributes to a newsfeed is based on your own subscription, but the user will still attribute this problem to Facebook. The comment problem is another thing, but most people don't comment and just click "Like," so I don't think it's that serious. I would like to focus on the too much content problem if you agree.

INTERVIEWER: Go ahead.

CANDIDATE: All right. I can think of a few solutions to this:

- **Filtering**. We could add tags on the side. For example, we can filter by closest friends, pages only, and other options. The trick is getting the filters right. If we have too many it's essentially repeating the problem since the user can't decide. If it's too late, it's somewhat pointless to have this feature in the first place. Ideally, the user can pick, say, "closest friends," and view what his closest friends are up to. We'll also have to define what a closest friend is in the algorithm.
- **Auto Sorting**. Auto Sorting is similar, except it is automatic. So this is an option where the user can opt-in, and display news by relevance instead of time. Obviously, you still need to segment based on time, so probably auto sort news by day. The trick is finding what is the most relevant to the user. I think a lot of this could be based on how long users stop on certain posts, his interactions with it, and how often he talks to certain friends to determine this. The drawback is that this requires the users to opt in and they may not know of this option.
- **Better Organization**. The feed could use a bit of organization. Right now, it's just based on time and there's no differentiation unless I look at the poster. We could differentiate by color-coding, and don't forget to consider colorblind users. We also need to make sure the colors are chosen carefully, because we don't want to make the page too colorful. That would be stressful on the eyes. I think a little colored box on the corner of each post would be a good start. We can differentiate between shares, original content, and pages.

If I were to actually roll these out, I would A/B test them on a subset of users before rolling them out. I would see if this would lead to more engagement and retention. If they work, users who usually check occasionally would be engaging with more posts. Hardcore users would probably have a decrease in session length but their engagement should be about the same. A danger here is that we are getting less session length and engagement, so we want to look out for that.

Screenshot / *PM Interview Questions* and Facebook

Improve Facebook Mobile

Redesign the Facebook Newsfeed for Mobile.

Things to Consider

- Use the CIRCLES design framework.
- Ask the interviewer if you can refresh your memory and look at Facebook on your phone. It'll trigger your brainstorm: both for pain points and new solutions. It will also preserve your credibility by not recalling, incorrectly, how a feature works.

Common Mistakes

- Mumbling and/or speaking too quickly

 Spending too much time with the CIRCLES design framework such as too much time spent talking about goals or personas.

- Coming with unimpressive solutions because the candidate forgot to ask for time to think.

Answer

CANDIDATE: Let me look through Facebook and see if I can spot any problems.

Candidate looks through Facebook on his phone.

CANDIDATE: I notice a few problems I would like to tackle:

- **No ads**. The mobile version simply does not have enough real estate to show ads. This is a monetization problem.
- **No Messenger**. This is a problem I want to point out that Facebook has not been able to solve yet. This is also a Facebook app problem and not exclusive to the timeline. This is because the app would simply be too big if the messenger is added. I can think of a few ways to remedy this though. This is an engagement problem.
- **Friends & Photos are not seen on mobile**. This is both a limited real estate as well as engagement problem.

Is there any specific one you want me to tackle?

INTERVIEWER: Let's see how you solve the ad problem.

CANDIDATE: All right, sure. Can I get some time to brainstorm?

Candidate takes one minute.

CANDIDATE: I can think of a few solutions:

- **Geolocated coupons**. Trigger discounts based on businesses around you. For example, get a $1 off a Starbucks Frappuccino or one quid off McDonald's.

- **Geolocated stickers and emoticon packs**. Allow users to earn special stickers or emoticon packs, based on their geolocation. To make it more interactive, have the user perform an action at that location such as answer a trivia question based on what they see or tag items in real-life a la Pokémon Go.
- **Small ads below your post.** Say you posted something about going to a burger joint, a small ad inside the post shows the viewer's local burger restaurant. It's hidden and not as big as before. It's also nice because it's relevant to the topic at hand. Again, it can upset and confuse some people.
- **Top Banner.** Kind of like ads in most apps. There's a banner on top, which is always there and you can keep switching ads. The problem is that it's extremely irritating. With iPhones having a small space as it is, that top banner is just annoying. It's going to drop the user experience. People might also accidentally click it when they don't want to, so that's bad for them and for the advertiser since they are most likely paying for clicks.

Back to what I said earlier, a lot of these stem from the lack of memory on a phone. I feel like we can alleviate this somewhat if we only allow these ads to show up on larger format phones, such as the iPhone 6 & 6S Plus and the bigger Android phones.

INTERVIEWER: Interesting. Which on would you recommend?

CANDIDATE: I would recommend the top banner. The other two feels like it's invading your personal experience a bit too much. If I am reading my own timeline or someone else's, seeing an ad really feels out of place. But the banner on top? It's annoying but it gives out the appearance that it's not part of the timeline so we avoid this problem.

INTERVIEWER: How would you determine if this feature is worth it? As in, where do you draw the line that you are willing to sacrifice user experience for monetization through this feature?

CANDIDATE: It would really depend on the data. I would definitely roll this out to a small subset of users first, and of course limit to bigger screen phones like those that I said earlier so the experience isn't too painful. I think Facebook probably has thought of this before and is not doing it for a reason. I think the retention and engagement drop would have to be several times smaller than the monetization increase to be worth it, because you are really sacrificing your long-term gain for a short-term gain. I could spend time to calculate this number if you want.

INTERVIEWER: That's fine. I think that's all the time we have.

Improving Pinterest

How would you improve Pinterest?

Things to Consider

- Use the CIRCLES design method.
- Do not forget to clarify the purpose of the product improvement.
- Do not get defensive if you get push back from the interviewer.

Common Mistakes

- Damage credibility by proposing a seemingly innovative solution, only to have the interviewer explain that Pinterest does that already.
- Proposing unimpressive features that in the better, faster category.
- Incorrectly assuming a complete and accurate understanding of how Pinterest works.

Answer

CANDIDATE: Let me first think about what kind of users Pinterest attracts. In my experience, the following users are huge Pinterest fans:

Candidate writes the following on whiteboard.

- **Social**. *These people use Pinterest as a form of social media and share pictures on it.*
- **Photographers**. *These people love taking pictures and using filters.*
- **Artists**. *They like posting their work, but most of all, use Pinterest to find art pieces to reference.*
- **Sharers**. *These people using Pinterest as a place to upload and store pictures.*

The artist persona really interests me, so I would like to focus on that if you agree.

INTERVIEWER: Please, go ahead.

CANDIDATE: So why are we improving Pinterest? We could target several metrics. I think engagement, retention, and revenue would be the three. There are also other things we could focus on, including customer satisfaction. I am thinking along the lines of customer satisfaction.

I am proposing these ideas.

- **Better Tags**. Currently the tags are actually bad for artists to find pictures. An example of this would be trying to find digital painting of a casino dealer. It would form the tags of "Digital," "Painting," "Casino," and "Dealer." You end up getting results you are not interested in. This makes for a bad user experience, and thus lower customer satisfaction.
- **Picture Types**. Artists mostly look for a certain type of pictures, such as concept drawing, pencil drawing, cell shading, 3-D modeling, texture, etc. Pinterest currently does not support this directly. It rolls it into tags. I propose that there is a special type you can mark your picture with when you upload it. You can also filter your search with this so you can find what you want easier.

- **Picture Quality.** Artists not only look for types, but also how finished the picture is. For example, highly finished vs. different stages of work in progress. A highly finished picture is very different from a concept design. Right now these are rolled into tags, and again, hard to find. I propose that there is a special quality you can mark your picture with when you upload it. You can also filter your search with this so you can find what you want easier.

I personally think Better Tags would take a while to get the details right and some engineering effort. It would also need a lot of A/B testing. Picture Quality is not as useful as Picture Types, so I think I would recommend Picture Types.

INTERVIEWER: It's an interesting idea for sure, but a bit impractical don't you think? We can't just add a special type in the search bar just for artists. If we do this for every type of users, we would end up with a clutter.

CANDIDATE: I agree with that sentiment. I think it would be good to label what type of pictures you are uploading. If you are uploading a drawing, then this tag can be an option. Otherwise, if you are uploading, say a photo you took this weekend, you won't get this option. If we want it to be even more convenient, we can have Pinterest be able to detect that this is an art piece and show this special labeling option.

INTERVIEWER: Fair enough. But you do know your idea only works if people are actually tagging and labeling their uploads right?

CANDIDATE: This is true, but so is the regular tagging on Pinterest. I think it's safe to assume this isn't really a new problem.

INTERVIEWER: Fair enough. Let say this feature is launched. How would you tell if it's effective?

CANDIDATE: I would track data. What is the average time an artist spends finding a picture he wants before vs. now? If it takes a lot less time now, then we know our feature is working. We can also check if artists are actually tagging and/or labeling their pictures correctly. The filtering would only work if the users are tagging and labeling them correctly. We brought this point up earlier.

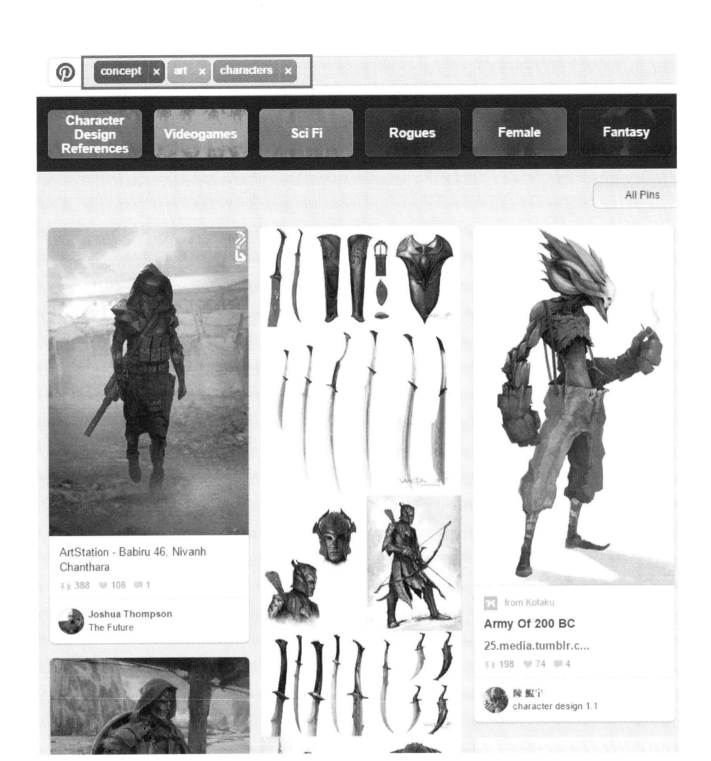

Improving Amazon

How would you improve Amazon?

Things to Consider

- Use the CIRCLES method.
- Amazon has a lot of products and features. Clarify with the interviewer which product he or she would like you to focus on.

Common Mistakes

- Not clearly describing suggested ideas.
- Suggesting an idea that already exists.
- Assuming revenue is the only goal and being perceived as very business focused rather than product (or customer) focused.

Answer

CANDIDATE: When you say, "Improve Amazon?" are you referring to the core product experience?

INTERVIEWER: Yes.

CANDIDATE: The core Amazon.com experience can be improved multiple ways: engagement, retention, revenue, and acquisition. Which one do you want me to focus on?

INTERVIEWER: Which one do you recommend?

CANDIDATE: I would like to focus on retention. Right now, there is no reason for people to come back unless they intend to sell something, which is why the only way Amazon is boosting this is through sales. I feel like by getting people back on Amazon more often, it would indirectly lead to more revenue.

INTERVIEWER: Sounds good.

CANDIDATE: Can I brainstorm for a bit?

Candidate takes one minute.

CANDIDATE: I have a few ideas in mind:

- **Items Just for You**. Every few days or a week you get a list of items (e.g. 8-10) that is recommended to you with a deal. The items will be generated based on what other items this user will most likely buy. This will give the user a reason to come back to the site, or at least if we are only doing this in a personalized newsletter, a reminder about Amazon.
- **Daily Ratings**. Every day you can log on Amazon to look at some pre-selected products. These are products that are not selling well for some reason, and we want user feedback. The user will take a look at the entire product page and write down what they think needs to be improved. Is the price too high?

Are the pictures bad? Users will then get a stacking 3% off. This can be stacked up to 10 times and be used as a coupon. This not only boosts retention; it would also give us feedback.

- **Return Coupon**. If a user hasn't been on Amazon for a long time, or hasn't purchased anything for a while, a special coupon will be given to him (10-15% off). This can be applied to any item. If the percentages are too high, we can make it only applicable to items over a certain price range. This will encourage users to come back to Amazon and buy something.

INTERVIEWER: Out of all of these ideas, which one would you recommend?

CANDIDATE: I would recommend the items just for you. I believe we already have most of these data, so we can just offer a sale based on the profit margin (e.g., Item X has a profit margin of 20%, so give a 10% off). It would be easy to implement. Obviously, we need to test this on a small subset of users first.

INTERVIEWER: If these are items that similar users will buy anyway, wouldn't this cut into our profit margin?

CANDIDATE: There is always this concern, yes, but most of the time it works out well. There are a few reasons why:

- When users buy something, they usually buy other things too. In some cases, they may buy unnecessary items to qualify for the $35 super saver shipping threshold. It's likely we won't be offering sales on expensive items through this anyway, since most people don't buy expensive items on a whim.
- This will most likely increase sales. More sales, at a lower profit margin, mean more profit. Isn't this the motto Amazon heralds?
- We can offer items that don't sell as well but still might be relevant to this user's purchase data. We can offer bigger sales to items that don't sell well and smaller sales to items that do sell well. Obviously, we won't offer very popular items on sales. These can all be fine-tuned when we have actual data.

Improving Dropbox

How would you improve Dropbox? Which feature is still missing?

Things to Consider

- Use the CIRCLES design framework.
- Think of adjacent areas beyond file sharing such as:
    - A more robust UI for specialized file types. Think: photo, music and video sharing.
    - Document version control. Think: GitHub for Microsoft Office documents.
- Use the SCAMPER brainstorm frameworks. For example, what happens when you combine Dropbox and:
    - Airbnb?
    - Facebook?
    - Microsoft Outlook?

Common Mistakes

- Not showing enthusiasm, making the answer boring.
- Choosing to talk about a persona that the candidate is not familiar with.
- Not using the whiteboard to help the listener better visualize a proposed improvement.

Answer

CANDIDATE: Are there any constraints to this problem?

INTERVIEWER: No constraints.

CANDIDATE: Okay. Can I get some time to brainstorm?

Candidate takes one minute.

CANDIDATE: I can think of three features that I think Dropbox would need.

- **Chat**. Dropbox currently does not support chat. I think having chat would be nice. When users are collaborating on the same projects, they can instantly chat with each other to solve problems.
- **Revert**. Dropbox does not have a revert option. Therefore, if someone changes a file, there is no way for anyone else or even that person to revert to a previous version. This could be problematic, especially in big teams.
- **More Information**. Currently, if I am working on some files with a few people. There is no way for me to know who changed what file. Thanks to Dropbox and Microsoft Office integration, I can preview the file. However, it would be even better if I can see who is working on the file. It'll minimize the opportunity for conflicting changes. I don't want to touch files that someone else is working on.

INTERVIEWER: Interesting. What solutions do you have in mind for revert?

CANDIDATE: I can think of a few solutions:

1. **A revert option, storing previous versions locally**. The good news is that we would not incur cloud infrastructure costs. The bad news is that users may not like that we're occupying their limited local storage. We could hide the fact that we're using local storage, but if they find out, the users might be unhappy.
2. **A revert option, storing previous versions to the cloud**. The good news is that it doesn't occupy the user's precious local space. The bad news is that it'll cost money. We could minimize cloud costs by simply saving incremental changes vs. entire files, which will save space.

I would recommend option #2. There are some costs to it, but it'll be a better user experience.

Improving Google Play Store

What would you change in Google Play Store?

Things to Consider

- In addition to user needs, consider how Google Play is different from equivalent offerings such as Apple's ecosystem.
- Scope the question appropriately: Google Play can refer to Apps, Music, Movies, Books, etc.
- In addition to the user experience, consider the developer experience as well.

Common Mistakes

- Incorrectly thinking that it's only the structured thinking process and not the answer that matters.
- Raising common or superficial improvements such as improving the recommendation algorithm.
- Claiming the UX can be improved, but neglecting to draw how it can be improved on a whiteboard.

Answer

CANDIDATE: I would like to approach this from the point of metrics. Why do we want to change the Google Play Store? I am thinking in terms of retention and engagement. Specifically, I am thinking of making it more convenient to use to boost these two metrics.

INTERVIEWER: Okay.

CANDIDATE: Can I get some time to brainstorm?

Candidate takes one minute.

CANDIDATE: I can think of a few things:

- **Screenshots**. This is a mobile issue. Screenshots may come in as portrait or landscape. Most users browse through a portrait view, so when they see a landscape screenshot the first thing they do is tilt their phone. What Google Play Store doesn't do is that it doesn't lock the screen. It should, so the screenshot doesn't change display. Otherwise, it's a really bad user experience. There is no point in changing due to tilting anyway. Why would the user want to change it?
- **Search**. Search is a huge thing for the Google Play Store, since it searches based on keywords and ranking. The problem, though, is when you are searching for an app that is named exactly that, and it shows some other apps. Because the app you are looking for is not that popular, it doesn't show up first. I understand the practicality of this, since it is ranked search, but it's still an annoying user experience.
- **Prediction**. Whenever I go to Google Play on the browser, it always shows me the latest music or movie. The thing is, I never buy these on Google Play, so why show me them? I understand the need for advertisement, but ads that do not interest the user are seen as annoyance. I mostly download games on Google Play, so why not show me a personalized news and only show me games?

INTERVIEWER: It's interesting you mentioned search. Do you feel the better user experience outranks the ad revenue?

CANDIDATE: From my understanding, you are saying there are two things that show up:

- **Sponsored Ads**. These show up first and they have a little yellow icon "AD" on the bottom right.
- **Better-Ranked Apps**. These show up because they are popular. If we don't show them up front, they might be less interested in promoting on Google Play.

Let me address both issues. First, I think the yellow "AD" one can stay. Only two show up anyway, so it's all right. You see at least 4-5 apps on the first row. The better-ranked apps are the ones that have to go. It's the bulk of the problem. Google Play has the most users anyway so people are going to be promoting on Google Play. I also want to add, that someone knowingly search for a specific game title is a rare case, so it won't affect that much.

INTERVIEWER: If it's an unlikely scenario, why focus on it?

CANDIDATE: Because it's the details that matter sometimes. Google Play Store is already pretty good, so why not make it perfect?

INTERVIEWER: Okay, on to the next question. For your prediction idea. Don't you think showing the ads is more important? For example, how would Google Play get you to try buying music or movies if we never show you any ads related to them?

CANDIDATE: I understand where you are coming from. Being able to show ads to users is Google's core strength. However, I've been using Google Play for years. If I haven't done this for a while, I am not going to do it. What Google Play should do is show me a splash screen for ads I am interested in. Steam does. Sure, you may say Steam only sells games, but it sells lots of games. Steam has personalized ads and deals for every user, and will only show you ads for games you probably want based on your playing history (so genre in this case). This makes for a better user experience, and you can drive more sales. It makes each ad more effective. Isn't that the whole point to contextual ads?

Improving Google Hangouts

How would you improve Google Hangouts?

Things to Consider

- Brainstorm several ideas, not just one.
- Give your ideas memorable names.
- Be clear on how your suggested solutions work and why they are important.

Common Mistakes

- Afraid of suggesting dumb ideas.
- Being unwilling to draw how the feature might work.

Answer

CANDIDATE: Google Hangouts doesn't really monetize right now, so I am thinking of improving toward engagement metrics. I don't think retention is a problem, because of Gmail. I think if we improve engagement it'll bring retention up as well. With your permission, I would like to focus on engagement.

INTERVIEWER: Okay, go ahead.

CANDIDATE: Can I brainstorm for a bit?

Candidate takes one minute.

CANDIDATE: I can think of several things:

- **Find New Friends**. One of strengths of Google Hangouts is that it uses the contacts from your Gmail. You have a set of friends to start, which is one of the challenges of instant messengers. Something lacking is that Google Hangouts has no way for you to find friends. You have to do this from Gmail. It's a relic from the past because Hangouts was built as a feature in Gmail. I am thinking of a system where it can help you find friends based on your criteria (age, gender, etc.) and proximity. Also, introduce friends your friends know, kind of like a social network. This will increase its engagement.
- **Status during Image/Video Sending**. Whenever you send a large content like images or videos over, Google Hangouts never tell you the status. All it shows is, "Sending…" If it fails, it just tells you failure. What it should do is tell you the upload percentage. This makes for a better user experience, because otherwise this is a bad user experience.
- **Personal Status**. Google+ is not doing well as a social network, partially because nothing happens on there. This idea draws on Tencent's QQ and WeChat, which started out as instant messengers for the PC and mobile, respectively. By offering a simple personal status, we can add a bit of flavor and life. This is similar to a status on Facebook. While nothing may come of this, this could be the first step toward turning Hangouts into a social network. A simple status is a great opener for any conversation. This will increase engagement.

INTERVIEWER: Interesting. Which idea do you recommend?

CANDIDATE: I would say personal status. It should be the second easiest to implement out of the three ideas, and it has the greatest potential.

Monetizing Google Maps

How would you monetize Google Maps?

Things to Consider

- Use the CIRCLES Method.
- Although the question prompt revolves around Google Maps, reflecting upon the shortcomings of its' competitors' can help (e.g. Apple Maps and Waze).

Common Mistakes

- Having trouble suggesting monetization ideas aside from ads.
- Not being thoughtful in the recommendation.

Answer

CANDIDATE: I'm going to tackle this question in three steps.

1. Explore pain points with Google Maps, especially ones with monetization potential
2. Brainstorm solutions
3. Make a recommendation

INTERVIEWER: Sounds good.

CANDIDATE: Let's start with monetizable pain points. Here's what comes to mind:

- Not sure which mapping application has the best directions, whether it's Google Maps, Waze or Apple Maps.
- Drives can be boring, especially long road trips.
- When driving, I see interesting things, like lakes, castles and mountains. I wish I could Wikipedia for more information, but my hands are busy. Or if my hands aren't busy, it will take too much time to complete the search.
- When I travel to a place with no cellular data connection, I can't pull up directions.
- To get offline maps, I need to download it in advance. However, I never know when I need to download offline maps in advance.
- I'm looking for the best-priced gas station along my route, without having to backtrack.
- I'm worried about getting a ticketing for speeding.
- I don't know why a person has bad driving behavior. The person is tailgating me, cut me off or won't let me into his or her lane. Is there a way I could communicate and tell him or her to stop it?
- I hate it when ads show up while I'm driving on mapping apps, especially on Waze. To clear the ad, I have to close it. I have to look down and take my eyes off the road. In addition, the close button is very, very tiny.

CANDIDATE: Can I get some time to brainstorm some ideas?

Candidate takes one minute.

CANDIDATE: I can think of several ideas:

- **Advertisement.** This one is a simple idea. When a user is looking for something like, "Nearby Italian restaurants," Google Maps would show this information. The first two or three could be sponsored restaurants. Another use would be highlighting sponsored shops, companies and even billboards on the GPS as the user is driving past.
- **Open API.** Open our API to extend to other apps or third parties. For example, an app to send alerts about commutes or even opening our entire API for others to build customized maps. It could be for book, movie or game interactive maps. A strong example would be allowing services like Uber to track mileage.
- **Sightseeing.** Tourism provides huge revenue, and this Google Maps can tap into this. Travel sites can build companion travel map guide apps that will guide the tourists on a tour around the city, all powered by Google Maps.

INTERVIEWER: Which one would you recommend?

CANDIDATE: I would recommend sightseeing, actually. Ads can harm the user experience. Sites that show ads can get criticized about it (e.g. Yelp). Open API could work, but I think sightseeing is more specifically focused on one industry. It would be easy in terms of both business development and technical focus.

Disney Experience with Your Phone

Create an experience around Disney theme parks using your phone.

Things to Consider

- Use the CIRCLES method.
- Unlike the previous question, you are not constrained by using Google products.
- To help you get started, here are some pain points to consider:
  - What to do?
  - Where is my kid?
  - Where can I find good bargains?
  - How do I minimize my wait times?

Common Mistakes

- Making a common, tired suggestion like a Disney theme park map that provides the optimal route to maximize rides.
- Suggesting an auto recommender feature and hand waving the implementation by saying machine learning is the solution, without going into details.

Answer

CANDIDATE: Can I get some time to brainstorm?

Candidate takes one minute.

CANDIDATE: I can think of a few ideas:

- **Automatically edit your photos.** Whenever you take a picture, the app will suggest photo edits. The app will indicate characters and objects related to the place you are capturing (e.g. Aladdin and his flying carpet appears next to his palace). The app will also recognize if individuals in a photo are wearing costume based on Disney characters.
- **Look through your phone.** You can look through everything through your phone's camera, and get information related to the Disney film this is from including the relevant characters. You will also see real time edits similar to the feature mentioned before.
- **The characters calling you.** Whenever you walk to a place, you'll get a phone call from the major characters related to the place. For example, if you walk near Aladdin's palace, you'll get Aladdin or the Genie to call you and talk to you.

INTERVIEWER: Which ideas do you think will offer the best experience?

CANDIDATE: I think the auto edit idea is the best. People naturally take photos during a trip to Disneyland, especially selfies. This will make their experience immersive, which is the big driving point of Disney. In addition, it requires no additional upkeep besides the technology itself. Finally, these can be shared on the social network to find likeminded people to discuss about this.

Mobile App Design for Nest

Design the next product that Nest will offer, focusing on mobile app design.

Things to Consider

- To increase your chances of getting one impressive idea, brainstorm at least three solutions.
- Explain why you suggested certain ideas.

Common Mistakes

- Answering casually.
- Giving a stream-of-consciousness answer that is hard to answer.

Answer

CANDIDATE: Hmm, can I get some time to brainstorm?

Candidate takes one minute.

CANDIDATE: I have a few ideas in mind.

- **Smart Garage Door.** I am thinking of a smartphone app that reports your position to the garage door opener. It would then check traffic based on Google Maps and estimate how far you'll be from home. It will then have the door open by the time you get home. The inverse happens when you leave: it would automatically close the door when it detects that your car has left the driveway based on the location of your iPhone or when you lose WiFi connectivity.
- **Smart Water Heater.** This is similar to the smart garage door. If you want to shower as soon as you get home, it would boil the water so that it's not only ready for you when you're home but also conserving energy. If you shower in the morning or some other time, you can schedule a time on your phone. It would remind you that the water is ready by sending you a phone notification.
- **Smart Pet Feeder.** You can set a pet feeding schedule. If your pet is also hungry and starts banging on the machine, you'll be notified. With a phone swipe, you can dispense food remotely.

There's a similar theme for all three product ideas: monitor and control your home while your away, giving you peace of mind. I feel this is Nest's mission statement.

INTERVIEWER: Which idea do you recommend?

CANDIDATE: Based on market potential?

INTERVIEWER: Yes.

CANDIDATE: If I had time, I would build a profit forecast to understand the business impact to the company. Did you want me to do a back of the envelope calculation now?

INTERVIEWER: That's not necessary. Just go ahead and tell me which one your gut says has the most market potential.

CANDIDATE: Based on my gut, the smart garage door has the most potential. There are many homeowners in the United States, and they are worried about their home safety. By having a device that monitors whether a garage door is open or closed gives them peace of mind. The smart water heater provides conservation but not safety benefits. Lastly, the smart pet feeder, while it is cruel to have a loved pet go hungry, it is unlikely to drive as much peace of mind comfort as a smart garage door.

Local Service Recommendation Engine

How would you design a better local service recommendation engine? We want it to be better than Yelp. The recommendation engine will cover everyone from pediatricians to plumbers. Answer this from a consumer, not small business perspective.

Things to Consider

- Use the CIRCLES design framework.
- Build a customer journey map to help uncover pain points.
- Push yourself to come up with big, innovative ideas.

Common Mistakes

- Oversimplifying the solution.
- Proposing a magical solution without going into the implementation details. For instance, "Yelp will magically find the best local service for our customers. It will be so easy that you just have to press 'I'm Feeling Lucky' button and voila – Yelp will suggest the perfect service."
- Not picking a specific scenario and / or customer problem, leading to generic solutions.

Answer

CANDIDATE: Can I get one minute to brainstorm?

Candidate takes one minute.

CANDIDATE: I am a Yelp user; I usually use it for restaurants, so maybe my perspective is a bit different. Since we are going for all types of stores, it's hard to break down our users into segments. Therefore, I think it's easier to talk about users in general.

I can think of several problems with Yelp that I encountered during my use, and I think they are relatable.

- Not enough information about store environment and cost
- Not enough information about parking and directions
- No closest match or "what others who like this service also likes"

For the first one, Yelp doesn't actually tell you what the environment is like. For example, how do you know how you need to be dressed for a particular restaurant? You don't. You end up having to flip through pictures just to spot how other people are dressed. This is the same thing with cost. They give you a five $'s marker, which starting from two $'s it could be $11 to $30. That's a big range.

For the second one, you never know what's up with parking in this place. You have to scour through the customer comments in order to find it, assuming someone commented on this. A picture of where the parking is would also be great. Sometimes stores have parking away from the premise. Another thing is directions. A map is not enough. I want a street view of what it looks like so I don't miss it.

For the third one, if you are looking at a store and you don't like it, I have to go back to the search and look at the next one. Why doesn't Yelp offer me a suggestion about stores like this? This way it would save me a lot of time.

All of my problems are related to customer convenience. Boosting these should increase retention. In the last problem's case, it would increase monetization through ads.

INTERVIEWER: How would you improve it if you were making a similar product?

CANDIDATE: I would address the problems above. Let me provide solutions for them all.

For the first one, I would have more information. I would ask the store to fill this information first. For the environment that's easy to do. For the price, a manual upload of the menu and averaging the cost would be good. Customers could also verify this. The problem would be getting stores and customers to engage and fill in, but that's an existing problem on Yelp anyway. I think by providing a field for it, people would be more likely to fill it in.

For the second one, I would see if I could grab Google Map's street view. That would solve both problems. If you don't see parking in front of the store, then that's when you need more information. I would ask customers or stores to fill in. As long as we have a field for it people would be more likely to fill it in.

For the last one, we just need an algorithm to do this. We can track based on what others like. We can rank based on how many users like restaurant B who also like A. We rank every restaurant that is related to A this way, then present the best. We can also display restaurants that are advertising through us on this which will increase our revenue. Obviously, these need to be within the proximity too. I know Yelp currently has something similar, but it's more weighted toward proximity as far as I know.

INTERVIEWER: Your suggestions are geared toward restaurants but not other types of services.

CANDIDATE: I can't deny that, but I feel like many services would benefit from this as well. Numerous services require parking and could benefit more from a more accurate pricing. They could definitely also benefit from street view. I can't tell how many times I've gotten lost because a store or a clinic is hidden behind several buildings.

INTERVIEWER: Which one would you recommend?

CANDIDATE: I think the last one is the one I would recommend doing. It directly boosts our revenue and customer satisfaction. It would be the hardest technically, but it requires no user adoption which means it just depends on how fast we can do it.

INTERVIEWER: How would you track if it's working?

CANDIDATE: I would see how many users are actually clicking on them and how many of those users come back with feedback. There is obviously going to be a low conversion factor, since most people who go to restaurants do not comment back on Yelp. However, there is no other way to attribute. Another way would be to see if our ad revenue is going up. If sponsored restaurants saw a business increase, then they would decide this is cost-effective and spend more marketing dollars with us.

Lego

If you were the CEO of LEGO, what new product line would you come up with to increase revenues? Why? Who is the target customer? How do you reach them? How does the product function and what does it look like (UI/UX)? What's the potential market size?

Things to Consider

- While this prompt has many sub-questions, tackle it in two parts. Part 1 is a product design question. Part 2 is a market estimation question.

Common Mistakes

- Not wanting to make calculations because the candidate is insecure about calculating numbers.
- Feeling overwhelmed with the multi-question answer and reacting with a hard-to-follow, poorly thought-out response.

Answer

CANDIDATE: Can I get some time to brainstorm?

Candidate takes one minute.

CANDIDATE: I am thinking of targeting adults who have played with Legos in the past. In other words, let's capitalize on nostalgia. Nostalgia drives sales in many consumer-oriented industries including video games, movies and books. You often hear people talking fondly of playing with Legos. Another data point: the popularity of *The Lego Movie*, especially with adults, shows that nostalgia can be profitable.

- **Pre-built sets.** Sell nostalgic pre-built sets for adults. Therefore, these would be famous and popular Lego sets from the past that come pre-built. Adults can buy them and place them around home. I recommended pre-built because adults have no time to play with Lego either building them from scratch or tinkering with them.
- **Lego-fy**. This lets you buy pieces that you can use to Lego-fy your home. Examples would be cup-holders or utensil holders in your kitchen. This has become a trend lately and would work well in nostalgic adults.
- **Adult Sets.** Try to sell it to adults who got a little bit more time and want to really reminiscence. This would sell them Lego sets that are a bit more complicated, but not too different from your standard Lego. I know Lego has tried this in the past, and it didn't really work well precisely because they were too different from the standard Lego. They would come with very detailed instruction booklets (think Ikea) and videos (we can also host them on YouTube). Adults can follow it step by step if they want since they might not have a lot of time to explore. Those with more time can play around and try to do it on their own.

INTERVIEWER: Which ideas do you recommend?

CANDIDATE: Pre-built sets seems to take all the fun out of Lego. That is, building the sets and having a sense of accomplishment was almost the entire benefit of Lego for me, as a kid. Lego-fy is an interesting trend, but I'm not sure how big that market is. Therefore, I'd recommend the adult sets. I think Lego grown-ups would love Lego sets that are adult-themed.

INTERVIEWER: How would you market to these people?

CANDIDATE: I would probably market them in the same channels as I market to the kids first. When kids buy Lego, adults are the one paying for it, so they'll see it. Adults who played Lego are most likely going to have their kids play them. We can also market it on things like TV shows only adults would watch. In addition, we can sell bundles where it includes one set for the kids and one set for the adult. This is especially nice in physical Lego stores when parents come in with their kids.

INTERVIEWER: Can you identify the potential market size?

CANDIDATE: Sure.

Assumptions

- US Population is around 300 million.
- US Life Expectancy is around 80 years.
- Lego's adoption rate is probably around 30%.
- Lego's history is around 25 years.

Calculating Potential Market Size:

$$Market\ Size = \frac{US\ Population}{US\ Life\ Expectancy} * Lego\ Adoption\ Rate * Lego\ History$$

$$Market\ Size = \frac{300\ million}{80\ years} * 0.3 * 25\ years$$

$$Market\ Size = {\sim}28\ million$$

CANDIDATE: The potential market size would be around 28 million people.

INTERVIEWER: Why did you divide the US population by life expectancy?

CANDIDATE: I assumed that the US life expectancy ranged from 0 to 80 years old. I also assumed that the age distribution was uniform; in other words, there's an equal number of people in each age range. To find out how many people are in a single one-year range, we divide 300 million people by 80 years, which is 3.75 million people per year.

INTERVIEW: Ah, got it. And why did you multiply the adoption rate and how long Lego has been in business?

CANDIDATE: I'm assuming that 3.75 million people each year, for 25 years, had an opportunity to play with Legos. I'm assuming that the number of people who actually did so was 30%, which I call the Lego adoption rate.

INTERVIEW: Thanks for the explanation.

Better Starbucks

Design a better Starbucks.

Things to Consider

- Use the CIRCLES design framework.
- Rant to get some hard-hitting pain points.
- Brainstorm many ideas to increase your chances of having a memorable and impactful idea.

Common Mistakes

- Taking the question too casually such as blurting out, "Just make the coffee better."
- Not empathizing with the customer deeply enough, limiting your ability to come up with innovative ideas.
- Copying competitor's innovations like Blue Bottle's cold-drip coffee makers below and being perceived as an unoriginal job candidate.

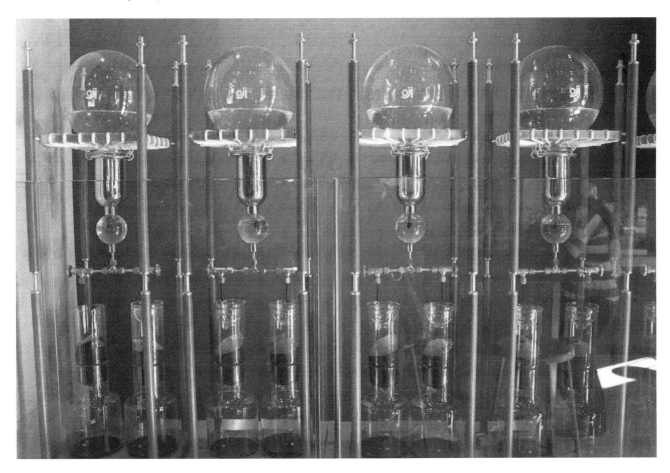

Screenshot / Business Insider

Answer

CANDIDATE: Are we talking about improving Starbucks as in generating more revenue, getting more customers or just improving customer satisfaction?

INTERVIEWER: What would you recommend?

CANDIDATE: Revenue would be straightforward. I think customer satisfaction would be a bit harder. I would like to go for that.

INTERVIEWER: Confident, are we? I like that. Okay, go ahead.

CANDIDATE: Can you give me some time to brainstorm?

Candidate takes one minute.

CANDIDATE: I think it's important we first think about what problems Starbucks has. Once we figure that out, we can tackle them and offer solutions.

INTERVIEWER: All right, sounds fair.

CANDIDATE: I can think of a few problems.

Candidate writes the following on whiteboard.

- *Long Lines. Starbucks usually has a long line, and waiting could be annoying.*
- *Crowded. Sometimes it is hard to find seating when there are so many people.*
- *Limited Electrical Outlets. Many Starbucks' customers bring their laptop. There are not enough outlets.*
- *Poor furniture. Chairs are comfortable, especially for those who are spending hours at Starbucks trying to study or get work done. The tables are too small, making it awkward to have anything more than a laptop or a single book on the table.*
- *Small food portions. I understand the need for healthy eating, but I would never consider Starbucks food for anything more than a light snack.*
- *Expensive prices. Some Starbucks beverages are so expensive. Instead of a Starbucks' Grande Frappuccino, I can buy a complete meal, beverage included, at McDonald's.*

INTERVIEWER: Which problem do you think is the most severe?

CANDIDATE: I would say long lines would be one.

INTERVIEWER: What is your solution for it?

CANDIDATE: I can think of a few solutions.

- **Waiting Area.** Have a special area where customers can wait for their orders. Comfortable sofa with a TV and some magazines would be a start. Customers can relax while waiting for their drinks.
- **Store Status.** Check your local store's status on Starbucks' mobile app and website. Get information like estimated wait time for a line. This way you can decide if you want to go or not. You can also add in additional features like checking the inventory of the other items that may be out of stock.
- **Reservation.** Allow you to reserve tables. The store can then gauge how many users are coming in over the next hour and give you a warning if you are reserving for an hour that is already flooded with people. It can show an estimated wait time so you can decide if you want to reserve it for this hour.

If I have to rank them, I would say Store Status is probably the best to do. I know Starbucks already has an app and this would be easy to do technically. However, there is the problem of getting stores to comply and actually update information. Reservation would not be bad either, and it could be an add-on for Store Status. Waiting Area is great, but that's an extra space taken away from sitting customers. Probably a bit difficult as that's a lot of housing space wasted and it'll cost too.

INTERVIEWER: Let say your ideas are implemented. How would you know they are working?

CANDIDATE: If we are doing Store Status, the store already has to update information about lines and estimated wait time. Starbucks should already have data on the estimated wait time now. We can just compare the two. If the wait time has gone done while the business (i.e. revenue) has not, then this is working.

Favorite Product

Tell me your favorite product. How would you improve it?

Things to Consider

- Get on the same page on what constitutes a favorite product by sharing your criteria.
- Compare with alternate products to help the interviewer appreciate why your chosen product is special.
- If necessary, explain what the product is, in case the interviewer is not familiar it.

Common Mistakes

- Not providing a scorecard upfront.
- Choosing a product that the interviewer is unfamiliar with, causing the interviewer to get bored.
- Picking a trite example such as iPhone.

Answer

CANDIDATE: Can you give me some time to brainstorm?

Candidate takes one minute.

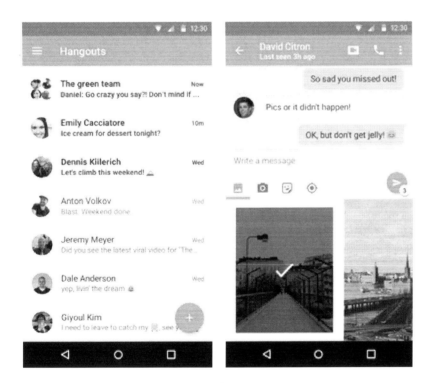

Screenshot / Google Hangouts

CANDIDATE: My favorite product is Google Hangouts. It's my favorite because it satisfies my three requirements for a good product. That is:

- Is it useful?
- Is it innovative?
- Is it easy to understand and use?

Let me go into more detail.

First, Google Hangouts is extremely useful. I use it every day to talk to all of my Gmail contacts. Since Gmail is the primary email most people use, it's useful to have all of your contacts in a chat program.

Second, Google Hangouts is innovative. Sure, the concept of an instant messenger isn't exactly new, but who built one in their email? Google does this, and it works. One of the biggest requirements for an instant messenger is the user base, both for the company if they want to launch one, and for the user if they want to enjoy using one. Google Hangouts achieved this because Gmail already has a huge number of users.

Third, Google Hangouts is easy to use and understand. The UI is intuitive, and the users can easily find it since it's right there in your Gmail. No tutorials or walkthroughs needed. Simple and easy.

To summarize, I like Google Hangouts because it's useful, innovative, and easy to understand and use.

INTERVIEWER: How would you improve it?

CANDIDATE: Can I get some time to brainstorm?

Candidate takes one minute.

CANDIDATE: Google Hangouts is mostly for engagement purpose. To break it down, it's for customer satisfaction. It doesn't serve ads so it has no monetization. I would like to improve the customer satisfaction by making it more convenient. I can think of a few ideas.

- **Status when sending videos and images.** Whenever you send an image or video right now, it just says "sending…" on Google Hangouts. I can't tell how much longer I should wait or if the system is stuck. Sometimes it fails for no reason, which is frustrating. I would like to know the current upload status to minimize my anxiety.
- **Friend finder.** Google Hangouts is built on Gmail contacts. Still, I think some people would love to find more friends. A way to find people by location would be good. This would increase engagement. I think it also needs a way to be able to find your business contacts. Google Hangouts is mostly used as a social app, and no one really uses it for business purposes like Skype. By allowing you to search or add a user by entering some information, such as their phone number or name, Google Hangouts could start capturing the business sector.
- **Status.** Google+ isn't working out, and Google, I am sure, would love to get in social networks. We can start small by adding a status on your Gmail. Think of it like the status on Facebook, or a more aptly comparison would be status on AIM. This allows you to share a bit of yourself. If people really like this feature, we can add more and grow it one-step at a time to a social network.

INTERVIEWER: Which idea would you recommend?

CANDIDATE: I think the sending image/video status would be the easiest to do, but besides making the experience a bit better, it's not as good as the other two. Friend finder is nice, but I think I like Status a lot more. I think we have a real opportunity to grow Hangouts into a social network. I currently use an app called WeChat that is made by Tencent. Tencent has QQ, an instant messenger in China. WeChat is similar, but more for the mobile experience. By having something that is a bit more complex but not too much than status, WeChat is a growing social network. I think Google Hangouts with something small like the status has the same potential.

Favorite Website

What's your favorite website and why?

Things to Consider

- First, establish your criteria for what would qualify as your favorite website.
- Then, explain what the website is.
- Lastly, explain why the website meets your criteria.

Common Mistakes

- Neglecting to draw what the website looks like. Pictures are more effective than words. A low fidelity sketch, taking no more than a few minutes, will suffice.
- Not being clear or having different expectations on what constitutes "favorite" website.
- Not explaining (or explaining poorly) what the website is because the candidate assumes the listener knows the product that they are talking about.

Answer

CANDIDATE: Can you give me a minute to brainstorm?

Candidate takes a minute.

CANDIDATE: When I think about my favorite website, it has to meet these three criteria:
- How useful is it?
- How innovative is it?
- Is it easy to use and understand?

The first website that comes to mind and meets these criteria is Splitwise. Splitwise is a website where friends and roommates can track bills and other shared expenses. It's useful because it's hard to remember who owes whom and for what reason. It's even synced with PayPal and allows friends to pay each other back. Therefore, it meets my usefulness criteria.

It also meets criteria number two: innovative. I haven't found another website that offers a similar solution. I admire Splitwise because it fixes one problem well and in the simplest way possible.

Lastly, Splitwise meets my last criteria: it is easy to understand and use. As soon as you enter the website, it shows your payment history in the main panel and a big red "Add a bill" button. You can click on any payment and see more details. It doesn't surprise me that there's no first-run tutorial because it is so intuitive to use.

To conclude, Splitwise is my favorite website because it satisfies my requirement for a good website: useful, innovative, and easy to use.

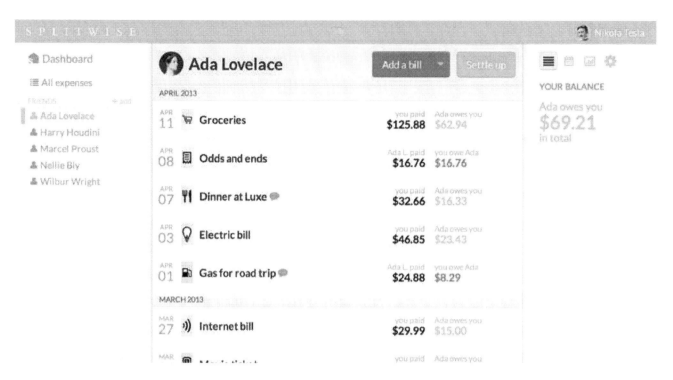

Screenshot / Splitwise

Car for the Blind

Enumerate and prioritize use cases for a self-driving car targeted for blind people. Justify everything with sound logic.

Things to Consider

Although the question starts with "Design a car," the interviewer is actually just looking for the candidate to first articulate the use cases and then prioritize them. It's a reminder to clarify with the interviewer if his or her intent is unclear.

Common Mistakes

- Using the full CIRCLES method when the interviewer only wants a subset.
- Not mentioning safety issues

Answer

CANDIDATE: I would first actually think about the constraints this car is put under. Are we limited by tech?

INTERVIEWER: What do you mean by tech?

CANDIDATE: Can we make these self-driving cars? I don't really see any other way blind people can drive around otherwise. Even with self-driving cars, we might have some legal issues.

INTERVIEWER: Let's say we can do self-driving cars, and we don't have legal problems.

CANDIDATE: Okay, then I would first think about our users. I'll then think about our use cases. I'll list out the gaps and address them through new features in our car. I'll then prioritize them.

INTERVIEWER: Okay, go ahead.

CANDIDATE: Our users are going to be both blind people and their friends, relatives and caretakers. I can see a few use cases:

- **Drive.** You can break this down to very specific use cases, like switch lanes and stop at red lights. Either way, the car needs to do it automatically. We already have self-driving cars for that. The only problem is that one, California requires self-driving cars to have the driver put at least one hand on the steering wheel. They do take traffic laws seriously and according to traffic laws, blind people can't drive. But we negated this earlier. Two, there is no way for the blind person to react to anything, really, since they can't see what's going on. What we can do is alleviate this with audio feedback. For example, the car is now turning left or the car is stopping at a red light. This way the blind person can know what's going on. The car also needs to tell you the speed, and the blind person should be able to provide audio input (e.g. speed up or slow down).
- **Park.** The car needs to auto-park. I am sure the typical self-driving car already has this. All we need is more audio feedback. For instance, you are now parked at a spot facing west.
- **Location Information.** The driver could find alerts on their location to be helpful. The driver may also want to share this location data to his friends, either for monitoring or for a rendezvous.

- **Additional Information.** Outside of location information there may be some additional information the driver or passengers might find helpful such as which direction the blind driver is facing or whether the blind driver should be careful when exiting the car, especially if he or she is parked parallel to the curb and there's oncoming traffic.
- **Safety.** In instances where either the car or driver is unable to drive effectively, the car should have the appropriate safety features so that the driver and others are not harmed. Options to have the car pull over and stop or perhaps allow a remote person control the vehicle, like a drone operator, would be helpful.

Driving, parking and safety would be my top two use cases, followed by providing location and additional information.

Phone for the Deaf

Design a phone for the deaf.

Things to Consider

- The interviewer is testing your ability to empathize with the target persona, even if you may not be deaf yourself.
- While you may not be familiar with what it's like to be deaf, you will be surprised with what you uncover, if you take the time contemplate their needs.

Common Mistakes

- Instead of answering the question, responding with a process that you'd use to approach this problem in real life.

Answer

CANDIDATE: Are we talking about a cellphone or a home phone?

INTERVIEWER: Cellphone.

CANDIDATE: A smartphone or flip phone?

INTERVIEWER: A smart phone.

CANDIDATE: Our primary users are going to be deaf people. I would also say their relatives and friends will also be secondary users.

Let me think of some use cases and their flaws:

- **Call someone.** A deaf person can't tell what the person on the other line is saying.
- **Receive a call.** A deaf person can't tell if the phone is ringing. They also can't hear what the person on the other line is saying (same problem as above).
- **Alarm.** Can't hear the audio part of the alarm.
- **Apps.** Some apps are not going to be useful because they may require hearing. Examples would be Spotify and sleep pattern apps.

We can solve these problems with the following features:

- **Vibrate.** We definitely want to increase the magnitude of vibration on the phone so deaf people can tell if a call is coming in or the alarm is sounding.
- **Haptics.** Similar to Vibrate, Haptics is great tactile feedback but a little subtler than vibrate. Haptics typically has more programmability depending on the function or alert. You could allow for several different patterns of haptics or vibrate to signal a phone call or different alerts for apps.
- **Lights.** We need to make sure the phone lights up more when a call is coming in or the alarm is sounding.

- **Voice-to-text.** We need voice-to-text for calls. So when someone is talking with the deaf person on the phone, anything they say is displayed as text on the screen.
- **Calling Keyboard.** It's possible that a deaf person cannot speak, so we need to have the option to have a keyboard show up during a call so the deaf person can input.
- **Text-to-voice.** On the other end, the other person probably doesn't want to read and instead want to hear voices during a call. For this reason, there is an option to have the phone voice the text the deaf person typed during a call.
- **Specialized App Store.** We need a section in the app store where only deaf-friendly apps can appear or deaf-friendly version of existing apps.

ATM for the Elderly

How would you design an ATM for elderly people?

Things to Consider

- Use the CIRCLES Method.
- Rant to get deeper and more insightful customer pain points.

Common Mistakes

- Spending unnecessary time further defining the persona, given that the interviewer already selected the persona.
- Going straight into solutions and not discussing pain points first.

Answer

CANDIDATE: Would this ATM be used by others as well?

INTERVIEWER: Assume that it will.

CANDIDATE: Let me think about some of the pain points elderly have with ATMs:

- Can't see the text
- Get tired standing up
- Potential confusion on whether the ATM card should be swiped or inserted
- Get startled when the machine beeps when I'm taking longer than usual
- Unclear why I can only deposit cash sometimes but not at other times
- Concerned when there's a long line of customers waiting behind me

CANDIDATE: All right. Let me think of some features that addresses the needs of the elderly while not taking out features that would make it hard for other people to use as well.

- We have to make sure it's placed inside the bank. It might get windy and cold outside.
- The text on screen needs to be big because elderly people might have difficulty seeing.
- The sound need to be louder, because elderly people might have trouble hearing.
- It should be an ATM that allows you to sit down.
- The ATM should allow wheelchair access.
- The lines for it should have chairs. It's not good to let elderly people stand while waiting.
- The ATM should have supports below for the elderly to rest their elbows on. It's also good for counting money.
- There should be a big, noticeable button to ask for help.
- Have a sign noting that the elderly or handicapped have priority for this ATM and that they should be encouraged to go before others in line for this ATM, similar to signs on reserved seats on busses.

Lastly, it goes without saying, ATMs for the elderly should have all the features of regular ATMs such withdrawing and depositing money.

Physical Product

What is your favorite physical product? Why? Also, give me big ideas on how you would increase its revenue by three times.

Things to Consider

- This is a combination question. Part 1 requires you to identify a favorite product and explain why. Part 2 asks you to brainstorm ideas.
- For part two, use the CIRCLES Method.
- In your answer, don't forget to connect your ideas with the goal: increasing revenue 3X.

Common Mistakes

- Coming up with ideas that don't meet the 3X revenue objective.
- Answering part 1 and not part 2. Or vice versa.
- Failing to come up with a big, game-changing idea.

Answer

INTERVIEWER: Tell me a physical product you like and why.

CANDIDATE: Hmm, my answer is somewhat weird, but I am going to stand by it. My favorite physical product is a water boiler I have. It fits my three great criteria for a good product. It does its job well. It's also convenient, easy to understand and easy to use.

First, the whole point is the boil water. I don't need it to flavor water, I don't need it to make water cold, and I definitely don't need it to look good. It looks like a plain water container, and all it does is boil water. The purpose to the product is clear, and it isn't littered with functions I don't need.

Second, it's convenient. What does that mean? It means it makes my life easy because the creator has thought of everything. One, it automatically turns off when the water is boiling so I don't need to keep an eye on it. Two, it sits on top of a cooker like thing that is attached to the power cord. The container itself can be taken off instantly, so I never need to worry about the power cord again. Three, it's designed to be easily carried with its handle that allows for a strong grip. Four, it's designed for pouring water, so the opening is small and direct.

Third, it's easy to use. It has two components. The first component is the cooker-like thing which has a power cord. You hook it up and place it on a flat service. The second component is the container itself. This is also easy; you just place it on the cooker. The cooker-like thing has only one button and lights. You press it and the light turns on because it's telling you it's cooking. When it is done boiling, it makes a sound and the light turns off. Easy and simple to understand.

To conclude, the water boiler I have is my favorite physical product, because it does its job well and nothing else, it's convenient, and it's easy to understand and use.

INTERVIEWER: How would you improve it with some big ideas to increase its revenue by 3 times?

CANDIDATE: Hmm, give me some time to think. The challenge of this is I don't want to add big ideas that'll defeat the first point of why I like it in the first place: it does its job and nothing else.

Candidate takes one minute.

CANDIDATE: I can think of a few ideas.

- **Water Quality Inspector.** Now that I think about it, the reason why water needs to be boiled in the first place is that I don't trust the water quality. If the container can check for water quality, it would serve that purpose. I can think of three different scenarios where this is a good idea. One, I am trying to cook water that is already good quality. Two, even after I cook the water, it's still not good. Three, the water that was good has been sitting inside for too long and probably gone stale.
- **Water Drinking Reminder.** Sometimes I am not drinking enough water, and this water boiler would be a great medium to tell me that. It should monitor how much water I am drinking by measuring how much water is being poured.
- **Water Temperature Keeper.** Some people like hot water, some people like cold water, and some people like something in between. This boiler should be able to tell you the temperature. It should be able to keep the temperature if you want it to. That would make it useful.

INTERVIEWER: Which idea do you propose and why do you think it'll make 3 times as much revenue?

CANDIDATE: I think I would propose the water temperature keeper. I think it's the most inexpensive feature so far. We don't want to make our boiler way too expensive compared to other water boilers.

I think it'll make 3 times as much revenue because it's a feature that is commonly needed. Remember this is not only for water. This can be used to make soup or tea. These things are best served hot, and this allows the boiler to be multi-purposed. This will give it a competitive age when compared to other water boilers. At the very least, it can tap into a new market.

INTERVIEWER: Earlier you said you like this product because it does its only job and nothing else. This idea goes against that. How do you address this?

CANDIDATE: I specifically pointed this out earlier too. Anyway, my first idea was going with this. For the last two ideas, I went the other direction. Sometimes big ideas will take your product into another direction. This is true in product design. Since our goal is to increase revenue, that means we need to either make the existing crowd more likely to purchase or find new crowds to attract. The last two ideas went toward attracting newer markets, so it makes sense that the water boiler does more than its one job now.

Chapter 15 Metrics: Brainstorming Exercises

Metrics for eCommerce

What are top metrics you would track for an eCommerce website?

Things to Consider

- Examples of top e-commerce websites include:
    - US: Amazon, Wal-Mart, Apple
    - India: Amazon, Flipkart, Snapdeal.
    - China: Tmall, JD, Suning
    - Europe: Tesco, Zolando, Otto
- Consider sales, marketing and website metrics

Answer

Acquisition

- Number of new customers
- Cost per acquisition (CPA)
- Cost per click (CPC)
- Cost per impression (CPM)
- Top search terms
- Mailing list click through rate
- Mailing list open rate
- Mailing list conversion rate
- Mobile app downloads

Activation

- New registered users

Retention

- Conversion rate
- Recommendation engine conversion rate
- Shopping cart abandonment
- Shopping cart size

Monetization

- Revenue per customer
- Lapsed customers
- Purchases per year
- Revenue per click

- Cost of sale (ad spend / revenue)
- Lifetime value

Other

- Cost of goods sold
- Shipping time
- Stockout
- Market share
- Margin

Metrics for Two-sided Marketplaces

What are top metrics you would track for a two-sided marketplace?

Things to Consider

Examples of two-sided marketplaces include:

- Ridesharing: Uber, Lyft, Kuaidadi
- Lodging: AirBnB, Booking.com, Expedia
- Peer-to-peer marketplaces: Craigslist, eBay, OfferUp
- Talent: Indeed.com

Answer

Buyer side

Acquisition

- Mobile app downloads

Activation

- Users with at least 1 search

Retention

- Searches
- Searches with 1+ Matches
- CTR for search result
- % satisfied transactions
- Net promoter score

Monetization

- Revenue
- Avg. transaction size
- # of transactions

Seller side

Acquisition

- Sellers
- Seller growth rate

Activation

- Sellers with at least 1 listing

Retention

- Listings per seller
- Net promoter score

Monetization

- Gross marketplace volume
- % fraudulent transactions

Other

- Seller concentration, that is % of revenue generated by the top X% of sellers
- Marketplace as a % of overall channel sales

Metrics for SaaS

What are top metrics you would track for a Software as a Service (SaaS) application?

Things to Consider

Examples of SaaS applications:

- CRM: Salesforce
- Messaging: Slack
- Financial and human capital management: Workday

Answer

Acquisition

- Leads
- Virality

Activation

- New registered users

Retention

- Daily active usage
- Time onsite
- Interval between logins
- Churn

Monetization

- Conversions
- Deals
- Renewal rate
- Monthly recurring revenue
- Revenue per user
- LTV

Other

- Uptime
- Renewal rate

Metrics for Mobile Apps

What are top metrics you would track for a mobile application?

Answer

Acquisition

- # of mobile installs
- Cost per install

Activation

- # of accounts created, after mobile download

Retention

- Daily and monthly active usage
- Time in app
- Star rating
- Session length
- % of users that rate the app

Monetization

- % of paid users
- Lifetime value
- Average revenue per user
- Churn

Metrics for Publishers

What are top metrics you would track for a publisher's website?

Things to Consider

Examples of publishers:

- News: New York Times, India Times, Sina.com
- Sports: ESPN
- User-generated content: Reddit, Quora, Medium.com

Answer

Acquisition

- Unique visitors per month
- Sessions per month
- Monthly page views

Activation

- # of registrations

Retention

- Pages per visit
- Time on site per visit
- Monthly minutes on site

Monetization

- Display ad rates (per thousand)
- Banners per page
- CPC ads per page
- CPC (Cost per Click)
- CTR (Click through rate)
- Total CPC ads shown
- Total Clicks
- CPA ads per page
- Total CPA ads
- CPA (Cost per Acquisition)
- CTR on CPA Ads
- Total Clicks on CPA Ads
- Conversion Rate (on CPA Ads)
- Total Conversions

- Average Sale
- Total Sales
- Affiliate Percentage

Metrics for User-generated Content Website

What are top metrics you would track for a user generated content website?

Things to Consider

Examples of user-generated content websites include Reddit, Quora and Medium.com

Answer

Acquisition

- Visitors
- Returning visitors

Activation

- Registered users

Retention

- Voters or Flaggers
- Commenters
- Posters
- Moderators

Monetization

- See items from the answer, Publisher Metrics

Metrics for Support Tickets

What are top support tickets metrics you would track?

Things to Consider

- What are the business goals?
- Which metrics correlate with saving money?
- Which metrics correlate with increasing customer satisfaction?

Answer

- # of customer tickets
- # of customer tickets by type (email, call or chat)
- Average resolution time
- Concern classification
- Net promoter score
- First call resolution
- Average # calls per resolution

Uber KPIs

Based upon what you know about Uber and its business model, what are some of the KPIs (key performance indicators) that you would want to focus on to judge how a market is doing overall?

Things to Consider

- From a business goal perspective, what's more important to Uber: revenue or market share?
- From a marketing perspective, what's most important: awareness, interest, trial or purchase?
- What are the most important recurring usage metrics?

Common Mistakes

- Not getting familiar with the topic beforehand, considering how widely Uber's business model and metrics are covered by mainstream business press.

Answer

CANDIDATE: Hmm, I can think of a few KPIs:

- **Number of rides per day**. The more, the better.
- **Average miles of each ride**. Are people actually taking rides for long distances or short distances? If it's mostly long distances, it might be a temporary thing. Short distances mean it's probably more stable.
- **Average rating across all Uber drivers**. Are our drivers good in our customers' eyes?
- **Surge pricing as a % of total time**. How often do customers have trouble finding an Uber ride? While drivers make more money when there's surge pricing, it turns off customers. We need to find a healthy balance.
- **Number of new drivers who get at least X amount of rides each time**. Are we getting new drivers who are appeasing the market? Are they finding decent work every day?

Chapter 16 Metrics: Prioritization Exercises

Most Important Metric: Two-Sided Marketplace

What is the most important metric for a two-sided marketplace like Uber?

Answer

CANDIDATE: Supply-side capacity is the most important metric for two-side marketplaces. For Uber, supply-side capacity is the number of drivers. For eBay, it's the number of seller listings. For AirBnB, it's the number of apartment rentals.

Take Uber for example. The more drivers there are, the more likely Uber can:

- *Cover a geographic location,* especially an area where there's demand
- *Increase the likelihood of matches,* improving customer satisfaction. Uber calls this minimizing zeroes. Zeroes are situations where a passenger fires up the app and can't find a driver.
- *Minimizes customer wait times.*
- *Minimize usage of surge pricing, improving number of completed transactions*
- *Increase word-of-mouth recruiting for drivers,* especially if current drivers tell potential drivers about the compensation possibilities

While it may feel that addressing customer demand could be as important, consider the following:

- Uber riders need drivers more than the drivers need the riders. In other words, the drivers can find alternative and similar ways to make money, whereas the alternative to Uber rides, whether it's taxi (not enough coverage, poor service) or public transportation (inconvenient, unreliable) is significantly poorer.
- If the riding experience is not of sufficient quality (largely controlled by the drivers), riders are unlikely to adopt Uber's service.
- If the riding experience is of sufficient quality but unavailable (not enough drivers in a geographic area), then riders cannot adopt Uber's service.

Most Important Metric: Mobile App

What is the most important metric for a B2C mobile app like?

Things to Consider

For B2C mobile apps, common ways to generate revenue are advertising, app purchases, subscription fees and in-app purchases.

Answer

CANDIDATE: For most mobile apps, the most important metric is growth in ad revenue. Here are the reasons why:

- Revenue will matter eventually, whether the company is large or small.
- Growth also matters for both companies big and small. Shareholder value will not appreciate if the company is not growing.
- Compared to mobile app purchases, advertising is the preferred and dominant method for generating mobile app revenue. Consumers are conditioned not to pay for mobile apps, given the copious number of free apps available.

I've sketched out the key drivers of mobile app revenue below. Looking at the issue tree, the most critical drivers of ad revenue, in my opinion are # users and time spent per user. These two metrics, which have a heavy impact on ad revenue, is based on how compelling the mobile app is coupled with how much usage that app drives with its audience.

If I could pick three metrics, I'd pick growth in the following metrics: ad revenue, # of users and time spent per user. But I know you wanted one metric, so to recap, I'd choose ad revenue growth since that metrics embeds the two other metrics I find important: growth in users and time spent per user.

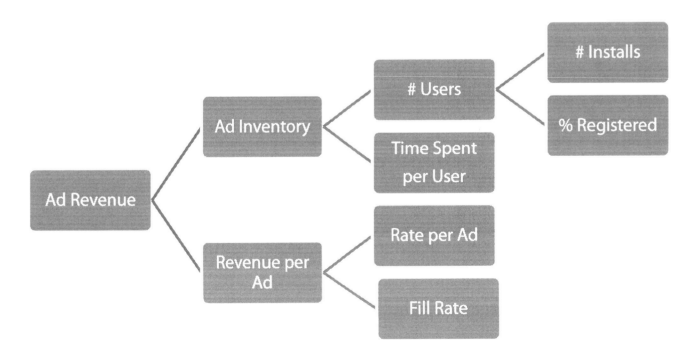

Most Important Metric: eCommerce

Let's say you are a venture capitalist. What would be the most important metric you'd want to see if you're considering an investment?

Things to Consider

- Venture capital is a high-risk and high-reward business. In other words, they're looking for opportunities where they can make billions of dollars.
- For an eCommerce to be worth of billions of dollars, they will have to dominant the industry, like Amazon. By dominating, they can enjoy the economies of scale benefits such as super brand, logistics infrastructure and negotiation power over suppliers.
- Gross merchandising volume represents the total sales volume, in dollars, flowing through an eCommerce site.

Common Mistakes

- Giving a short, uninspiring response (e.g. "I'd go with profits.")

Answer

CANDIDATE: There are several eCommerce metrics to choose from including:

Conversion Rate	Customer acquisition cost	Site traffic by source
Average order size	Margins	Gross merchandising volume
Shopping cart abandonment	Site traffic	Newsletter subscribers

If I were to choose one metric, I'd choose gross merchandising volume. Here's why:

- As a venture capitalist, I'd like to know how big the business could be. Gross merchandising volume (GMV) can give me a sense of how the large the business might be.
- From GMV, we can compute the revenue, whether the eCommerce site is based on extracting a commission like eBay or deriving gross margins by selling goods like Amazon.
- GMV is also driven by important metrics such as traffic, conversion rate and average order size.
- GMV is also a proxy for market position.

As much as I like the GMV metric, there are a few drawbacks:

- GMV does not factor in customer acquisition cost.
- GMV does not consider cost of sales or other margin information.
- GMV may not be correlated with cash flow.

Chapter 17 Metrics: Diagnose Exercises

Shopping Cart Conversions

The number of shopping cart conversions is down. What things would you check to diagnose?

Answer

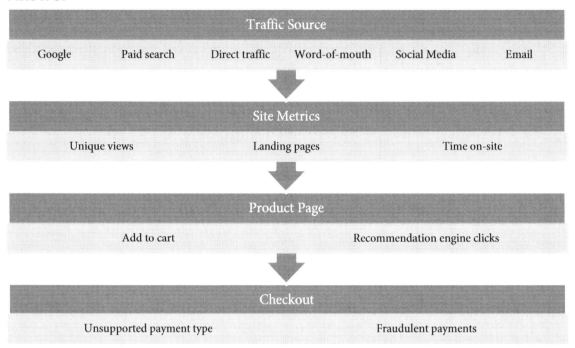

Mobile App Ratings

The number of mobile app ratings is down. What things would you check to diagnose?

Answer

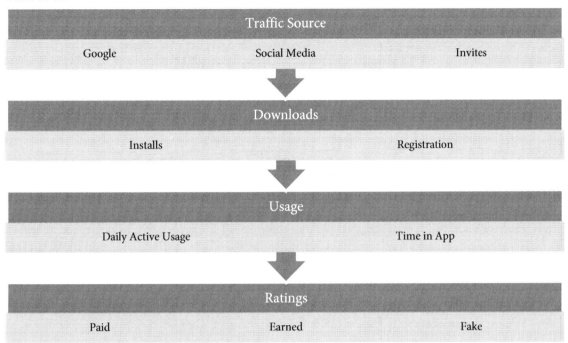

Reddit Posts

The number of Reddit.com posts created is down. What things would you check to diagnose?

Answer

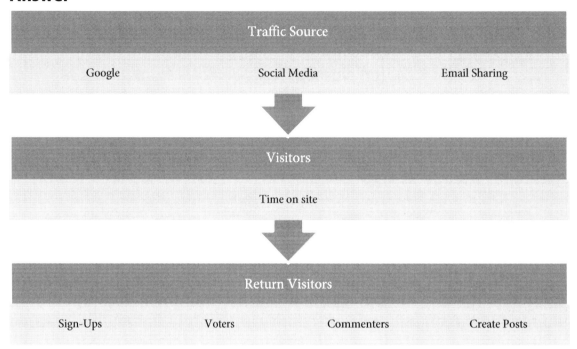

Chapter 18 Metrics: Putting it Together

Your Favorite Google Product

What is a Google product you love? Imagine you are responsible for one of its features. How would you monitor its use, and how would you measure its success or failure?

Things to Consider

Use the AARM metrics as a starting point

Common Mistakes

Not committing to a particular goal

Answer

CANDIDATE: My favorite Google product is Google Hangouts. It has the following features:

- **Voice Call.**
- **Video Call.**
- **Send/Receive Messages**. Including text, images, and videos.
- **Group Chat**. Add or remove from group.
- **Voice Message**. Leave a voice message.

Which feature do you want me to focus on? I would pick send/receive messages.

INTERVIEWER: Why don't we go with that?

CANDIDATE: All right. Here are a few metrics I would track:

- **Session Length:** I want to see how often a player is on during a session. It's natural for someone who is chatting to log on and off. I want to see if people are actively using this feature. This tells me how engaged our users are with our product. If the original intent is one way and data shows something else, that is a failure.
- **Session Frequency:** How often are users coming back throughout the day? If they rarely do, our engagement is low.
- **Retention:** I want to see whether a user actively uses our feature as days go by.
- **Push Notifications (Mobile):** Are users actually allowing push notifications for our product? If not, then that means they are not active users. How many users are coming back because of a push notification? If not, then our engagement is low.
- **Messages Sent:** How active are the users?
- **Messages Received:** A user may be sending lots of messages but is not getting anything in return. That may mean the default contacts are not good enough for our product, and we need to figure out some way to introduce friends.

To conclude, I want to see how engaged our users are with our feature. Depending on what we find, we can improve engagement by improving or adding features.

Drop in Hits

There was an 8% drop in hits to google.com. Larry Page walks into your office. He asks you to think and list what the reasons might be.

Things to Consider

- Seasonality
- Server maintenance
- Changes in referrers
- Changes in website layout
- Changes in website content
- Changes in website loading times
- Software bugs

Common Mistakes

- Having a short, unsatisfying list of metrics.

Answer

CANDIDATE: I would first begin by examining if this is country or region specific. Maybe there is censorship happening or a country has problem with its network infrastructure, or maybe our servers for that area is down. If that's not the case, I would see if this is desktop vs. mobile. I would continue to check if it's platform specific (e.g. iOS, Android, Amazon, Windows Phone) if it's mobile or browser specific (e.g. Chrome, Edge, Safari, Opera) or even if it's OS specific (Windows, Mac, and Linux).

Since this is an 8% drop in hits, I would also check with our tracking. Maybe our tracking has gone awry. I don't think I need to ask about other technical problems (like search not working on specific terms) because if we have them, I am sure Google has all the necessary checks in place to detect this and we would be facing a different question.

I would then begin to see if returning users or new users are the culprit. If returning users, perhaps a recent UI redesign is causing people to dislike our page. Maybe our search algorithm has a problem and the results are not as good as before. Or perhaps we added annoying ads or our account system is doing something weird. These are all likely things that would cause recurring users to leave.

If it is not the returning users, it must be our new users. We can dissect this through direct or referral. For direct, as I said earlier, if google.com is down we would have known by now so I don't think that's the problem. We can look at referral. First, is our marketing suffering from problems? Maybe our budget was slashed, or the rate has gone up but we haven't changed it so our prices are no longer competitive. Or perhaps our targeting is off. Are we targeting people who have access to Internet and a computer?

Next, we can look at other sources of referral. Are the links to google.com still working for our other products? If there is a problem with that, that could be it. Or, if new users are getting to our page fine, we must dissect our user experience. Maybe we're driving new users away with a different UI, different search algorithm or perhaps annoying pop-up ads.

This is the process I would go through. Is there any specific ones you want me to focus on?

INTERVIEWER: You've got a great list. Let's move on to the next question.

Amazon Web Services Metrics in Sydney

Imagine you are the AWS PM in Sydney. What are the top three metrics you'd look at?

Things to Consider

- For those who aren't familiar with AWS, it helps to first brainstorm a list of potential metrics to make sure nothing is missed.
- From there, choose what you believe to be the top three metrics.
- Be prepared to defend your positioning with clear rationale.

Common Mistakes

- Blurting out three metrics and then changing one's top three after they realize something better. It comes across as wishy-washy.

Answer

CANDIDATE: Interesting question. Could I brainstorm for a bit?

Candidate takes 30 seconds.

CANDIDATE: I would look at these three metrics:

- **Profit.** I want to know how much profit our service in Sydney is making us. This is important, because we need to pour more resources into maintaining and expanding this. If we are not making profit, we need to think about why this market has more room to grow.
- **Companies that need similar services but are not using AWS.** I want to know why they are not using AWS. Are there local or global competitors? Are they using them over us because of pricing or maybe different policies or customer service? This would also give us the potential market we could get. If this market is very small and we are not making profit, then we need to rethink Sydney.
- **Companies that promote products outside of Sydney who are using the servers in Sydney.** How many companies are using our Sydney infrastructure who are promoting products elsewhere? If there are a lot, why are they not using products in these other areas? Do we have services in those areas? Why not? This would give us an idea on whether or not we should expand to nearby areas.

Amazon Operations' Employee Performance

Assume you work in Amazon operations. What metrics do you think we use to assess employee performance?

Things to Consider

- Productivity
- Attendance
- Peer satisfaction
- Safety and compliance
- Complaints

Common Mistakes

- Choosing a vanity metric that's easy-to-collect but not actionable.

Answer

CANDIDATE: I would think of the following:

- **Cost.** How much does it cost us to keep them?
- **Revenue Generated.** How much revenue does the employee generate? We contrast this with cost to get effectiveness.
- **Work Done.** For certain employees that cannot have their work measured in monetary value, we can measure in terms of work done. This could be packages shipped, bugs fixed, etc.
- **Peer Review.** Probably based on a 1-5 star rating and a short description.
- **Manager Review.** Similar to the peer review.
- **Managed Employee Review.** Similar to the peer review.

INTERVIEWER: Why did you include peer review, manager review, and managed employee review?

CANDIDATE: This is an all-encompassing rating system. First, your peers work with you every day, so they know if you have been slacking off or have been efficient. Your manager also has an idea of this, but from a more top position point of view. You may be a manager yourself, and I think we would want to know how effective you are as a manager.

INTERVIEWER: What if a manager is rated low but he is efficient?

CANDIDATE: I assume you mean he is efficient at managing his employees. Maybe he's a slave driver and that's bad because the employees are disgruntled. That isn't going to last in the long run so this would show he's a bad manager. Results are not everything for a manager. We want managers that know how to make his teamwork efficiently and is well liked, otherwise his employees are going to hate it and eventually leave. Leaving and replacing someone wastes a lot of time and resources, so it's better if we try to prevent it as much as possible.

Declining Users

Facebook users have declined 20 percent week over week. Diagnose the problem. How would you fix the issue?

Things to Consider

- For diagnosis, think about the root causes of a decline. Drawing out a root cause analysis tree can help.
- For fixes, this is a brainstorming exercise. Take a pause to brainstorm solutions.

Common Mistakes

- Jumping to conclusions that a competitor's actions is the cause and hence the company should react by releasing identical features.

Answer

CANDIDATE: Hmm, interesting question. I would first start asking if this is mobile or desktop. If it's mobile, is it a specific platform (e.g. iOS, Android)? If it's desktop, is it a particular OS or browser (e.g., Chrome, Edge, Safari)?

INTERVIEWER: Let's say it's an even distribution.

CANDIDATE: I am going to assume it's not a hardware problem, like with our hosting servers. Because if it is, I think we would have discovered this a while back. Is there a particular page or feature that is having problems?

INTERVIEWER: It is not.

CANDIDATE: Okay, then I can say it's not a technical problem. Could there be a general downturn? Like the whole tech industry is seeing a 20% decline?

INTERVIEWER: It's just us.

CANDIDATE: Is this specific to a certain country or territory?

INTERVIEWER: It's across the globe.

CANDIDATE: Is this a recurring user or a new user problem? If it's a recurring problem, maybe it is our web design or content? Did we redesign the website lately and causing recurring users to leave? Or perhaps our content is having problems. Maybe the feed is acting up and not delivering as much content as before, or maybe our chat is broken. We could also be having a problem with our internal search. Maybe users are not finding certain pages because our internal search is broken.

Is there anything wrong with our content or system? Or do we have a growing competitor on the rise?

INTERVIEWER: Nothing of that sort.

CANDIDATE: Then it must be a new user problem. What is the status of our marketing lately? Have we dropped our marketing budget lately? Or perhaps the user acquisition price has increased, but we are still using the same rates so we are not as competitive?

INTERVIEWER: Doesn't seem to be the case.

CANDIDATE: Or maybe it's our target audience. Are we targeting the right audience? If not, perhaps we are running out of first-rate audiences and we are targeting second-rate audiences so they are not as good in quality.

New users come from three sources: search, direct or referral. For search, are we indexed correctly on Google or other search engines? For direct, we already determined that our website is okay, but is there something up with the DNS lookup? For referral, is there something wrong with our ads on different sources?

INTERVIEWER: Seems to be our new user traffic. Specifically, it seems to be our referral ads.

CANDIDATE: Oh, then we can just track it down to the problematic website, and fix it. It could be our link is not set up properly, or maybe our ad message or materials are not displaying correctly. It could be that we need new marketing assets.

Engagement on Dropbox

What metrics would you use to track Dropbox user engagement?

Things to Consider

- Active users
- Upload frequency
- Download frequency
- % of storage used
- Upgrades from free to paid
- Referrals

Common Mistakes

- Not factoring one of the most drivers of Dropbox engagement: whether or not a new user uploaded a file.

Answer

CANDIDATE: Can I get some time to brainstorm?

Candidate takes one minute.

CANDIDATE: I can think of a few metrics:

- **Average Number of New Files by day.** This tells me how active a Dropbox user is.
- **Average Number of File Edits by day.** This also tells me how active a Dropbox user is. The more files they are editing, the more they are using Dropbox. We need to be careful though, this number might be skewed. We need to look at this in addition to other metrics. If someone is editing one file daily, that's good engagement. However, he would have less edits compared to someone who is editing every file once a week.
- **Average Team Size.** I want to know how many users on average work on shared folders. This will tell me how useful people are finding this feature. This is for the shared folder only.
- **Percentage of People who used Share Folders in the last 30 days.** I want to know the recent adoption rate of this feature. This is for the shared folder only.
- **Average Number of Edits Made by Team Member.** Only track edits made after another team member has made an edit. I want to know how engaged people are with this feature. This is for the shared folder only.
- **Average Number of Devices.** What are the number of devices that use Dropbox by the same person across our users? This will give me an idea if people are finding Dropbox useful. Ideally, this number will be greater than one.

INTERVIEWER: Which metric do you think is the most important?

CANDIDATE: I think the average number of file edits by day. This would give me an idea how active a user is. If the user is editing many files every day that tells me, he or she finds Dropbox very useful. Otherwise, why would he or put the files he or she is working on in Dropbox?

Support Metrics for Dropbox

What metrics do you want to look at if you were the support manager of Dropbox?

Things to Consider

- Number of customer tickets
- Time to resolution
- Support customer satisfaction
- Tickets handled per support member
- First response time
- Contact volume by channel

Common Mistakes

- Drilling down too quickly on very specific issue such as sync errors or billing issues.

Answer

CANDIDATE: Just to make sure I understand: the support manager is someone who handles all customer support right?

INTERVIEWER: Yes.

CANDIDATE: Can you give me some time to brainstorm?

Candidate takes one minute.

CANDIDATE: Here are a few metrics I would look at:

- **Number of requests per two weeks.** Since Dropbox probably rolls out new fixes quickly, I would look at number of requests within a two-week period. I want to see whether people are having more problems as time goes on, especially during new patches and updates. If we see this, that may mean our QA process for updates need to be more thorough.
- **Requests that are about the same problem, ranked by frequency.** I want to see if we have problems that are never getting fixed while customers are still having trouble with them. This will help us identify these problems.
- **Summary of categories by ticket count.** This will help me see which are the problem categories and if we need to focus more toward these areas.
- **Average response time.** How are we doing on our response time? If it's too low, we may have a labor shortage problem, or our solution procedure needs to be looked at.
- **Resolved vs. unresolved tickets.** This will help me gauge whether or not customers are generally satisfied with us.

INTERVIEWER: Which one would you say is the most important?

CANDIDATE: Probably the tickets closed with resolution vs. tickets not. This will help me understand customer satisfaction. While it would be preferable to have a quick response time, it would not make our customers happy if the quick response time did not fix our customers' problems.

Success Metric for UberPool

What should be the main success metric for UberPool?

Things to Consider

- # of UberPool requests
- # of UberPool matches
- # of UberPool trips, given a time period
- # of active UberPool users
- Reduction in city congestion, due to UberPool usage

Common Mistakes

- Choosing vanity metrics such as visitors and visits to the www.uber.com/ride/uberpool/ page

Answer

CANDIDATE: Hmm, UberPool is the one where you are carpooling with multiple people right? For one ride? And each rider is being picked up from different locations and going to different pickups?

INTERVIEWER: Yes.

CANDIDATE: Hmm, I would track these:

- Average number of people per UberPool. A pickup location might be two people instead of one.
- Average number of stops per UberPool.
- Percentage of UberPool compared to other Uber rides.
- Number of times people thought about UberPool, then gave up and chose something else.
- Average rating differences between UberPool experience vs. other Uber rides.
- Average number of UberPool trips per month by repeated users.

The main success metric is probably the percentage of UberPool compared to other Uber rides.

INTERVIEWER: You mentioned percentage earlier. What percentage do you think is healthy for UberPool compared to other Uber rides?

CANDIDATE: Hmm, I would look at historical data and see what data we were happy with before. If we don't have that and I have to guess within 10 seconds, probably around 10%.

INTERVIEWER: That's low. Why 10%?

CANDIDATE: Well, most people who take Uber do it for the convenience, but also a large sector of people use Uber because they need to get somewhere fast. Speed is of the essence here, so I don't think it'll be that popular. Sure, plenty of people want to save, but I don't think it'll be that high.

Metrics for Uber Pick-up

What metric would you measure if we were focused on improving the Uber pick-up experience?

Things to Consider

- Number of people opening the request page
- Number of people making a ride request
- Number of requests that are fulfilled
- Time to fulfill request
- Post-trip satisfaction

Common Mistakes

- Focusing too much on low value-add items such as whether the driver offers water to its riders or whether the driver is a good conversationalist.

Answer

CANDIDATE: When you mean pick-up, do you mean just the waiting period, or do you count the finding a driver part of the experience?

INTERVIEWER: I mean the whole experience.

CANDIDATE: Okay, I would track the following:

- How long does it take someone to get a ride?
- How long does it take the driver to arrive at the pickup location?
- Average rating of the drivers.
- How long the phone call is between the driver and the rider? I'm guessing shorter phone calls means a better rider and driver experience. This could be misleading though, so we need to look at this in conjunction with the other metrics.
- How many drivers do users look at before picking one?
- How many times surge pricing happened? Frequent price surges indicate higher rider fares and a shortage of drivers.

Slow Download on Kindle

How would you troubleshoot a slow download of content on a Kindle device?

Things to Consider

- Large Kindle files
- Slow user connection
- Slow Amazon connection
- Slow server performance
- Slow user device performance

Common Mistakes

- Not considering non-Amazon issues, such as slow Internet connectivity.

Answer

CANDIDATE: I would first determine if this is a global problem or a country or regional problem. If it's a country or regional problem, it could be our infrastructure or Internet in that area.

If it were a global problem, I would think about our devices. Is this on a specific model?

If that is not it, then maybe it's our own distribution servers. Judging from the wording of this question, I am going to assume not, because I am sure Amazon has checks in all these critical parts. So if there were a failure, we would know instantly.

I would then check the content next. Is this all content or specific category of content? Like are we talking about books or videos?

Once we determine that, we can see if certain specific content is causing the problem. Maybe it's a specific category of movies or videos over a certain length. If it's content, it's most likely an indexing problem on our servers.

Pinterest Metrics

Imagine you are a Pinterest product manager. What metrics would you track?

Things to Consider

- Pins and re-pins
- Visitors and visits
- Conversions and revenue

Common Mistakes

- Using the wrong terminology, such as calling a pin or save a retweet.

Answer

CANDIDATE: Can I get some time to brainstorm this?

Candidate takes one minute.

CANDIDATE: I am thinking of these metrics:

- **Pins:** I want to see how many people are pinning content every day. This tells me the quality of the content on Pinterest. If this number continues to go down, we got a problem.
- **Most pins:** What is the most pinned content on our website? This is the most interesting content. I would also dissect this by user type (based on their search and uploads) so I can see what kind of content are considered the most desirable by these groups.
- **Re-pins:** What kind of content is so good that it is brought up repeatedly? I would want to know. I would also be wary of this number, because if it's too high when compared to pins, then that may mean we do not have enough fresh content.
- **Uploads per day:** How often are we getting new content per day? If this gets too low, it may be a problem with our users churning or not engaging.
- **Number of searches per day:** How many people are actually searching on Pinterest? This is the same idea with uploads per day, except on people who only use Pinterest for finding content.
- **Average time of search:** How fast does it take someone to find something he or she is satisfied with? The bigger this number, the worse the user experience. Either we don't have enough content, or there is too much content and users are having a hard time filtering out the one he or she wants.
- **Transactions:** How effective are our ads? We could look at revenue, but that doesn't tell the whole picture. What if our users are not clicking on many ads but are still making big purchases?
- **Revenue:** How effective are our ads?

Rehabilitation in Irish Prisons

How would you measure the rehabilitation rate in Irish prisons?

Things to Consider

- Rehabilitation, as defined by Wikipedia, is the "re-integration into society of a convicted person."
- Some metrics to consider include:
  - % arrested after reintegration within a defined timeframe
  - % arrested by offense type such as drug trafficking, fraud or robbery
  - Sentence type and length for rehabilitated persons arrested

Answer

CANDIDATE: What do you mean by rehabilitated?

INTERVIEWER: I mean, they are no longer committing crimes and are capable of taking care of themselves.

CANDIDATE: I would check:

- How many of them are no longer in prison?
- How many of them have a job?
- How many are actively looking for jobs?
- How many of them have been arrested for a new crime?
- How many of them are mentally healthy?
- How many of them are suffering from addiction such as drugs and alcohol?

INTERVIEWER: I find it interesting that you want to track mental health. Why?

CANDIDATE: Some prisoners are depressed or have trouble controlling their anger. Poor mental health may increase the probability of someone committing a crime. Improved mental health may indicate someone who has successfully rehabilitated.

Go-To-Market and Success

How would you measure the success of a go-to-market strategy?

Things to Consider

- As a starting point, think about all the key pieces of the marketing funnel: awareness, interest, trial and purchase.

Common Mistakes

- Setting the wrong goals.
- Not setting sufficiently high goals.
- Not having the data or getting incorrect data, leading the team to make the wrong conclusions.

Answer

CANDIDATE: Hmm, this is an open-ended question. Let me first describe what a go-to-market is, and then I will ask some clarifying questions.

Go-to-market can probably be best explained as a marketing process. When you start, you should think about your customers. Who are they? Are we targeting consumers or businesses? What kind of consumers or businesses? Once we identify a target segment, we can think about what marketing campaigns can target this segment most effectively. For example, if we are targeting businesses, a direct sales effort is more effective, especially since business products are a high involvement process. Then we need to think about how they can purchase our service. Going back to the business example, they can sign contracts with us, or they can sign for our service on their own, using a credit card like a software-as-a-service business like Salesforce. Our account managers can then serve as first point of contact should our business customers encounter any problems.

INTERVIEWER: Thanks for the go-to-market explanation. So what success metrics would you look at?

CANDIDATE: I would measure various metrics:

- **Reach.** How many customers did we reach out to?
- **Conversion rate.** Of those that we contacted, how many purchased our service or product?
- **Customer acquisition cost.** How much are we spending to market our products and goods? I'd like to compare this by product line, geography and sales channel.
- **Revenue and profit.** Most tech companies care about revenue, especially since tech companies have significant fixed costs such as R&D labor that can't be easily assigned to a single P&L. However, it would be best if we can track profitability. Numerous companies have incorrectly sustained poor performing businesses because they allocated costs incorrectly.
- **Market share.** Market share is most critical for winner-take-all markets such as two-sided marketplaces like AirBnB, Uber and eBay.
- **Word of mouth.** How many customers come to us because of other customers? We can track this using the industry measure for virality, the K-factor.

Handling Client Feedback

How would you make sure all client feedback is gathered and acted upon?

Things to Consider

- Since this is a hypothetical question, the first part of your response should be a hypothetical answer.
- Apply the rule of three in your hypothetical answer.
- Simply having a hypothetical answer may feel unfulfilling. So start with a hypothetical answer, roughly about 30 seconds in length for your part I. For part II, share an anecdote where you handled client feedback in accordance with the process you indicated.

Common Mistakes

- Giving answers that are short, ambiguous and vague.
- Not including an anecdote or example, making your hypothetical answer becomes perceived as "textbook."
- Sharing an example that doesn't necessarily follow the best practice process you offered.

Answer

CANDIDATE: First, we need to understand client feedback comes from different channels. For example, we could have a feedback from our mobile and web client. We could also get feedback through forums, email and social channels.

Next, we need to think about organizing feedback. We can start by grouping based on feedback type. Potential categories include praise, complaints, requests for help, and all encompassing "everything else" bucket.

Then we need to think about prioritizing based on urgency. We would prioritize the most urgent ones, perhaps measured in terms of revenue or PR impact, first. Furthermore, asynchronous communication channels, such as phone calls and live chat, may have to be addressed immediately.

It is useful to group again into symptoms and problems. A lot of client feedback could be referring to symptoms, not problems. For instance, a single problem may be the cause of both a customer complaint about the website doesn't work and nothing shows up on my screen.

Then we can consider the investment required to fix. Some issues are just questions that can be answered instantly. Some could be a minor fix that a user can address, provided they know what to do. Others may take hours, days or even weeks to do. When considering fixes, we need to consider our own schedules. We cannot respond to all complaints by asking all developers to drop what they're doing.

Lastly, we need to figure out a response to each piece of feedback. Ideally, we would love to report that the issue is fixed, but at the very least, we should be responsive and let them know that we are working on it.

INTERVIEWER: How would you track the effectiveness of your responses to clients?

CANDIDATE: I would implement a 1-5-star rating as well as a "Was your problem solved?" question from an account manager, business developer or customer service representative. I would also track the success rate by feedback. On a separate note, I will consider that some problems may not have a solution or that some solutions may take time to implement.

INTERVIEWER: I see.

CANDIDATE: Did you want me to give you an example of when I applied this client feedback process?

INTERVIEWER: Thanks for the offer. We are short on time, so let's move on to the next question.

Chapter 19 Hypothetical: Opinion

Creating Product Roadmaps

How do you define or create a product roadmap?

Things to Consider

- It is difficult to improvise an answer to this question, especially if you haven't put together a product roadmap recently.
- It's a great idea to plan what you're going to say, so that you don't provide an empty answer.
- An important part of roadmaps is the sequence of features, which imply tradeoffs and an understanding of critical path dependencies.

Common Mistakes

- Product roadmaps are innately visual, yet many candidates fail to draw the roadmap template that they use.
- Poor explanations on how product features are prioritized.

Answer

CANDIDATE: When I create roadmaps, here's my approach:

1. **Goals**. What are we trying to achieve? More customers or revenue? Or decreased churn?
2. **Brainstorm**. Create a giant list of every possible feature that I'd want to add. Creativity is a weapon. And one of the best ways to get groundbreaking, creative ideas is to brainstorm as much as possible.
3. **Prioritization**. Which combination of features will help us meet those goals, considering effort, cost (both labor and financial), and risk? Which ones have dependencies?
4. **Visual communications.** I'd put the roadmap on a slide so it is easier to communicate and get buy-in across audiences.

INTERVIEWER: Can you elaborate on how you would prioritize?

CANDIDATE: Sure, I would use a prioritization matrix. Here's an example:

	Benefit			Cost			Overall	
	Increase revenue	Customer value	Strategic value	Implementation effort	Operational costs	Risk	Score	Rank
Native iOS App	5	3	4	5	3	3	68	3
Referral Feature	3	4	4	3	2	3	84	1
New Dashboard	1	4	2	2	4	1	72	2

Source: Inspired by ProductPlan.com

INTERVIEWER: Can you draw out your roadmap?

Candidate takes a minute to draw

Acme X Roadmap	2016										2017
	Q4			**Q1**			**Q2**				
	October	November	December	January	February	March	April	May	June	July
Maximize Revenue										
Referral Feature										
Native iOS App										
New Dashboard										

CANDIDATE: I'd recommend we start building the referral feature in November. It's our most important feature, and it's expected to drive significant customer acquisition at low ongoing operational cost. The native iOS app work should start in January. I know the iOS app is ranked third in our list, but our Los Angeles engineering team has bandwidth to take it on then. They're also talented iOS developers. Lastly, the new dashboard work should start in March. We have a functioning dashboard today. It's not the most user friendly dashboard in the world, and it has some awkward manual workarounds. But I think we'll live if we have to wait three to four extra months.

Product Roadmap Best Practices

What are some product roadmap best practices?

Things to Consider

- A satisfactory best practice (and interview answer) makes the interviewer feel smarter after hearing your response.
- A strong best practice example is also novel and new.
- An anecdote, featuring a best practice insight from a recent book, article or workshop, would work well. It shows that you keep up with industry and indicates that you have a propensity for self-improvement.

Common Mistakes

- Answering the question by offering only a definition when the interviewer is expecting best practices.

Answer

CANDIDATE: I would be happy to share product roadmap best practices, but can you provide more details on what you are looking for? I looking for general advice, product roadmap templates or something else.

INTERVIEWER: Ah, sorry. I'm looking for a product roadmap template that I can use for my executive presentation next week.

Candidate is momentarily perplexed, but quickly regains composure.

CANDIDATE: When I put together roadmaps in the past, I've used three different format types: timelines, roadmap without dates, and Kanban. Would you like me to walkthrough these three types and discuss the pros and cons of each?

Interviewer nods eagerly.

INTERVIEWER: Yes, please.

Candidate draws on the whiteboard.

Timeline

Q1			Q2			Q3		
Jan	Feb	Mar	Apr	May	Jun	Jul	Aug	Sep

User Interface (UI)

| Conduct user interviews | | Interactive UI improvements |

| React framework |

Application Programming Interface (API)

| Define API specifications | | API Beta | | Rollout production-ready API |

Storage

| Agree on storage vendors | | Move entire product lines to new storage vendors | | Performance improvements |

Other Services Integrations

| Narrow down integration partnerships | | Complete integrations before EOY |

| Rollout first 5 integrations |

This format shows how initiatives relate to one another in the context of time. The advantage of this format is that it's clear when things happen, but the disadvantage is that it doesn't emphasize strategic importance.

Candidate draws on the whiteboard.

Roadmap Without Dates

People

Increase staff		Split groups in special task forces
	Onboarding & training	

Technology

Define SLA	Rollout three 9s	
		Increase to five 9s
Migration Plan	Migration implementation	

Security

Agree on security plan	Rollout must-haves	
		Meet production goals

This format shows initiatives relative to strategic priorities. In the example above, the strategic priorities are clearly people, technology, and security. The disadvantage is inverse of the previous example: the strategic priorities are clear, but it's not clear when these initiatives will start or end.

Kanban

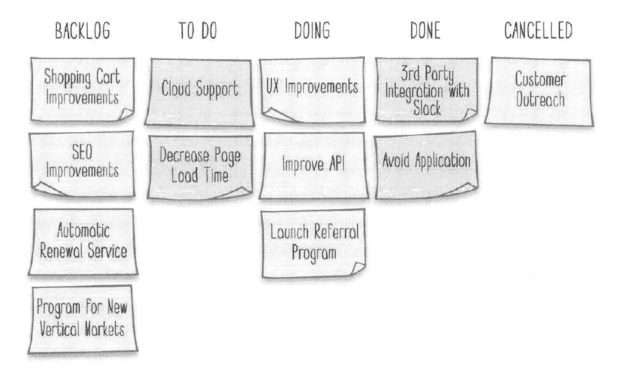

Screenshot / ProductPlan.com

A Kanban-style roadmap clearly indicates the status of individual initiatives, something the other two formats do not do. This format has two disadvantages:

- Start and end dates are not clear
- Strategic priorities are not clear

INTERVIEWER: Which one do you use?

CANDIDATE: I personally like the timeline method. I find that by having clear start and finish dates, we can be more goal-oriented in our approach. Management by objective (MBO) is one of the most effective tools is getting things done. Several high performing companies, including Google and Intel, have adopted MBO.

Prioritizing Requests

How would you prioritize requests, if you couldn't manage them all?

Things to Consider

- What is your criteria for prioritizing requests?
- How do you tradeoff between two requests that appear to be equally important?

Common Mistakes

- Giving a non-committal answer and implying that "one can do it all" by simply working longer hours.

Answer

CANDIDATE: It would depend on what type of product we are launching. Different products focus on different criteria. I would prioritize them depending on which ones we are focusing on:

- **Revenue Impact.** Which requests are projected to drive the most revenue? We could be working on a new ad SDK, and I would prioritize the most important ad space and features first. Our focus in this case is revenue, so if we don't launch with the biggest moneymaker it would deviate from our goal.
- **Customer Satisfaction.** Which requests will make our customers happy? Did we promise any features to the customers beforehand? What about critical fixes? These are things I would consider if I am working on, say a content website. If there are critical bug fixes or features we promised beforehand, not delivering them could result in a lot of negative feedback. As a product that thrives on customer satisfaction, that would be deadly.
- **Number of Customers Affected.** How many customers will each request affect? Let's say I am working on a social network. If a feature I launch would affect 90% of the users, I would prioritize that over one that would affect only 40% of the users. A feature that affects more users will most likely increase engagement, which will indirectly increase revenue and user experience.
- **Time to Resolution.** This is when we are trying to build breadth on our product or if we are doing bug fixes. Sometimes we are not going after the most critical feature, but trying to get as many features out the door as possible. How long it takes to deliver each becomes the measure for prioritization.
- **Technical Feasibility.** Everything is limited by if our engineers can do them. It won't make a lot of sense to prioritize features that are difficult technically.

In a real product, you are usually juggling more than two criteria. The criteria might be more specific or different from the above depending on your product and company goal. It's most important to consider your primary business goal, then your product and your team. Prioritize based on what you feel is the most important.

Good vs. Bad Product Managers

What are three characteristics of successful product managers? And three characteristics of bad product managers?

Things to Consider

- Use the Rule of Three
- For additional characteristics of good vs. bad product managers, refer to the following resources:
  - Ben Horowitz's famous essay, "Good Product Manager, Bad Product Manager."
  - Ian McAllister's Quora answer, "What distinguishes the Top 1% of Product Managers from the Top 10%?"

Common Mistakes

- Narcissistic responses.
- Answering the question by redirecting the interviewer to read another work such as, "Good product managers? You should read the essay that X wrote."

Answer

CANDIDATE: Successful product managers have three characteristics:

- **Ship products.** Some product managers obsess over details too much. As a result, their products take longer to ship than necessary. While making the perfect product is admirable, good PMs know how to balance time and quality.
- **Metric-centric.** Good product managers should have strong opinions. However, the best can analyze those opinions objectively and acknowledge contrarian viewpoints when necessary. Good product managers aren't obsessed with protecting their ego. They can let the data and metrics do the talking. And when it doesn't work, they are open to trying something else.
- **Motivate the team.** A good product requires a high performing team. Good product managers know how difficult and long it takes to make or improve a product. Sometimes teams will lose sight of the goal, but not teams with good product managers. Good product managers keep dreaming about the product; they will motivate the team to keeping marching. Nothing is impossible. They bring the burning ambition that fuels the team.

Bad product managers have the following characteristics:

- **Attempt to use authority.** Product managers manage the product, not the people. And product managers usually have limited authority. Even if they do have authority, using authority to get things done is a sign of weakness. Better product managers get things done through influence, usually through domain knowledge, data analysis and a proven record of accomplishment.
- **Married to their ideas.** Bad product managers grow attached to their ideas and will not let go, even if the data suggests otherwise. Good product managers take ownership of the product but never to a specific idea. Bad product managers don't understand this; they become offended whenever their ideas are rejected.

- **Have no goal.** Bad product managers don't have a goal or vision for their product. They get lost. They also have trouble articulating the roadmap toward the goal. They get distracted and jam everything into the product, confusing the team and delaying the schedule in the process. Bad product managers don't gather feedback and incorporate the feedback into the product. Their product becomes a cacophony of chaos.

Challenges for a PM

What are some of the challenges for a PM?

Things to Consider

Most common challenges for PMs include:

- Articulating product vision
- Convicting team on a certain course of action
- Figuring out ways to help the team do more in less time

Common Mistakes

- Complaining about unsexy tasks, such as taking notes and scheduling meetings.
- Complaining about being responsible even when the product is bad, marketing is poor, resources are limited or the engineering team is incompetent.
- Complaining about unclear executive priorities or not having enough time in the day.

Answer

CANDIDATE: The PM has a few challenges he needs to look out for:

- **Convince your team effectively**. As a PM, you have no official authority, so if you want the team to work on your ideas you need to convince them through proven success. This can feel frustrating because you may feel you know what's best. But know that even if you have authority over other people, using authority is a sign of weakness. Let your knowledge, charm, and proven record of success do the talking.
- **Strive to understand why**. Whenever someone tells you something can't be done the way you wanted it to be or that they don't understand your ideas, you need to have empathy. You need to see from their point of view why they don't agree, and see if you can address their needs to convince them. Usually, it's a simple case of misunderstanding. This is why you need to dig at the why. If you don't know the real reason why, how can you fix it? This goes for both working with a team and designing a product.
- **Beware of falling in love with an idea**. As a PM, you have a lot of ideas in your head, and not all of them will be good. This is why you work in a team and people can tell you how they feel about your ideas. Some people argue that as a PM, you are a trained professional who knows what you are doing. Engineers and designers can't possibly understand your vision. The truth is they don't need to. Every day users of your products won't care about your vision. They care about whether or not they find the product useful. When your team disagrees with you, sometimes they are actually right. Getting feedback is part of the design process. So don't be down. If an idea doesn't work, don't unnaturally force it. See if you can think of something better.

Mobile vs. Desktop Design

What are the differences between mobile vs. desktop design?

Things to Consider

- Use the Rule of Three.
- Backup your thinking with evidence.
- Further illustrate your point with examples, anecdotes or diagrams.

Common Mistakes

- Getting flustered.
- Identifying the right differences but going into depth.
- Giving up on answer and asking for pass because one is not a designer.

Answer

CANDIDATE: Can I brainstorm for a bit?

Candidate takes 30 seconds.

CANDIDATE: I can think of three things:

Space

There is less space on a mobile phone. As a result, you can fit less things into a mobile app. You can't cramp that many things into a screen either, since it would be a bad user experience. This affects both app design and language. Asian languages tend to do better because each character is the same size and a sentence isn't as long.

Desktop tends to be bigger, and things can take up a whole screen and be fine because users can easily resize to fit their needs. They can even attach a second monitor and have your product be on one screen. You still can't clutter that many things on one screen but this threshold is a lot higher compared to mobile.

Control

Mobile controls tend to reduce to only one thumb and just a press. To do other things you may use the other thumb, and have the user hold or use gestures. The thumbs or fingers you use also end up blocking what you are pressing. That's something you need to keep in mind as you design the UI.

A desktop user have the benefit of controlling software with two hands and two devices: both a mouse and a keyboard.

Habit

People tend to use mobile as a, "I have some time, let me check this out" attitude. They seldom stare at the screen for a long period. This is why things like push notifications are popular because it tells the user when there is something new happening. The advantage is that you can take mobile everywhere with you. With as little as 30 seconds to spare, you can check your mobile.

Desktop tends to be used for a longer period of time. You're usually sitting in front of a desktop in a comfortable position. When you're using a mobile, you're usually in a temporary position. So desktop software is optimized with this understanding. Clearly no one is going to pull out a desktop while waiting for a bus to come.

Emerging Technology

Talk about an emerging technology that you are tracking.

Things to Consider

- Voraciously read about latest technology trends if you haven't already
- Organize talking points for your favorite trends, preparing yourself to educate others on it

Common Mistakes

- Picking a cliché technology, which induces boredom
- Picking your own product or technology, which reveals lack of preparation
- Not explaining what the technology is or how it works
- Making a feeble attempt on why the technology is groundbreaking

Answer

CANDIDATE: I am actually tracking screenless display technology. Screenless technology, as the name implies, allows a computer to transmit visual information from a visual source without the use of a screen. There are three types of screenless technology today: holograms, retinal displays, and synaptic interface.

A hologram is self-explanatory. Retinal displays project images directly onto the retina perhaps with contact lenses. Synaptic interfaces bypass the eye and transmit images directly to the brain.

Here are three reasons why I'm excited about screenless technology, especially bionic lenses that provide retinal displays to the visually impaired:

- **Potential Market Size.** Think about how many people wear glasses today. This market is huge! Visually impaired individuals would never need glasses again and trust me glasses get in the way of everything. Most startups struggle to create demand; in this case, billions of nearsighted individuals provide latent demand.
- **Utility & Convenience.** Think of how useful it is to track everyone based on his or her eyes. Imagine walking around and have billboards display ads that are relevant to you. Sure, some might be concerned with privacy. But are smartphones not already tracking our every move? This isn't that different. Also, think about convenience. You no longer need to wait in line at the airport, and you can even have this tie to your payment information so you can just hop on the train or grab a meal without pulling out your wallet.
- **Health & Safety.** Having this technology would improve our safety and well-being. Nearsighted individuals would minimize the number of accidents that occur when they do not have their glasses or contact lenses.

To summarize, I am a big fan of bionic lenses because of the market size, utility, and contribution to health and safety.

Impact of Self-Driving Cars

What will be the impact of self-driving cars?

Things to Consider

- Better responses consider how the technology will create new industries or destroy old ones.
- Brainstorm an exhaustive list of things to consider such as the environment, urban planning, government agencies, customers and competitors.
- A before and after analysis can keep things organized.

Common Mistakes

- Limiting your answer to a few ideas. Interviewers expect many.
- Stating only obvious, commonplace answers such as taxi driver unemployment will go up.
- Not structuring the answer, making it hard to follow.

Answer

CANDIDATE: I can think of a few things:

- **More cars on the road**. People who didn't drive before will now drive. This includes people who didn't know how to drive, people who didn't want to be stuck in traffic and instead rode public transportation, and people who carpooled.
- **New laws related to self-driving cars**. Because there is now another class of driver, we need to update our laws regarding driving.
- **Oil prices will go up**. Now there is more people driving, which means more demand for oil.
- **Non-self-driving car prices will go down**. There is now something more convenient than normal driving; prices for cars that do not drive themselves will go down.
- **Shuffle in the car industry**. Depends on who is working with people with technology in self-driving cars, certain brands of cars may get more popular or decrease in popularity.
- **Increase in jobs**. We will need new roads, perhaps with different requirements. And new self-driving cars will be built. This means more jobs.

Favorite Android Apps

Tell us about your favorite lesser-known Android applications. Why?

Things to Consider

- The prompt is asking for "lesser-known" so stay away from popular apps like Yelp and Facebook.
- The reason this question is being asked: interviewer wants to be inspired and learn something new. They also want to feel that you are actively seeking out new applications to try.
- Don't forget to explain what the product is and why it's your favorite. Describing how it works is optional.

Common Mistakes

- Poorly explaining what it is.
- Giving lukewarm reasons on why an application is your favorite.

Answer

CANDIDATE: I can think of three:

- **Unified Remote.** It allows you to make your Android a remote for your PC. It's nice because people usually use it to play music or TV shows. Traditional TV is dying and Internet TV is taking over, but some people don't watch TV that often enough to commit to Internet TV. This services that sector because these people typically watch something on Netflix or Hulu on their computer that is hooked up to a huge TV. It has a lot of potential because if we can get the PC to send feedback back to the phone, we'll have contextual information on the user. We can push ads to the user (e.g. suggested music and movies).
- **RunPee.** This app lets you know when it is a good time to step outside for a bathroom break depending on the movie you are watching. It's a useful app because movie theaters, unlike watching movies at home, don't have pause buttons.
- **Hooked.** This app is fast food news. It's becoming more and more popular these days with people having less and less time. This is nice because there is a huge potential market here, and again, contextual ads. Let say you select your news based on your preference, we can show ads depending on your preference. If you like shoes, we can show you ads about where you can buy shows. Not only do we get user data, we can even contextualize ads based on the piece of content.

Product Management Definition

What does product management mean to you?

Things to Consider

- Answer by using the Rule of Three. It gives your answer depth; it also makes it easy to follow.

- Your hypothetical answer, in the best-case answer, would only take 30 seconds.

- I would recommend that after the first 30 seconds to offer an actual example where you behaved in accordance with the three principles outlined in your hypothetical answer.

Common Mistakes

- Giving a meandering, hard-to-follow response. This commonly happen when the candidate is trying to think and articulate their answer at the same time.

- This is a nit-pick, but many candidates unnecessarily stall by saying, "Great question." It is a filler phrase.

Answer

CANDIDATE: When I think about the role of a product manager, I think of three main pillars:

- **Serve as a team leader.** The PM serves as the hub for the entire team. Product development is becoming more and more complicated, and it's not strange for a team to have multiple departments within. The PM serves as the interface between all the teams and customers. This person routes resources, plans the steps, and fixes problems. The PM also ties the team together and march forward toward the goal with them. Lastly, the PM brings consensus and mobilizes the execution and success.

- **Define the goal**. The PM figures out the goal and the needs for the product. Which market are we targeting? What features do we need? Who are our customers? These are all answers the PM must answer. In essence, the PM is there to figure out the true north for the product, and this person is there guide the team. Whenever anyone is lost, the PM is there to remind that person what the true north is. This person builds expectations and drives the vision.

- **Explain the vision or game plan**. The PM needs to figure out why we are doing this product this way, and why. This person needs to figure out the prioritization of these features and why they are done in this order. The PM doesn't do this through sheer mental power. The PM also looks and pokes around the data and presents it to the team so they understand why. This person makes sure the team understands his point of view and addresses their questions or concerns.

Can I give you an example where I demonstrated all three pillars?

INTERVIEWER: Sure, we have some time.

CANDIDATE: Back in January of this year, I was in charge of the Amazon Web Services (AWS) Ireland project. We wanted to launch a new UI portal, and I was in charge of 20 service teams to get it released. In this role, I served as the team leader, determined the goal and explained the game plan to the team.

First, I determined the goal. We wanted to launch the new portal in four months, and I defined the key performance indicators (KPIs) for the project including meeting the deadline, service uptime, service availability and cross-team employee satisfaction.

Then, I communicated the process that included:

- Establishing a framework
- Streamlining work with our vendor teams
- Publishing documentation for the team's reference

Lastly, I prioritized our team's work items. I looked at three criteria including:

- Customer impact
- Urgency
- Strategic importance
- Projections of data center capacity

I am proud to announce that the UI portal launched two weeks ahead of time. Andy Jassy, the Amazon SVP who heads up AWS congratulated me and the team at the team meeting for a job well done. He told my boss that my leadership and my communication skills impressed him.

INTERVIEWER: Thanks for sharing the example.

What Do You Bring

What would you bring to the team that nobody else would?

Things to Consider

- Use the Rule of Three.
- Highlight personal attributes that reinforce your personal brand; that is, characteristics that make you special versus others.

Common Mistakes

- Choosing general, undifferentiated attributes like working hard and getting along with others.

Answer

CANDIDATE: I can think of three things:

- **Telemetry.** With project teams getting bigger and bigger, it's becoming increasingly hard for team members to understand what is going on around the company. As a PM, I would bring telemetry to the table. It's one of the core functions of the PM to interface with every team. I would route resources, plan the next step, and sync with everyone to make sure everyone knows what they need to push the product forward. My job is to point to the true north during our entire journey there.
- **Well-roundedness.** As a PM, my background and experience is well rounded. Engineering, product design, project management, user experience, and business are just some of the skills I have that will bring this team to its full circle. I bring to the team a unique perspective. Because I can understand every department's goals and views, I can see why they think the way they do and mold the team into one well-oiled machine.
- **Motivation & Teamwork.** Developing a product is hard business. Teams run into many roadblocks and frustrations. It's important the PM motivates them. Let them know it's okay to run into problems they can't seem to fix, that's why we are a team. Your problem is our problem, and there's nothing we can't fix by working together. As a team, we are an army that marches forth, and my job is to keep the army morale high.

To conclude, as a PM I would bring to the team telemetry, well-roundedness, and motivation & teamwork.

What do you like about being a PM

What do you like about being a PM?

Things to Consider

- Use the Rule of Three
- Acknowledge some of the keys traits of the role (design, product, and engineering), which preferably coincides with your strengths
- Be thoughtful

Common Mistakes

- Not having a good explanation on why you chose or transitioned into PM.
- Revealing character flaws that indicate not being suited for a PM role, such as a preference for working alone.
- Being overly enthusiastic, bordering on being pretentious

Answer

CANDIDATE: I have three favorite things about being a PM:

- **Intersection of Design, Product and Engineering.** As a PM, I feel lucky being able to stand at the intersection of design, product and engineering. I get to interact with everyone and get a hand in doing everything.
- **Teamwork.** I really enjoy the teamwork aspect of being a PM. I know everyone else is also in a team, but the teamwork experience is a lot more intense as a PM, since you are at the intersection. It feels great to work with a team to build a great product together. The togetherness builds camaraderie and fulfills my sense of community.
- **Iterative Design and Improvement.** There's a sense of accomplishment when you take something and make it better and better. You see the action firsthand, learn, suggest ways to improve, and repeat the process again. As your product gets better, the product gets more users. It is a virtuous cycle.

Challenges for a PM

What are some of the challenges for a PM?

Things to Consider

- Use Rule of Three.

Common Mistakes

- Only listing one to two challenges and unable to mention more, even when asked.
- Suggesting challenges that sound naïve such as too many meetings or too much politicking.

Answer

CANDIDATE: There are a few challenges I can think of:

- **No Authority.** The PM manages the product, not the people. As a PM, you have no direct authority over anyone. You can't ask someone to do something if they don't agree with you. Sometimes I imagine it would be easier if I could make everyone do everything the way I want. But remember, even if you had authority, using it is a sign of weakness. Not to mention deep down you know your ideas, without feedback, are nothing. When your team doesn't like your idea, it's a chance for you to improve it. Don't take feedback for granted; it's a gift.
- **Letting Go.** Sometimes it's hard to let go of your favorite feature or idea because it isn't working well. As a PM, you can't get married to your idea. Remember that if something doesn't work, that's a chance to switch gears and think of something new. That's exciting! You get to improve your product. What's not to love? What's the point of something that doesn't work well?
- **Doing Everything.** It may feel like you have to do everything no one else wants to do at times, and that makes you feel unfocused or useless. Remember that someone has to do these, so you are actually serving an important role. In addition, the focus is to make your product great. You want that, don't you? So let your false sense of pride go. You are a PM, and you are contributing to making your product great. What's terrible about that?

Chapter 20 Hypothetical: Problem Solving

Amazon and CEO of Lighting Company

Let's assume you're now in an elevator with the CEO of a lighting company, what would you say to her to convince her to list her products on Amazon?

Things to Consider

- Showcasing products on Amazon can improve awareness.
- Having products on Amazon expand the pie. That is, the lighting company will likely have greater overall profit, even if the company offers a unit discount on Amazon. (The unit sale increase will offset the price decrease.)

Common Mistakes

- Overestimating the effectiveness of rationale appeals. Appeals to emotion are just as important, if not more important.

Answer

CANDIDATE: Is there any specific reasons why she doesn't want to list her products on Amazon?

INTERVIEWER: She's concerned that listing her product on Amazon will cannibalize her own distribution channels.

CANDIDATE: Does she sell online?

INTERVIEWER: She sells it through her own brick-and-mortar shop and work with other distribution channels like Lowe's and Home Depot.

CANDIDATE: Hmm, that is probably a very common train of thought for vendors. I think there are various ways I can approach this.

- **Amazon's Market Share.** I understand she makes most of the profit if she sells it through her channels, but Amazon has the biggest buyer market. She would end up making more money even if she makes less on each purchase because of the traffic alone.
- **Different buyers.** The people who buy from her distribution channels and Amazon are not the same people. Most people that shop online probably don't want to go to a brick-and-mortar store to shop. She will be targeting a completely new market.
- **Just one of the channels.** If she's already selling her products to Home Depot and Lowe's, we are just another distribution channel. I mean, plenty of vendors, big ones too, sell through their own channels, brick-and-mortar stores, and Amazon.com. We are just another distribution channel. She is already working with others, so what makes us different?

INTERVIEWER: Which approach would you recommend?

CANDIDATE: Probably a combination of all three. If she's already open to the idea of working with brick-and-mortar stores like Home Depot and Lowe's, she's not trying to be exclusive. Revenue is her biggest concern and more channels can't hurt, especially since Amazon has the biggest market share.

Kindles on Christmas

You have 100,000 Kindles. There are three weeks until Christmas. The following vendors sell the following numbers of Kindles per week:

- Best Buy: 20K

- Walmart: 10K

- Staples: 1K

- Fred Meyer: 2K

- Amazon.com: 50K

How would you allocate the 100K Kindles that you have?

Things to Consider

- Profit should be the main consideration, but other considerations that may come into play including supplier relations, transportation contingencies and customer perception.

Common Mistakes

- Wasting time doing back-of-the-envelope calculations when the interviewer is looking for a simply qualitative discussion.

Answer

CANDIDATE: Is there a particular reason why some vendors are selling more than others? I want to know if this is because of the price difference, traffic or better presentation.

INTERVIEWER: What do you mean by those?

CANDIDATE: If there are two stores, A and B, and A is selling more than B, it could be because A sells it for cheaper, A has more or higher quality traffic or A presents the product better. For the last one, since it's a Kindle, maybe A lets people try them and B does not.

INTERVIEWER: If I have no such data, what would you infer?

CANDIDATE: Well, Best Buy is well known for selling electronics vs. an office supply store like Staples. Therefore, I would say Best Buy has better-matched traffic. Whereas Walmart has stores everywhere and tend to have more people. Fred Meyer is similar to Walmart, with a smaller retail footprint, based in the Pacific Northwest. Finally, Amazon.com just has a lot of people, lower price, and of course, more customers that like Amazon products.

INTERVIEWER: What other information do you need?

CANDIDATE: I actually want to know two more data sets. First, I am sure every store will discount the Kindle.. What's the discount for each store? In addition, do you have an estimated number of Kindles sold last year in each store? If not, the traffic flow last year for each store would also work.

INTERVIEWER: Let's just say Best Buy and Walmart has a 25% discount. Staples and Fred Meyer has a 15% discount. Amazon.com has 30% off. I don't have the sales figure from last year nor do I have the traffic information.

CANDIDATE: Okay, I think I would distribute it like this:

- Best Buy: 30K
- Walmart: 15K
- Staples: 2K
- Fred Meyer: 3K
- Amazon.com: 50K

There are several reasons I did this:

- **Last Minute.** People will buy gifts at the last minute, and they usually panic and go to local stores.
- **Brick-and-Mortar Popularity.** Most people prefer shopping in brick-and-mortar stores during the holidays. They can look at the Christmas displays and have kids meet with Santa and his reindeers.
- **Showrooming.** I still think Amazon wouldn't lose sales to the brick-and-mortar store. For instance, many of my friends will want to try a Kindle at a brick-and-mortar store and then purchase on Amazon.com. They're assuming that they'll get a better price and service if they buy directly from the manufacturer.

Overstocked Books at Amazon

Let's assume we don't have a system that tracks and manages our inventory levels (we do), how would you approach the challenge of overstock books?

Things to Consider

- Did you demonstrate your understanding of why overstock books is a problem for Amazon?
- What kind of clever ways can you turn overstock inventory into cash?
- What kind of clever ways can you turn overstock inventory into non-monetary value?

Common Mistakes

- Suggesting only obvious ideas such as discounting on Amazon or doing an Amazon Prime Warehouse deal.

Answer

CANDIDATE: Just to be clear, you want to know what I would do to get rid of them if I suddenly got a lot of overstock books right?

INTERVIEWER: Yes.

CANDIDATE: Do we have books of all different genres and types (e.g. magazines, textbooks, novels) or is there an overstock of a particular type?

INTERVIEWER: You have a mixture.

CANDIDATE: Okay, can I get some time to brainstorm?

Candidate takes one minute.

CANDIDATE: I can think of a few ideas.

- **Sales.** I would start a sale on Amazon.com just to sell these books. This would get rid of some if not all the books because of the warehousing costs for unsold inventory. A sale would also attract some new users (both new to Amazon and those new to buying books on Amazon).
- **Promotions.** I would run some sort of promotions. We can do one where we offer free books or lower priced books if you purchase select items. We can do free book giveaway events. We can even do bundle sells (e.g. buy two books and get the third one free). This gets rid of the books and has the potential of attracting new users.
- **Other Distribution Channels.** Since Amazon has no physical stores, I would see if I could sell these books to physical distribution channels like Barnes & Noble. Sure, they are technically a competitor, but this wouldn't strengthen them or anything. Of course, I would not offer any exclusive books as they are Amazon only, but this is a good way to get rid of overstocked books. The problem is that we don't really get any indirect benefits like more engagement or users unlike the other two ideas.

INTERVIEWER: Which one would you recommend?

CANDIDATE: Probably the promotional event. It can attract users both new Amazon customers and existing Amazon customers (that is, those that haven't bought books before). It can also influence Amazon customers to purchase other goods. And when people come buy something on Amazon, there is a good chance they'll purchase other things too. This drives up sales.

INTERVIEWER: How would you implement this?

CANDIDATE: To start, I would need some data regarding our profit margin on the books. I want to see how low I can sell the books without taking a loss. I would also want to see how popular these books are usually. That'll give me a good idea about which books to pair with which items. For items we are pairing with, I would also need their sales figure. I would pair popular items with not so popular books or books that are overstocked. This way I can get rid of them faster. Of course, these are all in preparation of these events. I would launch new deals as the event is going to react to real time sales figure. If a book that is not being sold as quickly as I like, I would either lower the price some more or pair it with other items as well. If a certain book were selling well, I would try pairing it with items that are not normally sold very well to see if this book is good at driving purchases.

Vendor Failure during Holiday Season

How you deal with a vendor's failure to deliver on large contract during the holiday season?

Things to Consider

- What is the impact?
- Who do it affect and to what degree?
- Why did this happen?
- How do we prevent this from happening again?

Common Mistakes

- Not holding the vendor accountable.
- Not suggesting an alternative plan.
- Not planning for this potential risk.

Answer

CANDIDATE: It depends. Are those products they produce things that will be center stage for our holiday sale?

INTERVIEWER: Let's assume they are.

CANDIDATE: That would be a big problem then. Let me list out some problems we'll face:

- People are expecting product X, and we are going to be out of stock on product X. That's a bad user experience, not to mention loss of revenue.
- People who buy product X might end up buying product Y and Z while they are here. Those are missed cross-sell opportunities.
- People who buy product X might end up seeing product A and B because they figured they might as well (for shipping, they are on Amazon anyway, etc.) Now that cross promotion is gone.

INTERVIEWER: That's a good analysis. How would you handle these problems?

CANDIDATE: I can think of a few solutions:

- **Don't offer discounts on product X.** Fewer people will buy product X, without the discount, but we'll hold onto more product before running out of stock. Some customers will be disappointed that there's no sale, but it's better than not being able to buy the product at all. It's not a permanent fix, but it's better.
- **Don't promote product X.** Same thing as the previous solution. We don't put it in the front page. Less attention means less buyers; less buyers means we can hold onto more product before it goes out of stock.
- **Limit purchases per account.** Just in case people want to buy multiple (this tends to happen with TVs on certain holidays), we want to limit maybe one or two per account. This delays the out of stock problem.

- **Contact other vendors.** See if other vendors can offer the same or similar products. This might not work out though, since it's likely this is something we are already doing for the holiday season. Even if there are, it will take time and we might not have enough time.
- **Offer similar products.** Offer similar products if we have this. Let say Samsung TV is product X. Maybe a TV from another vendor will suffice. Think about it, most people buy TVs because they want a TV, not because they want a Samsung TV.
- **Allow other stores to sell on Amazon.** This might be a long shot, but it's worth a try.
- **Purchase from other stores.** This is something extreme, but if we figured out that we will get a lot of lateral sales and cross promotions, we can actually buy this product X from other stores and sell at a loss. As long as we estimate correctly, we'll end up with a net gain.

INTERVIEWER: What if the ads for this product is already sent out to the users and everyone is waiting for this product to be on sale for a specific price?

CANDIDATE: I would stop promoting it right now and definitely not promote it on the website. I would also limit the purchases by account. While it will minimize the bad user experience, it won't completely solve the problem. I've actually encountered cases like this as a user and it's frustrating, but definitely less disappointing than the website just not offering the product or offering it at a much higher price than advertised.

INTERVIEWER: Of these solutions, which one would you propose?

CANDIDATE: Probably a combination of them. The first three would be easy to do on our end. Not a lot of work required. Everything else would be something we have to try as well. In terms of effectiveness though, if contacting other vendors and offering similar products work out, they are better solutions.

Not Hitting Deadline

You have to do feature X or launch product Y, which requires 10 engineers to finish on time. You only have five. What do you do?

Things to Consider

- Can you get more resources?
- Can you change scope?
- Can you gain more time?

Common Mistakes

- Not developing a structured framework that is easy to follow.

Answer

CANDIDATE: Can I get some time to brainstorm?

Candidate takes one minute

CANDIDATE: Anytime I'm faced with a tight deadline, I use the following six-point framework to consider my options:

1. **Recruit Engineers Externally.** Recruit more engineers externally to fulfill our requirement.
   - **Pros:** Solves the problem completely.
   - **Cons:** Might take time to recruit. Takes time for new engineers to get comfortable. We might not need extra engineers after this.
2. **Recruit Engineers Internally.** Recruit more engineers to work on this project within the company.
   - **Pros:** Solves the problem completely.
   - **Cons:** Might take time to recruit. Might not have engineers on standby. Takes time for new engineers to get comfortable. Need to switch back after which will take time.
3. **Change Implementation.** Maybe the way we've been doing it is a bit too complex. We can see if we can provide easier solutions first.
   - **Pros:** Might discover new solutions when reassessing the situation.
   - **Cons:** Might not be what users/stockholders want. Pushes the problem back because we might still need to implement the solution later.
4. **Change Scope.** Maybe we should scale back a bit and only implement partial functionality or more critical features, then update the rest later.
   - **Pros:** Is a very graceful way to fix this. Rather get the thing out and have users playing around with some functionality than not.
   - **Cons:** Might not be what users/stockholders want. Launching is going to take time so we are essentially doubling that. Still have to implement later.
5. **Push Deadline Back.** We can always ask to push the deadline back.
   - **Pros:** Fixes the problem completely.
   - **Cons:** Might not be doable depending on business strategy. Might lose out to competitor.

6. **Overtime.** We can ask the team to overtime.
   o **Pros:** Fixes the problem completely.
   o **Cons:** Bad for team morale. Team will definitely not be happy. Bad precedent.

INTERVIEWER: It's interesting you mentioned overtime in there. That's a very touchy issue for a PM to bring up to your team. How would you approach this?

CANDIDATE: I would first not tell the team about this. I want to approach the higher-ups first. Ask them if the team commits to overtime (I would estimate how long the team needed), could the team get some additional vacation time after the deadline? If higher-ups agree, I will then ask the team if they want to do this. If they say yes, I'll get back to the higher-ups and we'll schedule it this way.

INTERVIEWER: What if the higher-ups say no to vacation time and just want you to work extra hours?

CANDIDATE: I would have to assess the situation. Even if I know the feature is very important, losing the morale of the team is the bigger tradeoff here. Think about it. Sure, we were delayed or we only had partial features for a launch. However, that's nothing compared to the entire team being dissatisfied. We might even lose a few people over this and that's going to waste so much time and effort.

INTERVIEWER: So you would tell the higher-ups that it's not doable?

CANDIDATE: It's a hard question to answer because there is no win-win situation, so I have to pick a side. In most scenarios, I would side with my team. Besides the reason above, my team would also lose trust in me. I can't do my job properly as a PM if my team no longer trusts and respects me.

INTERVIEWER: You are saying you would spoil your team whenever they ask for something?

CANDIDATE: No, I would not. In this case, it's not spoiling. It's a tough situation to be in and I thought about the tradeoffs. I picked a side.

INTERVIEWER: But situations like this happen a lot. Are you going to do this every time? How can the company trust you as a liaison between upper management and the team?

CANDIDATE: If they trust me to be the liaison, they should trust my judgment. I get where they are coming from. I really do. However, sometimes we have to make sacrifices to make the team happy. Overtime is something that happens a lot, but who caused this anyway? Did we do badly on estimating how long we need? We need to perform an analysis on where we went wrong so we can prevent this next time. But for this current situation, we need to fix it this way.

INTERVIEWER: What if you were the one at fault for this? Would you still tell the team this?

CANDIDATE: Yes. I would own up to my mistake. There's no point in lying to your team. They'll find out anyway, and you should be honest toward your own teammates. If you aren't going to do that, then how can they trust you?

User Problems

Half the users have one problem. The other half have another problem. How would you resolve this?

Things to Consider

- What is the issue?
- Which issue is more important?
- Are there opportunities to resolve both with a single solution?

Common Mistakes

- Not demonstrating a willingness to investigate the issue deeply and instead, just reacting.
- Showing poor prioritization judgment.

Answer

CANDIDATE: I would start by seeing if these two problems are related. Maybe they are just two separate symptoms of the same problem.

I would then analyze if these two users were related or completely unrelated. If they are completely unrelated, maybe that's the key in solving it. For example, maybe one set of users have Windows, and another set have Macs. We are seeing problems related to their operating systems.

If these two sets of users are related, I would exclude factors until I can find where they are not related. Reason being it's probably like above.

INTERVIEWER: What are some reasons why two groups of unrelated users are encountering different problems?

CANDIDATE: Well, I can think of a few:

- They are using different operating systems.
- One set is mobile and another is desktop.
- They are using different platforms such as iOS vs. Android.
- They are using different browsers such as Chrome vs. Edge.
- They are A/B targets (unlikely, but maybe someone at Amazon really wanted to test something).
- They are trying to buy different things such as games vs. electronics.
- They are in different countries such as Japan vs. US.
- They are using different languages such as Japanese vs. English.
- They are using different payment options such as credit cards vs. PayPal.

Kindle Date Slip

It is March. You are on the Kindle Team, and the engineers tell you that the new Kindle due in September will not ship until January. What do you do?

Things to Consider

- If your first thought is freak out, you're not the only one. Resist the urge to start blabbing; instead, use your fight or flight impulse as a reminder to take a moment to calm your nerves and think about the situation before answering.
- Consider using the Five Whys technique to investigate the root cause of the delay.
- Many candidates become preoccupied with analysis that they forget to issue a recommendation.

Common Mistakes

- Not issuing a recommendation.
- Not going deep enough on the potential reason for the delay.
- Not suggesting a satisfactory solution.

Answer

CANDIDATE: I'm going to take a minute to collect my thoughts.

Candidate takes one minute.

CANDIDATE: I would first start asking him the reason why they are delaying it.

INTERVIEWER: They believe the product is not feature complete. If it launches in September, they believe it'll disappoint customers.

CANDIDATE: I would ask what features do they think are missing?

INTERVIEWER: Whispersync. It lets you synchronize your audio books with your regular books.

CANDIDATE: Is this a new feature or a feature carried over from the previous version?

INTERVIEWER: Does it matter?

CANDIDATE: Well, if it's something from the previous version of Kindle, users would feel the feature isn't complete if it doesn't show up here.

INTERVIEWER: It's a new feature for this Kindle edition.

CANDIDATE: Is there any reason why we never included it in the original spec?

INTERVIEWER: The team thinks that only a small percentage of users would find this useful, so they didn't feel justified to include it.

CANDIDATE: So what is the reason for including it now?

INTERVIEWER: The team researched the market again and realized it is a feature requested by 40% of the users surveyed.

CANDIDATE: How many users did the team survey?

INTERVIEWER: Around 50,000.

CANDIDATE: I am assuming the reason why the Kindle is slated for September is to get in the shopping seasons in November and December. If we delay it until January, the sales figures would probably go down. How many Kindles are we expecting to sell in the first month?

INTERVIEWER: Around 4 million.

CANDIDATE: Is this a software feature or a hardware feature? Meaning, can we patch this feature in after the Kindle has shipped?

INTERVIEWER: It is a software feature. We can patch it in after it has shipped.

CANDIDATE: Was this feature ever announced to be part of this edition of Kindle?

INTERVIEWER: Yes, it was announced recently.

CANDIDATE: Then I would suggest we do not delay the launch. I would project some data. For example, I think the months of November and December would increase our sales figure by 50%. So even if we lose 40% of the users because of this one feature (which we won't. The actual figure will definitely be lower than this) it'll be more than enough to make up for it.

We need to run a PR campaign about how we will be adding this after the launch.

For the engineering team, I would personally bring up this data to them. Obviously, the data I will present will be actual market research and not just an estimate I did. I would also assure them the first thing we do after launching the Kindle is adding this feature. I think we can still have the feature in by January, but we will just be launching the Kindle in September.

To have this conversation, I would first talk with the engineering lead. I would bring up the market data and see if he comes to the same conclusion as me. If not, I'll point this out and ask him if he thinks my conclusion is enough.

INTERVIEWER: Let's say you have this meeting. He agrees with your numbers, but he thinks we are disappointing a lot of our users and this will hurt our branding.

CANDIDATE: I would say that I would try to spin it to the users as we want them to get the Kindle earlier. As long as we deliver this update as planned, it will not be bad. We can tell them our plan of releasing in January, and how we are launching it early in September and the new feature will come in January so it will not be that different. Obviously not every user will understand, but I think in the end we will sell more units and when we launch the feature in January, everything will be all right.

Chapter 21 Strategy: New Market Entry

New Markets for Amazon

Let us pretend you are a brand new Product Manager at Amazon. Tell me how you would determine the next big thing for us and then walk me through your idea for it.

Things to Consider

- Start with Amazon's core competencies.
- Factor in the customer's needs.

Common Mistakes

- Getting defensive with interviewer asks clarifying questions or gives push back on an idea.

Answer

CANDIDATE: I would start from Amazon's core competencies. Ideas that start with a company's strengths are more sustainable in the long-term.

Here is a list of the Amazon products I can think of:

- **Amazon.com**. E-commerce. Lots of high-income customers with a propensity to spend. Good fulfillment infrastructure, selection, and customer service. Only limited to the Internet though.
- **Amazon Fresh**. Grocery purchasing.
- **Amazon Digital Services**. Lots of digital goods on Amazon including games, books and music.
- **Amazon Prime Video**. TV shows and movies on demand. Original content too.
- **Amazon Fire TV**. TV box.
- **Amazon Web Services**. Server infrastructure. Lots of enterprise customer relationships.
- **Amazon Advertising**. Servicing ads (with self-inventory) to other companies.
- **Twitch**. Game streaming website with lots of users and influencers. Great for advertisement and hosting tournaments.
- **Kindle**. Physical products and platforms for books, apps, music, games, movies, etc.
- **Alexa**. Web traffic data and analytics.

I don't think I missed any major ones.

INTERVIEWER: Okay.

CANDIDATE: I am going to think first about the strengths of Amazon, because it is always easier to build something that takes advantage of your strength. I then see what kind of areas Amazon is already powerful in, and see if there are any holes that need to be filled. If not, I think of new markets that could benefit from other strong markets that Amazon is already in. I also think of any possible threats and competitors Amazon might have, as well as past mistakes and not so successful products.

I also take into account of the users. There's no point in doing something if the market is not worth our time. I think about the market, revenue, and growth. I then think about how realistic the idea is. There is a huge difference being able to get somewhere in a year or two vs. ten.

Can I have some time to brainstorm?

Candidate takes one minute.

CANDIDATE: I can think of a few ideas:

- **Amazon Games.** We need something to attract developers to develop games for the Amazon platform, including Amazon Fire TV. Amazon has platforms that have great potential. Fire Phones didn't succeed because not enough developers adopted it, meaning not enough content. Fire TV is doing okay, and this could help it too. Most gamers on mobile are females who like casual games that seems to fit right in the market with Fire TV. With so many games being sold on Amazon.com already, this would be a great natural fit. Twitch would also contribute by streaming games and hosting tournaments.
- **Amazon Physical Stores.** Amazon is the #1 e-commerce website, but it lacks in physical stores. Some people are not used to the idea of online shopping, so they proceed to go to brick-and-mortar stores. And some goods are not sold through Amazon, for example big items like ovens and kitchen counter tops. Microsoft and Apple both have stores, and I feel like Amazon could benefit a lot from it too. First, it can sell those things I mentioned before that Amazon doesn't carry on the online shop. Amazon could also be selling Kindle. One of the failures of the Fire Phones is that most people can't try them out before buying, and there are not a lot of stores that carried them. Another thing Amazon could be selling are books. Barnes & Noble is starting to sell e-book readers in their shops, and I think Amazon can come in and smash that market.
- **Amazon Browser.** Amazon has a strong presence online, but it can magnify that with a browser. Google is a major threat to Amazon. By competing with a browser, we can weaken Google's data collection. With more data on our side, that can only improve our ads and analytics. We can start by making this browser the default on our Kindles and TVs.

Is there a specific one you want me to expand on?

INTERVIEWER: Why don't you walk me through the physical stores?

CANDIDATE: Okay. First, I thought of how Amazon actually benefits a lot from showing its products (like the Kindle) in physical stores. I heard about Target not carrying Kindles anymore because too many people were coming in to see the Kindle, then buying it online because it was cheaper (most likely through Amazon.com). Therefore, we can determine that showrooming does help e-commerce.

I then thought about Barnes & Noble. They are starting to do their own e-books in physical stores, and it has some measure of success. Amazon carries numerous e-books and even made Kindles just for reading them. This might be a direction we should go in the future. Even if we do not get any new markets, it'll be a defensive play. Let's also mention that not everyone is an e-book person. Some people love physical books, and while Amazon does carry them online, it's a completely different experience to walk into a bookstore.

So now, we got two points for showrooming. I then remembered how Fire Phones didn't work out, and a lot of it had to do with the lack of physical stores. Apple and Microsoft have their own stores, which creates another channel for trying and ultimately purchasing high-involvement physical products.

Finally, I thought of how much revenue brick-and-mortar stores make and how Amazon doesn't carry some of these items because they require showrooming or installation. These problems can be solved with a physical store. We can also carry third-party products like the ones we have on Amazon.com.

INTERVIEWER: What are the challenges to your idea?

CANDIDATE: The labor, cost and time would be significant. The cost would break down to things like setting up the store, hiring store clerks, and marketing. This marketing would be unlike anything we have done before. This would require us to establish local business connections (e.g. service companies that can install an oven). Maintenance would also be something we need to take care of. Expanding this business overseas would also be another challenge.

INTERVIEWER: What would the first year be like for your idea?

CANDIDATE: I would probably only implement this around Seattle first to test the water before rolling it out on a state-by-state basis. I would start by only selling certain goods like the Fire Phones and Kindles. Starting with ovens and kitchen counters would be difficult. We can see if we are making the revenue we are projecting and then decide if we need to expand our market, inventory, and continue.

Selling on Amazon

Amazon started as a place in which you can "buy" stuff, and they were doing really well. At some point, they decided to allow people to also "sell" their stuff. It was a very risky decision; they couldn't anticipate if it was going to be successful. Do you consider it was a good or bad decision to do so? Why?

Things to Consider

- What is the cannibalization impact?
- How did this shape customer satisfaction?
- How did this affect competition?

Common Mistakes

- Hindsight bias

Answer

CANDIDATE: I want to point out that in reality, Amazon must have done a lot of market research and some initial testing before they decided to roll it out to everyone else. But to answer this question I would say it was a good decision because of these reasons:

- **More Traffic.** You mentioned Amazon is a place in which you can "buy stuff". Allowing people to sell things would also promote this message. You end up getting more buyer traffic as a result. Also, Amazon wants to become synonymous with the word "online shopping," and providing more things to buy online will only reinforce this message.
- **Diversifying the Business.** Don't risk everything on one endeavor. This is another way for Amazon to diversify its revenue and that is always good.
- **More Profit.** This opens up a new revenue stream for Amazon. When people sell things through Amazon, Amazon naturally takes a cut. I would much rather they sell it on Amazon than somewhere else where we can't monitor and we can't profit off.
- **Defensive & Offensive Play.** Amazon had two big competitors outside of its direct competitors. These two are eBay and the resellers. By allowing people to sell stuff on Amazon, Amazon took a jab at eBay and defended its turf from resellers.
- **Monitoring & Data.** By having these transactions occur under Amazon, not only can we gauge the latest price points (so we can reprice accordingly), we can also get valuable data on user buying habits. We can see what sells and what doesn't, and if it's a big market that we haven't provided products for yet we can go ahead and do that. Also remember that data analytics is a huge part of Amazon's profit as well.

INTERVIEWER: Wouldn't this have the side effect of losing some of our revenue because some people on our website are not purchasing off someone else and we only take a smaller cut?

CANDIDATE: It would, but I think there are three good things about this. One, Amazon has always been about lowering profit margin for higher market share, so this goes with that spirit. Two, we get this revenue back through long term, because this increases the retention of our website because we are providing more options.

Three, there is no danger of this person taking our traffic elsewhere, because our users trust our website and they are used to buying from our website.

INTERVIEWER: What are some negative points you can think of?

CANDIDATE: Well, I have a few besides the one you just mentioned:

- **More Management.** We have to provide more management on our side. This is in terms of both customer service and legal. We are now the liaison between the customers and sellers. If something bad happens, let say a seller won't ship his product, the customer will be mad at Amazon.
- **Confused Business.** Some users may get confused because there is an "apply to be a seller" button or something similar. They may accidentally wander into that when they came into Amazon wanting to buy things. Although Amazon's current design has done away with this problem, but at the time this must have been one thing they considered.
- **Branding.** This is two things. It increased branding for some of our sellers because they are selling through Amazon. It may also lower our branding because some sellers provide bad service and the customers will blame us for it.

Google's TV Cable Service

Should Google build a Comcast-like TV cable service?

Things to Consider

- The phrasing is ambiguous, but this is a casual-sounding strategy question.
- When answering a strategy question, a thoughtful pros and cons list will do.
- Conclude your answer with a recommendation.

Common Mistakes

- Not wanting to take a stand, afraid to take the wrong position.
- Not wanting to ask the question, given lack of expertise in TV cable services.

Answer

CANDIDATE: So we are talking about actual TV content, with commercials and all that? We are not doing Internet-based TV?

INTERVIEWER: That is correct.

CANDIDATE: Let me brainstorm some ideas that utilize Google's strengths, and then I will analyze our market and decide if these ideas fit.

Candidate takes one minute.

CANDIDATE: I can think of a few ideas.

- **YouTube content delivery.** YouTube has a lot of content, and it is nice to be able to have a huge collection of content to show. The problem is it will cannibalize YouTube, and if someone is already a huge YouTube fan, it's somewhat meaningless for him or her. This will reach out to people who don't watch YouTube though, like old people.
- **Original content delivery.** The content makes the network or so they say. It's important we have original content to attract users. Now YouTube has started doing original content lately, so it might not be enough. If we launch this service, we are going to need more.
- **Streaming.** Streaming is another way to get endless content. YouTube is beginning to do a lot of streaming, although most of it is game related. This might be targeting the same crowd as YouTube.

I think the most promising feature is the YouTube content delivery, followed by streaming, and then original content delivery. Ideally, I want to have all three, but it might be more feasible to do just one to test. I want to make a note here that we are really just porting YouTube over to a TV format. It would be easier if we were doing Internet TV.

I also want to say I left out traditional TV content, because Google doesn't have any resources in that area. We can buy shows in the future if this kicks off.

INTERVIEWER: You described some problems before, but didn't really go into details. What are some challenges you think this will face if it is done this way? How would you solve them?

CANDIDATE: I can think of several challenges:

- **Cannibalization of YouTube**. This will cause a dip in the YouTube traffic. We are essentially regurgitating content, and might target the same people who are already using our services. We can't really solve this unless we have original content that is not available on YouTube. However, if we have these two distribution channels, why would we exclude one out? So this problem can only be alleviated.
- **Lower Ad Revenue**. I mentioned cannibalization earlier and it might seem like it won't matter when both networks are under us. The problem is YouTube allows for ad attribution, so any ads we run on there are going to do better. If some users are instead watching our TV network, we can't do that, and it might result in lower ad revenue. (On a side note, revenue from new users can mitigate loss from existing users.) Some commercials that previously don't do well on YouTube might do well on the TV, which can bring our revenue up.
- **Setting up**. It'll be hard to set up our service. I am not an expert at how to build a TV network infrastructure. I get the feeling that it is not something we can buy off-the-shelf.
- **Competition.** We are going to have to compete with traditional TV networks. With our lack of original content, this will be a challenge. Also, the Google brand may be a curse than a blessing. People know Google as a tech company, not as a TV network. I'd recommend we use YouTube's brand instead of Google's.

INTERVIEWER: What do you think of this idea overall?

CANDIDATE: If it were up to me, I would do an Internet-based TV box instead. I think Google is already doing that (Android TV). It's a growing market and our competitors are already in it (Fire TV, Apple TV). It would still have some of the problems I described earlier, but it would have a much easier time to set up.

Uber's Ultra High-End Service

Should Uber roll out an ultra-high-end service line? That is, should Uber offer ridesharing services using Rolls Royce, Bentley and other super luxury cars?

Things to Consider

- Is there enough demand?
- Will the new service cannibalize existing services?
- What are the challenges with super luxury cars? Availability? Impact on insurance premiums?

Common Mistakes

- Unfairly dismissing usage of super luxury cars due to preconceived notions of cost
- Overestimating the surcharge customers are willing to pay in a super luxury car

Answer

CANDIDATE: I would do several things:

- **Potential Market.** This would probably be very city specific. We can read off our own data and see if there are people who might be interested in similar services. They could be people who are very wealthy. Let's take cities like New York and San Francisco as examples. Wealthy people live there and are probably the markets with the highest demand for this service. Since cities have bad traffic, people will want to sit in a nice car but not drive themselves.
- **Enough Supplies.** Uber drivers are all personal drivers, so do we actually have enough drivers with these cars? Would these people want to be Uber drivers in the first place? Money might not be a motivation for them. It could be other motivations like showing off their new cars or even to meet new people. I would also consider businesses who actually do this already and see if they might be interested in collaborating with Uber.
- **Competitors.** I want to see if there are competitors. How they operate, how much profit margin they are making, and how much market share they own are things I would think about. It's good to learn from others' experiences in this case.
- **Customer Confusion.** This comes in two parts. Customers may be confused because we try to offer another service. Sure, it's similar to our core model, but would this add confusion to our story? It's something we need to be careful about as we implement. Another is the UI. We need to make sure it doesn't clutter up the UI and create too many choices for our users. They may not like it.
- **Test Launches.** We obviously want to test launch this in select cities. Assumptions and projections are nice to have, but nothing beats real data. This way we can be sure our price points and profit margins and other numbers are good for the actual launch.

INTERVIEWER: It's interesting you mentioned other motivations for some Uber drivers besides money. Let's say we roll this out, and some drivers with really nice cars are using this to meet wealthy clients One of Uber's mottos is safety, so wouldn't this actually go against that and make our customer experience worse?

CANDIDATE: I get where you are coming from, and I understand this is a touchy issue. The thing is this happens whether or not we acknowledge it, so why not use it to our advantage? In addition, for safety and

266

customer experience, we have a voting system on Uber for a reason. If someone doesn't like the driver, they can vote that driver down, and we'll know. We can punish drivers that go too far. If certain customers have no qualms about it, then I say that clearly they don't have a problem.

Next Country for Amazon Expansion

How would you determine the next country for Amazon expansion?

Things to Consider

- What is your criteria for country expansion?
- Why did you include certain criteria? Why did you leave out others?

Common Mistakes

- Not factoring shipping and fulfillment challenges.
- Not factoring in payment challenges.
- Not factoring in regulatory issues.

Answer

CANDIDATE: I can think of three major factors:

- **Potential Market**. How big is the potential market? There is no point if there isn't a market. This is separate from revenue. Often, we want to expand somewhere to gain market share and not immediate revenue. This can be broken down to competition (is there already a major competitor there? Might be worth it to target countries where there is little competition first), spending habits (some countries may not translate well to Amazon's model), and the wealth of the country (less developed countries might be something we want to keep an eye on, but not necessarily expand right now).
- **Feasibility.** How feasible is it for us to expand right now? That would certain limit some of our options. This breaks down to location (might be better to expand to Belorussia when we already have a huge presence in Russia because it's close by), local talent (can't really expand if we have trouble setting up office there), and budget (we might not be able to target large countries or countries with a huge competition if we are short on budget).
- **Opportunity Cost.** What is the most worthwhile country for us to expand on? We obviously want to get the most out of this. As we are grabbing market share right now, other countries are sitting in the open allowing our competitors to take advantage.

INTERVIEWER: For potential market, do you mean it's a bad idea to target a country if there is already a major competitor there?

CANDIDATE: It can be interpreted two ways. One way is we want to avoid competitor-heavy countries because it would be an uphill battle. It might be more effective (considering everything else is equal like wealth and spending habit) to target a country with little to no competition. The other way we can interpret this is maybe a certain country is a strong portfolio for a competitor. We may want to target that so we can strike at our competition.

INTERVIEWER: Another point I want to make is, do you feel like if a country's spending habit doesn't match with Amazon, it's a bad idea to expand?

CANDIDATE: It really depends on the situation. If a country has a spending habit that is different, it'll be harder for Amazon to go in for sure, but it'll also deter our competition away. This is actually an opportunity because if either we can adopt to the local spending habit or we make Amazon's model popular, it opens up the market for us. We can then also expand to countries with similar spending habits.

Dropbox in a New Market

How would you evaluate if Dropbox should enter market X? What problems will you encounter and how would you solve them?

Things to Consider

- Customer demand, technical capabilities, as well as sales and marketing capabilities.

Common Mistakes

- Not mentioning regulatory issues.
- Payment problems are also prevalent from country-to-country. Certain countries accept unique credit cards like Japan's JCB. Other countries or organizations may prefer check payment. Others may prefer post-paid vs. pre-paid billing.

Answer

CANDIDATE: Can I ask some clarifying questions?

INTERVIEWER: Sure, go ahead.

CANDIDATE: What is our primary goal in this market for the launch? I would assume market share, but I want to confirm this.

INTERVIEWER: Your assumption is correct. We want to grab as much market share as we can right now before a competitor enters the market.

CANDIDATE: What is the launch plan? I am talking sales, preparations like business connections and local partners, server infrastructure, and advertisement.

INTERVIEWER: We are starting with the usual advertisement channels through both social media, other online referrals, and offline marketing. We are not really working with any local partners. We are working with Amazon on server infrastructure and they have servers locally.

CANDIDATE: Are there any constraints in this market I should know before I proceed?

INTERVIEWER: What would you classify as constraints? Wouldn't these pose the problem the question is asking for?

CANDIDATE: Yes, they would be. I wanted to know if there is anything specific, you wanted me to know before I start. For the constraints, I can think of a couple:

- **Number of Computers Owned:** How many people actually own computers? If there are not many, we may not get a lot of users.
- **Internet Access:** How many people actually have Internet? If the Internet adoption rate isn't very high, there's actually not a lot we can do about it until it is. Dropbox requires Internet so I am sure we already have market research done on this before we decided to launch.

- **The Need for Cloud Syncing:** How many people actually need cloud synchronization? I included it here for completion's sake because I am sure this was already researched before we decided to launch.
- **Competitors:** Judging from your response earlier, I am going to assume there isn't a lot of competitor activity in the market. Usually we would have to see what the competitors are doing and see if we need to change our plan or match theirs to gain a competitive edge.
- **Internet Infrastructure:** Maybe the local market doesn't have a good Internet infrastructure (e.g., SEA), so their average Internet speed is quite low. This would make our user experience worse because our product depends on that. Maybe we need to lower our free storage size to prevent people from putting files in and complaining that it takes too long. Also, maybe the Internet isn't very stable and we should account for that as well. Although come to think of it Dropbox should have no problem with this.
- **Local Servers:** You already told me we have a local server, but in certain cases we may need to consider this if we don't have any. It really depends on how many users we are expecting to acquire in the market.
- **Languages & Customer Service:** We need to make sure our website, software, and customer service are in the local language. There may even be multiple languages in the region (e.g., Malaysia, Belgium).
- **Pricing:** Our prices may not match the purchasing habit of the market. I know Dropbox is a freemium model but maybe the local market usually doesn't do things this way.
- **Payment:** Maybe the local market doesn't use credit cards or PayPal, for example, and we would need to work with carrier billing, prepaid cards or even cash payment.

INTERVIEWER: That's a lot. If you had to pick, what would be your top three?

CANDIDATE: Barring those we should already know before we decided to launch in the market, I would say:

- **Internet Infrastructure:** Since we are going for market share right now, we need to make sure our user experience is top notch. This directly affects that.
- **Payment:** It would be pretty bad if we can't accept payment even though certain customers want to pay. It's important we get this right for a good customer experience.
- **Languages & Customer Service:** Acculturating to the local language and making them feel like we care are huge in customer satisfaction.

Chapter 22 Strategy: Launch Plan

Expedia and Train Tickets

Let us say Expedia.com wants to launch a new category: selling train tickets. You are in charge of launching this new category. What would you do?

Things to Consider

- Is there enough customer demand?
- Does Expedia have relationships with train travel providers? If not, can it easily obtain relationships?
- How can they get the data? Will the data be fresh?

Common Mistakes

- Not appreciating how hard it is to get train data.
- Not appreciating how hard it is to get fresh and accurate data.
- Not appreciating how complicated is to calculate possible trip permutations.

Answer

CANDIDATE: Since Expedia.com operates globally, I would start by focusing on countries that are big on consumer train usage. The US is not one of them.

INTERVIEWER: Do you know which countries are?

CANDIDATE: Unfortunately, I do not. It doesn't matter either way, as we can research it later. The idea here is to come up with a plan. I would first pick a country Expedia already operates heavily in with a lot of consumer train usage, and then do a launch there. From there, we can improve how we operate and open it up to the world country by country.

To pick such a country, we need to keep in mind multiple things:

- **Potential Market.** We're looking to maximize profitability and ROI. If the pilot country is a small market, that's okay, especially if our goal is to just learn about the opportunity. However, our subsequent roll out should be larger market. It'll let us see if success from a smaller market can be repeated in a bigger market.
- **Competitors.** What's the competitive landscape like? If the competition is non-existent or fragmented, then that means we can use our scale and brand power to win market share quickly. If the competition is strong and organized, we might have to take a more measured approach on how we want to differentiate from the incumbent.
- **Ease of Operation.** How easy would it be to operate in the target country? Do we already have a local presence? Is the local market easy to enter from a regulatory, supplier and labor perspective? Is it easy for us to access the target customer via local advertising or perhaps through a partner channel?

- **Synergies.** Can we use our strengths to our advantage? For example, Expedia has a strong assortment of air, hotel, car and cruise options. Can we construct a better end-to-end purchasing experience vs. competitors who focus strictly on rail?

INTERVIEWER: You mentioned competition. Would a strong competitor deter you from entering the market?

CANDIDATE: Competition wouldn't scare me outright, but I do think it's important to have first-mover advantage, especially when there isn't significant product or service differentiation between companies.

I can give you an example. Uber didn't operate in China for a long time, giving an opportunity for other firms to pop up. When Uber decided to enter the Chinese market, Uber had to spend billions to mount an attack. Uber responded too late. Their competitor, not Uber, became the number one player.

Although Uber recently left the market by merging with their number one rival, it was worthwhile for Uber to give the Chinese market a shot. They shouldn't just give up the world's largest market without even trying.

INTERVIEWER: Okay, keep going.

CANDIDATE: The next thing I'd consider is customer scenarios. Here's a list:

- **Holiday vs. Commuter Travel.** Some Expedia users will be train commuters. Other users might consider train travel only for holidays.
- **Discounts and Deals.** Yield management is a big concern, since train seats are perishable. We'll have to manage discounts carefully to help train operators maximize revenue.
- **Long vs. Short Distance.** Consumers traveling a short distance place a higher value on being on time. Consumers traveling a long distance may be slightly more lenient about arriving on time.

INTERVIEWER: Can you tell me more about yield and revenue management?

CANDIDATE: Sure, every train has a set of operational costs when it makes a journey. It includes labor and fuel. There are other fixed costs such as:

- Depreciation
- Cost of capital
- General and administrative costs
- Insurance
- Marketing expense
- Train yard operations
- Maintenance costs for trains, railway structures and signals

Since train operators incur these expenses, regardless of how many passengers travel, every single passenger ticket a train operator can sell will help pay for these upfront costs. Discounts are an effective way to generate revenue (and pay off these costs) because the incremental cost of carrying and servicing an additional passenger is close to zero, as long as the train is below capacity.

INTERVIEWER: Got it. How would you address the holiday travel scenario?

CANDIDATE: The problem with this is that there are simply too many people wanting to use trains during a short time window. In some countries, I've seen scalpers purchase multiple tickets and attempt to resell them at a higher price. I propose these solutions:

- **Reactive Pricing.** As soon as the tickets become available, people who buy them as soon as possible will get the best price. As time goes on, the prices will increase. The price increases will help us manage yield. And yes, we'll attach fees for canceling or rescheduling, minimizing the likelihood of empty trains.
- **Limited per Person.** Limited ticket sales per ID. This will stop people from purchasing multiple tickets and reselling them at a higher price.
- **Season Pass.** A season pass will give us the flexibility of collecting revenue upfront and minimizing demand risk. As an extra benefit, season pass holders can pick trips and seats earlier than those who don't have a season pass.

INTERVIEWER: Which idea is your favorite?

CANDIDATE: The season pass one is my favorite. We get to collect revenue upfront. And for season pass holders who don't show up, we can resell their seat to someone else, effectively selling the seat twice.

New Uber Product in City X

How would you go about launching a new Uber product in city X?

Things to Consider

- Is there sufficient driver supply? Customer demand is important, but driver supply is a bigger problem for Uber.
- What is your marketing plan?
- How will you manage tricky PR issues such as passenger safety and driver employee relations?

Common Mistakes

- Disorganized discussion
- No thoughtful plans
- Missing critical dependencies such as driver availability

Answer

CANDIDATE: I would do several things:

- **Potential Market.** What's the market for this city? Do we have enough customers? We have to consider the city's traffic patterns. That is, when are rush hours? Where are the popular commute regions? How much demand is there for each region? How much are the consumers willing to pay? Finally, will consumers be comfortable with this form of transportation?
- **Product.** What parts of the default Uber mobile app can we keep? And what parts should we add or remove? Potential things that can be localized include different forms of:
  - Payment
  - Transportation
  - Computing infrastructure (e.g. allow the app to work when there's limited or no connectivity)
- **Driver Supply.** Do we have a sufficient supply of Uber drivers? Are there people interested in being Uber drivers? How does working for Uber as a driver compare with alternative jobs? Do prospective drivers have their own vehicles?
- **Competitors.** How we price the product, relative to the competition, affects our demand. Studying the competition can also help us understand effective driver recruiting tactics, challenges working with the city, and marketing best practices. Studying our competition can flatten our learning curve.
- **Payment.** What are acceptable forms of payment in the local market? Unlike the United States, many places around the world do not use credit cards. For example, citizens in developing countries are more familiar with pre-paid cards or carrier billing as forms of payment. Other alternative forms of payment include Alipay and WeChat Payment in China.
- **Pricing.** On the one hand, we will have to determine a price that is acceptable to prospective customers, factoring in market-rates and cost of living. On the other hand, we have to maintain an acceptable margin given our operational costs.
- **Legal.** We will consider regulatory issues, including licenses and taxes.
- **Public relations.** Uber is a new form of transportation for many parts of the world. As a result, Uber's arrival can threaten the status quo. Taxi cab drivers reacted negatively when Uber entered the Brazilian

and French markets. We also need to consider consumer reactions; many have heard about Uber's business practices or alarming headlines about passenger safety.

INTERVIEWER: You mentioned localizing the Uber app and possibly the experience. Wouldn't the customizations increase our operational overhead?

CANDIDATE: It would, but different places have different habits. If we don't adjust our product accordingly, our product would not meet the local market's needs. If we don't meet the local market's needs, then we will create an opportunity for our competitors to serve our customers better. When that happens, we lose market share.

INTERVIEWER: How would you decide whether we should launch Uber as-is vs. waiting to launch with a more localized, customized version of Uber?

CANDIDATE: I'd do a gap analysis. As part of the gap analysis, I'd see how the gaps affects revenue and profit. A great example is accommodating local payment solutions. What's the point of launching Uber in China, if the expected forms of payment such as Alipay isn't available?

INTERVIEWER: Would you refrain from entering a market where there's a large and successful competitor?

CANDIDATE: That's a hard call. On the one hand, we want to be efficient with our limited resources. If there's an untapped market with no competitors, it's hard to turn that down. But market size matters; we shouldn't give up a large, important market, just because it has an established competitor. We should act fast. Otherwise, it might harder to enter that large, competitive market and be successful if we delay.

INTERVIEWER: I'm not going to let you hedge like that. How would you make the decision?

CANDIDATE: I'd build a spreadsheet model with an ROI analysis. The ROI analysis would include a 10-year pro forma analysis that includes:

- Potential revenue
- Costs, both fixed and incremental
- Cost of capital, to factor in opportunity cost

INTERVIEWER: Thanks.

Chapter 23 Strategy: Other

Cutting a Microsoft Product

If you were the CEO of Microsoft, what product would you cut?

Things to Consider

- Use the Rule of Three.
- Be prepared to defend the opposing viewpoint.
- Consider the goal. There may be considerations other than declining profits or revenue.

Common Mistakes

- Not taking a stand.
- Only having one reason.
- Taking a timid position such as cutting a universally hated or already deprecated feature such as Microsoft Clippy. Timid positions come across as underwhelming and cowardly.

Answer

CANDIDATE: Can you give me a minute to think about this issue?

Candidate takes a minute.

CANDIDATE: I'm sure many candidates have told you that Microsoft should cut Windows Phone. Or others have suggested cutting the Bing search engine, which appears to be in a losing war against Google. Or avoid the question completely by suggesting humorously that Microsoft should kill Clippy, the Office Assistant, if Clippy still exists.

But to make it interesting, I'm going to suggest a more controversial decision: Microsoft should kill Microsoft Project. I'm guessing not many interview candidates have asked you to kill off successful, decades-old products like Project. But here's my reasoning:

- Limited growth opportunity
- Keeping it impedes Microsoft's innovation
- Opportunity costs

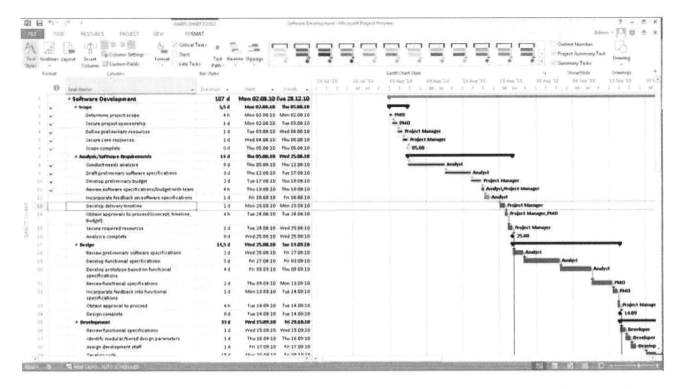

First, I'm not privy to your internal data, but I'm guessing Microsoft makes more than one billion dollars a year from Microsoft Project. While that seems attractive, as you can tell from the screenshot above, Microsoft Project's interface is optimized for waterfall project planning.

While waterfall is used by many industries such as construction and heavy manufacturing, the methodology is losing popularity over time. Agile methods have been more popular in the last 10 years, as more companies embrace lean innovation and production methods. Microsoft is probably seeing the impact from the shift from waterfall to Agile as competitors, like Trello and Asana, grab market share from Microsoft.

To summarize my first argument, Microsoft should not be putting resources in stagnant or declining projects. Microsoft Project is firmly rooted in an outdated trend, waterfall planning.

Second, while killing off a multi-billion dollar cash cow may not make sense, I would argue that keeping it around would be symbolically detrimental. Addicted to its revenue-generating potential and surrounded by Project employees who want to keep their jobs, Microsoft will likely fall prey to erroneously rationalizing the existence of Microsoft Project, even when consumers and competitors disagree.

I believe Microsoft CEO, Satya Nadella, would agree with me if I said Microsoft failed to take seriously the following trends: the rise of Mac after Apple's bankruptcy and the dominance of Google Apps in enterprise. Had Microsoft weaned itself from the revenue dominance of Windows and Microsoft Exchange and Outlook sooner, Microsoft may have adapted to those threats more effectively.

Third, there's opportunity costs involved with Microsoft Project. While it may feel like Microsoft has infinite resources, both in terms of money and people, Microsoft still needs more resources to fight for key battles in

Windows, Office, and other core businesses. By cutting Microsoft Project, Microsoft can apply its resources to other battles, which may have the opportunity for greater returns than the stagnant Microsoft Project market.

Defending a Microsoft Product

Now you are the CEO of Microsoft and the board wants to cut the product you chose above. Defend it.

Things to Consider

- Use the Rule of Three.
- It is okay to shift to the opposing position, but it's not a good idea to present contradicting logic or arguments.

Common Mistakes

- Withdrawing arguments or bashing logic that a candidate previously presented.

Answer

CANDIDATE: Ah, you tricked me! Okay, let's give this a shot. Give me a minute to brainstorm.

Candidate takes a minute.

CANDIDATE: I can think of three reasons why I would want to keep Microsoft Project. They are:

1. Cash cow
2. Convenience
3. Increases the perceived value of the Microsoft Office bundle

Reason number one: Microsoft Project is one heck of a moneymaker. Why kill a product when it's generating cash? If we were forced to kill a product, let's kill one that's not only hemorrhaging cash but one that's not predicted to generate profits now or in the future. Windows Phone, anyone?

Reason number two: having Microsoft Project included in the default Microsoft Office installation process makes it convenient for users. No need to first research project management software choices, then purchase and finally setup and install. It sounds trivial, but you will be amazed how much users value having software pre-installed on their machine, ready to go. If Trello and Asana could be pre-installed on a user's computer, they would absolutely be thrilled.

Reason number three: Microsoft Project is desktop-based not cloud-based. In other words, Project is fully functional off-the-grid whereas cloud-based alternatives are not. I can think of many scenarios, including construction, where a project manager may not have access to the Internet.

Reason number four: including Microsoft Project in the Microsoft Office bundle increases the bundle's perceived value. The additional value, even if the customer doesn't use the Project part of the bundle, may increase purchase conversions, leading to more revenue. Cutting Microsoft Project from Office would decrease its perceived value, possibly hurting Office bundle sales.

Dropbox in US vs. EU

What are the differences between new Dropbox users in the United States vs. Europe (EU)?

Things to Consider

- Don't give up on this question if you're not familiar with one or both geographic regions.
- Talking about a geography you're not familiar naturally makes one feel uncomfortable. Good leaders routinely are in uncomfortable situations, and they have to courage to feel that discomfort and trudge forward.
- This is also a test of customer empathy. Let's say you're unfamiliar with users in Europe. Can you accurately guess how their behavior might be different?
- Pause to think about the differences, and you'll be surprised that you've come up with a decent list.

Common Mistakes

- Pushing the interviewer to explain how Dropbox's European usage, making the interviewer feel that he or she is answering the question for the candidate.
- Begging the interviewer to move on to the next question, given one's lack of familiarity between the two regions.

Answer

CANDIDATE: Can I take some time to brainstorm?

Candidate takes one minute.

CANDIDATE: I can think of several factors:

- **Languages.** There are a lot of languages in the EU while the US is mostly English. This could affect indexing and compressions.
- **Population.** There are more people in the EU compared to the US.
- **Infrastructure.** The server infrastructure is different depending on the country you are in. Western Europe tends to be more developed. This affects connection speed and could be a better or worse user experience.
- **Favorite Software.** Different countries probably have their own popular software. This could affect what type of files are usually stored. US doesn't have this problem for the most part.
- **User Habits.** This could be how much space they typically use (e.g. one country might find 2 GB plenty when another does not) and what types of files they typically store. Countries in the EU would have different user habits.
- **Pricing.** Even though most countries in the EU uses the Euro, the spending habit is different. A single Euro could have different purchasing powers depending on the country you are in, so it may not be feasible to provide one price for the entire EU.
- **Business Relations.** Different companies and providers are popular in different countries. In the US, we can work with a few, but for EU there is probably a wide spectrum of them.

- **Ads.** Where ads are most effective, and style would be something different by country. This would make it harder in the EU. It's hard to use one or few images with translated text when different culture likes different things.

INTERVIEWER: What do you think are the top three problems with Dropbox?

CANDIDATE: I think pricing would definitely be one. It's easy to find the pricing point, but would be harder to do sales and perform customer service. Languages is another. This means we need to expand our customer service department by a lot. Infrastructure is another one. This means we need to understand the changes in infrastructure and see if we can avoid bad user experience by mitigating slow Internet speed.

Microsoft Product Strategy

How would you characterize Microsoft's product strategy? Should we wait to release a perfectly finished product, and risk delays, or should we ship an unfinished product to meet deadlines, and make updates/changes as we go? Can you cite some examples of products that fit either of these categories, and would you call them successes or failures? Lastly, how does your recommendation compare with your personal philosophy?

Things to Consider

- This question tests your ability to weigh tradeoffs between getting things right vs. getting things done.
- A good response objectively weighs both points of view, using examples to illustrate.

Common Mistakes

- Choosing poor examples.
- Not objectively weighing both points of view.

Answer

CANDIDATE: Do you have a specific department or sector in mind or just in general?

INTERVIEWER: In general.

CANDIDATE: Wow, that's a lot of questions! Give me one second to write them down.

Candidate takes 20 seconds.

The answer is it depends. Starting with my personal philosophy, I believe it's better to make updates and changes as we go. Like Mark Zuckerberg, I believe perfect is the enemy of finished. And thanks to client-server models, we can push out a release – whether it's a web product or mobile app feature – and easily update the server (or release a new mobile app) faster than before.

Just imagine back in the 1990s, if Microsoft accidentally launched a buggy version of Windows OS, think about the headache involved. They'd have to alert their OEMs, Dell and HP, to issue a recall. Then they have to reach out to consumers as well as IT managers to download and apply patches for a critical bug. It could take months or possibly years for the ecosystem to fix a bug. That's not the case with today's client-server technologies, especially with browser-based applications.

While Microsoft can adopt this philosophy for its web and to a lesser extent, mobile products, Microsoft has to have a more careful stance with its shrink-wrapped software products. A new release of Microsoft Office needs to be tested carefully before shipping for the reasons I mentioned before.

In addition to the productivity hassle, shipping unfinished shrink-wrapped products can affect PR. For example, Windows Vista is an example of product that while might have been complete, was considered unusable and hence unfinished to many customers. Even after Microsoft patched it to fix the problems, the negative PR backlash didn't go away. Many users stayed away from upgrading to Windows Vista, choosing a more cautious approach to stay on Windows XP. Not only did this delay significant upgrade revenue for Microsoft, it also coincided with the rebirth of Apple's Mac OS. These days, we see Apple dominant market share among new PC buyers, especially in the college market.

Windows 10 is a product that I'd considered launch complete. It's been on the market, and the perception has been very favorable. I'd also consider the Microsoft Office suite as well as Xbox as two other products that I'd consider as finished.

App for Apple TV

Should Microsoft build an app for the Apple TV?

Things to Consider

- Question asks the candidate to defend their position, so use a pro and cons analysis.

Common Mistakes

- Misinterpreting the question as *what* app should Microsoft build? vs. *should* Microsoft build an app? If there is any uncertainty, clarify with the interviewer.

Answer

CANDIDATE: It really depends on what type of app it is.

INTERVIEWER: Let's say it's a popular Microsoft app like Skype.

CANDIDATE: I know the two companies have an intense rivalry. Let's assume that Apple wouldn't be petty enough to ban whatever app we build for Apple TV. Now that I've addressed that, here are a few reasons why we should build for Apple TV:

- **No Competing Platform.** Microsoft is not currently building an Apple TV competitor. The most notable competitors today are Google's Chromecast, Amazon's Fire TV and Roku. Xbox can be considered a competitor, but most consumers think of it as a video game console first and a digital media player second.
- **Big Market.** Despite the rise of non-TV devices, such as computers, smartphones and tablets, consumers continue to spend a lot of time-consuming media on a TV. According to the latest Nielsen stats, Americans, for example, are watching five hours of TV a day. Having a foothold in this market is key. With TV continuing to attract strong usage, there's an opportunity to sell additional digital media and services through the TV platform.
- **New Customer Segment.** Even if consumers are using the Xbox and Apple TV for similar use case scenarios, our audiences are likely to be different. Xbox owners are more likely to be hardcore gamers. Apple TV users are less likely to be hardcore gamers. By building applications for the Apple TV platform, we tap into a new customer segment where we can introduce Microsoft products and services.
- **Growing Market.** Digital media players is a nascent market. The last figure I saw showed 25% ownership among TV owners.
- **Customer Demand.** We've heard consumers really enjoying using Skype in the living room via Xbox and Kinect. However, not everyone has an Xbox and Kinect. Adapting Skype for Apple TV might be a good idea.

INTERVIEWER: If our app turns out to be popular, wouldn't that promote Apple TV?

CANDIDATE: We could live in fear of helping Apple. However, we have to believe that competition is ultimately healthy for not only the market, but also Microsoft. Building an app allows us to dip a toe in the water. If it happens to gain popularity, we will be well positioned to compete. Our involvement might also lead us to consider whether we should get into the standalone digital media player business too.

INTERVIEWER: What would be a product you would recommend for the Apple TV?

CANDIDATE: Skype is the first product comes to mind. We can also tap into Microsoft's strong video game brand and adapt legendary Xbox games, such as Halo and Forza Motorsport, for Apple TV.

INTERVIEWER: I'm pretty partial to Solitaire myself.

CANDIDATE: You'd make Bill Gates happy.

Microsoft's Threats

What do you think will be the main threats to Microsoft's continued success in the future and why?

Things to Consider

- What are key consumer trends that can affect Microsoft?
- Consider trends in Internet, mobile as well as virtual and augmented reality.

Common Mistakes

- Focusing on Microsoft's most recognizable sources of income, Windows and Office, and forgetting other businesses such as Windows Server, SQL Server, Exchange, Xbox or Bing.
- No mentioning less obvious threats such as government regulations, distribution access, customer loyalty and network effects.

Answer

CANDIDATE: Can I brainstorm for a bit?

Candidate takes one minute

CANDIDATE: I can think of several threats to Microsoft.

- **Browser**. Microsoft is losing the browser war; I read that Chrome's market share worldwide is somewhere between 42 to 52 percent. This is terrible news for Microsoft, given that Chrome just launched in late 2008. The browser is a very important platform for Microsoft. While the traditional OS is still strong, the browser is emerging as a very important platform, given that many Internet applications are OS independent. By losing out in the browser fight, several Microsoft's online products, which rely on the browser, will be affected. This includes Bing.com, online advertising and Outlook.com, formerly known as Hotmail.
- **Mobile**. Microsoft's Windows phone is not doing well. Its market share is in the single digits. Mobile is a very powerful platform; it's the only computing device that we carry with us wherever we go. Mobile app revenue is growing; Google and Apple get a lucrative 30% commission anytime a developer sells an app through their app stores because they are the default app store on Android and iOS platforms respectively. Microsoft, by not owning a dominant platform, misses that revenue opportunity.
- **Console**. Microsoft is slowly losing against Sony in the current generation of console wars. Aside from the profit implications, Microsoft's Xbox plays a critical role in introducing the Microsoft product family to young adults, beyond just video games. Xbox helps build the perception that Microsoft can be hip, when they are generally not perceived as such.

Overall, Microsoft is losing out in the platform war on multiple fronts. While it remains strong in the OS race, Microsoft struggles to be relevant in the fast-growing, emergent markets.

Buying OfferUp

Should Facebook buy OfferUp?

Things to Consider

- Does OfferUp utilize Facebook's core competencies such as the social graph or the Audience Network?
- What synergies can Facebook unlock so that the resulting value is greater than the purchase price?
- Did you organize your thoughts in a framework so that it is satisfying, feels comprehensive and is easy to follow?

Common Mistakes

- Not citing the benefit of faster time to market.
- Not mentioning how acquiring OfferUp might distract Facebook from its core business.

Answer

CANDIDATE: Just to clarify, OfferUp is Craigslist on mobile, right?

INTERVIEWER: Yes, it is.

CANDIDATE: We have two options: buy them outright or build our own OfferUp-like solution. I know that they recently concluded their series B at around $20 million. So buying them outright could probably cost us around $200 million.

To figure out if it's worth spending $200M, we'll have to consider how much it would cost to build an equivalent solution on our own. Assuming a team of one PM, three engineers, two designers, one marketer and one data scientist, it would probably take us about three to six months to build it. I'll be conservative and go with six months. With an average annual salary of $150,000, it would be around $8 * \$150,000 / 2 = \$600,000$.

But that's not all! We have to think about marketing expenses such as cost per install (CPI). Let's shoot for about one million users, with an average CPI of $3, which is $3M.

Even with $3M, we can get new installs overnight. It'll probably take us six months to do so, which we'll continue to pay salaries for our core team of eight. So that's another $600K. In total, that's 12 months at $3M for marketing and another $1.2M for salaries, which brings us to a total cost of $4.2 million.

After a quick run of the numbers, let's think about some qualitative pros and cons:

Buying

- Pros:
  - Saves time
  - Pre-existing user base
  - Don't need to recruit a new team
- Cons:
  - Costly

- o Might have features we don't want
  - o Integrating a new team may be difficult, especially if there are cultural differences

Building

- Pros:
  - o Cheaper
  - o Can build it exactly the way we want it
  - o Tighter integration with Facebook assets such as prominent placement in the newsfeed and cross-promotion on WhatsApp and Instagram
- Cons:
  - o Takes time
  - o No existing users
  - o Need to recruit our own team
  - o Facebook doesn't have eCommerce experience
  - o Success is not guaranteed

This is not a clear-cut decision. There are benefits and risks to each approach. However, if I were asked to choose, I would choose to build vs. buy. Assuming my back-of-the-envelope calculation is reasonable, I'd much rather pay $4.2M, or even 10X that, than to part with $200M.

iPhone Exclusive Partnership

Do you think allowing AT&T to be the exclusive carrier of the Apple iPhone was a good or bad idea?

Things to Consider

- What are the benefits of exclusivity to AT&T?
- What are the benefits of exclusivity to Apple?
- What are potential outcomes if Apple did not grant exclusivity?
- Are there non-exclusivity examples from other countries? That is, based on outcomes elsewhere, we may infer what could have occurred if Apple did not grant AT&T exclusivity.

Common Mistakes

- Defending the exclusive partnership as being best, even though the alternative is unknown.

Answer

CANDIDATE: That was a while ago, no? I don't remember the details. Can you remind me?

INTERVIEWER: Sure. When the iPhone originally launched in January 2007, AT&T was the exclusive and sole provider in the United States. That agreement expired. Today, consumers can purchase iPhones from any wireless carrier in the US.

CANDIDATE: Got it. Okay, let me collect my thoughts.

Candidate pauses to think for 20 seconds.

CANDIDATE: I'm sure Apple received a healthy fee in exchange for exclusivity. However, I'm not in favor of the deal. I believe there are several drawbacks including:

Reduced Market Share

I believe it was important for Apple to prioritize market share first. By doing so, it would have given Apple more customers to sell complementary goods and services like accessories (such as headphones and smartphone cases) and App Store purchases (where Apple gets a 30% cut) later.

This is called the razor-and-razorblade model. You've probably heard of this term. It's when companies sell a platform for a low price and generate profits later by cross-selling complementary goods. Platform examples include the Windows OS, PlayStation video game consoles, HP printers, razors and of course, the Apple iPhone.

Giving AT&T exclusive distribution rights limited Apple's initial market share. In the US, there are four major wireless carriers: AT&T, Verizon, Sprint and T-Mobile. If each carrier had an equal share of the market, AT&T would have 25 percent. However, I feel that AT&T was one of the market leaders, so let's assume that AT&T had 35 percent market share.

While 35 percent sounds substantial, it prevented Apple from accessing the remaining 65 percent of the market. Apple would like to think that users could freely switch from competing carriers to AT&T, attracted by Apple's compelling smartphone offering. However, back in 2007, multi-year customer contracts prohibited short-term mobility between carriers.

Encouraging Anti-Apple Activity

Losing customers to AT&T couldn't have sat well with competitive carriers like Verizon. Verizon, and others, probably fought with vigor. This probably meant millions of marketing dollars to promote Android phones. Furthermore, it was not likely that they spoke favorably about the iPhone in their advertising campaigns.

Increased Freeloading

Since AT&T was the only way customers can get the iPhone, AT&T may have been lazy with its sales and marketing efforts. That is, thanks to the exclusive partnership, why would AT&T invest additional sales and marketing dollars when the coveted phone sold itself?

INTERVIEWER: Would you say all exclusive deals are bad?

CANDIDATE: I feel exclusive deals are bad. Both consumers and businesses benefit from competition.

INTERVIEWER: That sounds like a cop out.

CANDIDATE: Okay, you've pushed me to think harder about the issue. Let me think about it.

Candidate takes 10 seconds.

CANDIDATE: Giving it more thought, some exclusive deals could be a win-win. In business school, we learned that some companies would award exclusive distribution or retail rights, especially when there are significant upfront costs.

For example, a small business owner wants to license a McDonald's franchise in a particular location. To start a McDonald's store, the small business owner would have to invest roughly $1M to $2.2M. That's a large sum. If McDonald's allowed another small business owner to start a franchise one block away, the initial small business owner would be very unhappy. It'll affect that small business owner's sales, affecting the ROI and payback period of her startup investment. Had she had known that McDonald's would be so unpredictable in awarding franchise rights, she wouldn't have bothered to invest.

Her decision would have affected McDonald's immensely including one less store, reduced franchise fees, reduced monthly service fees, and missed opportunity for increased brand awareness.

And one last point, here's the critical difference between McDonald's and Apple: McDonald's, on the one hand, was faced with an all-or-nothing scenario. That is, if McDonald's didn't award exclusive rights, small business owners wouldn't open franchises, given the sizable upfront investment. Apple, on the other hand, wasn't in an all-or-nothing scenario. They wouldn't have been deterred from selling the iPhone without exclusive rights. Carriers set a precedent of selling and promoting phones without exclusivity.

INTEVIEWER: That's a good example. Thanks.

Chapter 24 Technical

Load Balancer for google.com

Design a simple load balancer for google.com. What data structures would you use? Why? Define access/delete/add order of complexity for each data structure and explain your choices. Design an algorithm to add/delete nodes to/from the data structure. How would you pick which server to send the request? Why? Why not?

Things to Consider

- Clarify definitions, if they are unfamiliar to you
- Inquire about goals and constraints
- To get going, work out a simple example

Common Mistakes

- Not being familiar with queue data structures
- Not understanding order of complexity concepts

Answer

CANDIDATE: Hmm, my understanding is google.com is a global website. So let's say you are using google.com in the US. It would be logical to first select the closest server group for you based on your region (e.g. California), then pick a server that has available computing power. It might be more tiered than this (based on city), but that's the general idea.

I am also guessing if in the event that the entire California cluster is full, I would have no choice but to reroute the request to a nearby cluster like Nevada. It is a bad user experience, but better than waiting until an empty "slot" opens up in California.

Based on this, I would say this probably needs round-robin or some variation of it. Based on my understanding of round-robin, this uses a queue. So how it works is that envision we have 10 available slots (a slot would be a node in the queue) from 1-10.

1,2,3,4,5,6,7,8,9,10

When user 1 comes, the load balancer grabs the first available slot for him. Since we are using a queue, the dequeue would give him 1, because it's FIFO:

2,3,4,5,6,7,8,9,10

Then user 2 comes, and he would get 2:

3,4,5,6,7,8,9,10

Let say user 1 is done, and node 1 becomes available again. It would get enqueued:

3,4,5,6,7,8,9,10,1

So if we are going by the double-tiered system I described earlier (states->individual slots), we would have two queues. The first queue would be states. The second queue would be individual server clusters.

But remember for our states, we need to pick the closest states if your current state isn't available. The round robin algorithm in that case would be weighted. Meaning the queue would be sorted each time so that available servers in your closest states would show up first when you need it.

The complexity for access is O(1), since the closest available server is always on the head.

The complexity for delete is O(1), since it's dequeue.

The complexity for add is O(1), since it's enqueue.

The algorithm is quite simple. A queue is basically a list where you only have three functions:

peek(); enqueue(node newNode); and dequeue();

peek() returns the current head of the list: return list.head;

enqueue(node newNode) adds the newNode at the end of the list: list.end.next = newNode;

dequeue() returns the current head of the list and deletes it off the list:

      node headNode = list.head;

      list.head = headNode.next;

      return headNode;

Something we have to node is that there is a switch in the round-robin algorithm. The slot becomes available again after some set amount of time even if the process is not complete. So if user 1 takes too long with slot 1, slot 1 stops working on the process, and goes back to being available again (enqueued). The next available slot (slot 3 in the above example) is used to continue the job. This prevents starvation, which is where a task is continually denied access to a resource. In this case, it's when a request is continuously denied because there are no server slots left each time it requests.

A more complex model would probably be using Level 4 and Level 7 load balancers. I've heard of them but have not really delved any deeper. I know they balance based on network and application layers, respectively, instead of just based on physical location like my simple version.

Dictionary for Scrabble

How would you design a dictionary lookup for Scrabble?

Things to Consider

- What's the optimal data structure to store this data?
- How would indicate if a sequence of letters is a valid word?

Common Mistakes

- Picking the wrong data structure
- Algorithms which are inefficient or finds duplicate words

Answer

CANDIDATE: Are we using English?

INTERVIEWER: Yes.

CANDIDATE: I am imagining using a Trie. It's a data structure built perfectly for the English language. When we think about this, we are thinking we got a "rack" of letters (e.g. A, B, E, E, G, S, X) There are a few attributes I am seeing:

- We can have repeated letters.
- This is out of order.
- We might have anagrams.

Let's keep these in mind and brainstorm our solution. An ideal function would probably look like this:

String[] lookup(char[] letters) {};

What this does is that it takes an array of letters and return an array of strings. These strings hold solutions to the problem. It could also return an empty array when there are no solutions. Let's explain this with an example. If letters is {A, E, S, T}, we can get this as our string array:

Seta, tea, sea, set, east, …

Ideally it should probably return points associated with each word, but that's the easy part.

So how should we do this with a trie? Let's try a naïve approach. What if we just add all letters of the alphabet into a trie? It doesn't sound so bad when you realize the longest word in Scrabble is 8 letters. Even if we play with an extended board or something, there is a max length.

So here is what each node in the trie looks like:

Class trieNode {
    char letter;
    boolean endOfWord;

```
        List<trieNode> children;
};
```

- letter denotes the current letter (e.g. A)
- endofWord denotes if this is the end of the word in the trie
- children is the list of trieNodes that come after

What does this trie look like? The head would be a random symbol that is not a letter, e.g. ^, which represents the empty string, then the head would have the children A-Z, while its children A would have the children A-Z, and B would have the children A-Z, and etc. We do this up to depth 8. In total, we have 26^8+1 nodes, and each node has relatively little memory but it does get up there. With the pruning next though I think we will reduce it by a lot.

Can we improve this? Yes. There are certain paths down the tree that doesn't make any sense because they don't contain words, and we can prune those out. For example: aaa is not a word, so we can prune out the entire branch. We only have to do this one time and output the result to a file that we can use next time. We can just look up a dictionary database somewhere.

Once this trie is done, given a rack of letters, we can input it into the function and go through the rack of letters. Going back to example {A, E, S, T}, we can:

- Look up A, then see if E, S, and T exist as branches.
- You are now at AE, see if S and T exist as branches.
- You are now at AS, see if E and T exist as branches.
- ...
- Look up E, then see if A, S, and T exist as branches.
- ...

Each word look up requires $O(N^2)$, where N is the length of the word. Space complexity wise, it's 26^8+1 node, with each node essentially being 2 (char) + 1 (boolean) + 8 (object reference) = 11 bytes in the worst case scenario. The average case scenario is probably small enough to fit into memory.

Statistical Frequency Analysis

How would you perform statistical frequency analysis on a random raw data source?

Things to Consider

- Clarify if you do not understand the question. The original question was phrased as follows, "How to perform statistical frequency analysis on a random raw data source to get a set of results that are most relevant to humans?"

Common Mistakes

- Confusing correlation with causation
- Forgetting that data analysis is about meaning or decision making rather than just extracting and presenting data

Answer

CANDIDATE: Do you have sample data you want me to use?

INTERVIEWER: No. This is a general question. Do you know what frequency analysis is?

CANDIDATE: Yes.

INTERVIEWER: Can you describe it to me?

CANDIDATE: It's basically where you get a lot of data, and you are trying to make sense out of it. So maybe you are trying to find some sort of pattern, so you begin separating all the data into elements. Then you see which elements show up the most frequently and least frequently to get a sense what this data is, and what results we can gather from this.

INTERVIEWER: Can you give me an example?

CANDIDATE: Sure, so cyphers use frequency analysis a lot. For example, if I give you a paragraph of English, the most frequent letters are probably going to be A, E, T, and O. The least frequent letters are going to be Q, X, and Z. So let's say instead I give a modified paragraph (e.g. cypher, I switched A to B, and B to C, and C to D, etc.), I can find the most frequent occurring letter and it's probably going to be either A or E. It may not be those two, but it gives me a really good starting point. I can do the same with the least frequent letters as well. I can test different matches and see which ones end up displaying a coherent English paragraph.

INTERVIEWER: What if you don't know it's English?

CANDIDATE: Well, it's most likely going to be one of the spoken languages we know or something like Morse code. We can try out each language. As long as we have the frequency analyzed, it gives us a good starting point. We'll first do frequency analysis on the language we want to try matching to, then do the same thing I described earlier. If this language doesn't work, we try another one. Eventually we'll find one.

INTERVIEWER: That doesn't sound very effective.

CANDIDATE: It feels that way, but imagine if we didn't do this. We just try to blindly match something. It'll definitely take a lot longer starting from scratch.

Google Search Services

Design the Google search service including the essential pieces and logic. Also explain key design decisions and tradeoffs.

Things to Consider

- Step 1. You'll need a web crawler to collect web pages and follow links.
- Step 2. You'll have to store a copy of those web pages.
- Step 3. Show relevant results, based on a user query.

Common Mistakes

- Waste time specifying non-software requirements including the need for servers, firewalls, load balancers and an Internet connection.
- Avoiding a detailed discussion by telling the interviewer that one would use an open-source package like Nutch, Scrapy and Heritrix and modify from there.

Answer

CANDIDATE: When a user types a query in Google search, Google will try to understand the search string first to get an idea what type of websites it should look for in the results. If there are misspellings or similar searches (e.g. "that blue social network" -> "Facebook") it would also find that. Then it will find all the results (in the form of website pages) and rank them based on the most relevant one for this search query.

Another essential thing is the user account. I can think of five parts:

- If the user has searched for similar things before, it will be taken into account.
- If the user has searched for related things before (e.g., he searched about programming before, so when he asks about C, he's probably talking about the language, not the letter), it'll be taken into account.
- If the user has watched a lot of strategy game videos on YouTube or similar things on other Google services, if he's searching about Terran he's probably talking about StarCraft..
- If the user lives in Mountain View or is searching from Mountain View (based on his current location), and he's searching for "nearby restaurants," it's best to show up restaurants near Mountain View.
- If the user has data showing he likes hamburgers, and he's searching for restaurants nearby, we should show up ads related to burger joints nearby.

There are probably many more, but these are the ones I can think of right now. The point of all of these is to provide context. This allows:

- Searches to be more accurate. Better user experience, obviously.
- Searches to be more relevant. Better user experience since the user can find what he or she needs in the shortest amount of time.
- Ads to be better targeted. More revenue if a user clicks on an ad that he likes.

Google search also has other essential pieces that have to do with context. For example, if a user writes a string like, "3*5+10" Google will pop out a calculator showing the result. If the user writes a string like, "What is the population of the US?" Google will tell you 300 million.

After the server receives the search string and context, it looks for the "correct" results. It then ranks them based on multiple criteria. I don't know the criteria, but I am guessing it has to do with:

- **Amount of times someone entered a similar search string and clicked on this link as the correct result**. In other words, he didn't go back and click on another. Makes it more accurate, which means better user experience.
- **Amount of times someone searched one thing, didn't find what he wants, then searched for something else similar, and found what he wanted and it is this thing**. More accuracy means better user experience.
- **Time**. An example of this is if someone typed "best TV shows," the webpage that talks about the latest TV shows will come up first (because of its upload time and recent traffic) instead of a webpage about the best TV shows from 10 years ago. More relevant information means better user experience.
- **Third party sponsoring**. Let's say if you type out "buying flowers," the vendors that pay Google ads will show up first. This means more revenue.
- **Google affiliates**. Let's say you type out "map," you'll see Google Maps and not Yahoo! Maps or Bing Maps. This means more revenue or cross promotion.

Another piece to Google search is filtering. There are many reasons why Google may want to filter results:

- Offensive results, including bad language
- Illegal results, such as sites that violate the country's hate speech laws
- Malicious results, including phishing sites and those that install malware
- Sexually explicit material, especially for users under the age of 18

The last intriguing topic is the inclusion of ads. Many think that Google's ads clutter the website, but it's a necessary sacrifice for a free service. However, like any computer-based algorithms, the Google search results algorithm is not perfect. Human intervention is necessary to fine-tune results. Google's ads provide that opportunity for humans, outside of Google, to offer their opinion on what (paid) results deserve to be on the search results page. The inclusion of ads is one of those rare business decisions where it's a win for the user (more relevant results) and a win for Google (paying for what is seemingly a no-cost service).

All-in-all, these decisions lead to a more complex and resource intensive algorithm. However, all of it serves to provide Google better search results and a better user experience.

Bayesian vs. AI

When are Bayesian methods more appropriate than artificial intelligence techniques for predictive analytics?

Things to Consider

- What is the Bayesian method?
- Which artificial intelligence method is the interviewer referring to? Machine learning? Rules-based?

Common Mistakes

- Quitting due to one's lack of familiarity with either Bayesian or AI methods
- Not coming up with plausible, cohesive reasoning on why Bayesian is better

Answer

CANDIDATE: Hmm, I am not too familiar with both of these, but I have some rough ideas. Let me kind of explain what both of these are:

- Bayesian methods use statistical methods to predict probabilities based on existing information. Compared to artificial intelligence, which I am assuming in this case involves machine learning, this is a much faster way of doing it because it's simpler.
- Artificial intelligence, in this case, involves machine learning. This means it tries to gather enough information to formulate a scenario and match with pre-existing patterns so it can know what to do next. It tends to be more complex.

With these thoughts in mind, I can think of three scenarios:

- We don't have enough data. Thus, we can't predict anything with a more complex method.
- The decision making isn't complex enough. For example, we only have to make a choice between "Yes" and "No." Bayesian would probably get the same accuracy even though it's simpler, because it's an easier problem to solve.
- We want to avoid overfitting. This happens when we try "too hard" to figure out a pattern because we have so much data that we end up corrupting our results with noise.

Reducing Bandwidth Consumption

How would you reduce global bandwidth consumption for Google search?

Things to Consider

- How does website complexity and content affect bandwidth consumption?
- What repetitive pieces of information can be left out?
- What information can be obtained from a non-Google source?

Common Mistakes

- Jumping into solutions without diagnosing problems

Answer

CANDIDATE: Hmm, we should think about why bandwidth consumption is high first so we can better solve our problem. It's probably due to:

- **Complex Websites and Content.** Flashy animations and complex CSS look nice, but they take up bandwidth.
- **Images and Resolution.** High resolution images would be a concern.
- **Videos and Resolution.** Same as images.

I have a few solutions in mind:

- **Browser Cache.** Up the amount the browser caches content to reduce bandwidth. Realistically we can only do this with Chrome, which isn't the most used browser in certain countries (e.g. countries in Africa).
- **Cache Policies.** If we detect the user is from a certain country, we ask their browsers to cache more.
- **Smaller Result Sets.** We don't have to display 25 results per page anymore. We can do 10 or even less.
- **Less Detailed Results.** We can show less details for each result. For text this means smaller context paragraphs, and no links except to similar/cached. For images and videos, we can display in a lower resolution, and definitely cache the thumbnail (which is probably already being done).
- **Standard File Compression.** This is probably already being done.
- **Minimize, Uglify, and Remove.** We should minimize animations, CSS, and even sound. The website still has to be readable, but it doesn't need to look as good.
- **Targeted Minimization.** Find the largest usage of bytes like HTML, images or JS. Optimize these.

INTERVIEWER: It's interesting you mentioned uglifying the webpage. Wouldn't that make the user experience worse?

CANDIDATE: That is true, but so would taking too much bandwidth and the users not being able to view webpages or won't because of bandwidth.

INTERVIEWER: Which one would you recommend?

CANDIDATE: The fastest ones we can use is probably Cache Policies and Smaller Result Sets. These won't require too much effort and will make a big impact. There are a few that could really make a huge impact but would take too long. I do want to mention that while cache policies are probably okay, smaller result sets would cause a different user experience depending on what country you are from. I would allow users to add in a specific tag to always return 25 results per page regardless of where they are from.

Racing 15 Horses

You have 15 horses that run various speeds. You also own a racetrack where you can race the horses; this track holds a maximum of 5 horses per race. If you have no stopwatch or other means of telling exactly how fast the horses are, how many races would you need to run between the horses to be absolutely sure which horses are first, second, and third fastest?

Things to Consider

- Work out the base cases.
- Prior distributed computing background might help in solving this problem.

Common Mistakes

- Not taking into consideration that horses from one heat can be faster than another.

Answer

CANDIDATE: Let's define our 15 horses as 1-15. I would first race each batches of 5 horses. So 1-5, 6-10, and 11-15. We have now done 3 races. Let say the results are: 1-5, 6-10, and 11-15.

We can observe some things about each of these 3 races:

- If a horse is #1, it may be in the top 3 spots. Up to 2 other horses (the #2 and #3) from its race can be in the top 3 as well.
- If a horse is #2, it may be in the top 3 spots. Up to 1 other horse (the #1 from the race) from its race can be in the top 3 as well.
- If a horse is #3, it may be in the top 3 spots. No other horses from its race can be in the top 3.
- If a horse is #4 or #5, we can eliminate them completely.

We can now eliminate these horses: 4, 5, 9, 10, 14, and 15 because of the last observation. We are now left with 9 horses.

Then I would race 1, 6, and 11 on one track. This is our 4ᵗʰ race. Let's say the results are: 1, 6 and 11.

We can now safely eliminate these horses:

- 8, because 6 is #2 in this race. Only 7, which was 2ⁿᵈ place in the race between 6-10, can be in the top 3.
- 12 and 13, because 11 is #3 in the race. None of the horses in its race (between 11-15) can be in the top 3.

We are now left with these 6 horses: 1, 2, 3, 6, 7, and 11. We only need one last race to determine this, because we do not need to race horse 1. It's already confirmed to be #1.

We race 2, 3, 6, 7, and 11. Let's say the result is in this order as well. We now know the top 3 horses are: 1, 2, and 3.

The last race could turn out differently, let's say: 6, 11, 7, 2, 3. Then the top 3 horses would be: 1, 6, 11.

The point is it doesn't matter how the last race turns out. The first 2 spots in the last race will always be 2nd and 3rd place.

This took a total of 5 races.

Racing 16 Horses Instead

Follow up to the previous question, now you have 16 horses. How many races would you need to conduct to find first, second, and third?

Things to Consider

Check your solution for 15 horses. See if there's an extra racing slot where you can put the extra 16th horse.

Answer

CANDIDATE: Still 5 races. In race 4, I only had 3 horses in the race. We can just add horse 16 in there. Then let's say the result is: 1, 6, 11, and 16. We can just eliminate 16 because it's the number 4. There is no way it can be in the top 3.

If horse 16 comes in any place but last, then we eliminate the last place horse (either horse 1, 6 or 11) and instead include horse 16.

Chapter 25 Traditional

Why Amazon

Why Amazon?

Things to Consider

- The interviewer is evaluating whether you are passionate about the company.
- The hiring manager is afraid that, you, if hired, will leave for a better paycheck.
- Using the Rule of Three can convey credibility and sincerity.

Common Mistakes

- Getting lazy and not customizing a response for each employer.
- Putting limited thought into the question.
- Failing to see the company's future, fixating on what happened to Amazon in the past and present.

Answer

CANDIDATE: Why Amazon? Three reasons.

One, Amazon has the best customer service on the planet. As a product manager, what the customer wants is something I take to heart. Working in a company that treats customers as the biggest boss in the room, which is a story Amazon is well known for, is not only a great fit in terms of culture, but also the correct way to run a business. As an employee, I want to make sure my company succeeds, and if it already is doing the right thing it makes it much easier.

Two, Amazon is at its heart a tech company. Everything is powered by tech. As a tech nerd this makes it a natural fit for me. One of my dreams is working on tech that affects millions of people, and Amazon is a prime example of a company that embodies this idea.

Three, Amazon makes a big impact. It has many ambitious projects that services millions of people. What else is more exciting than that for a PM? I want to work on big projects that affect millions of people. Any decisions I make can improve the day for millions of people. If that's not job satisfaction, I don't know what else can be.

To conclude, I want to join Amazon because of its customer-centric approach to business, its focus on technology, and its ambitious projects that serve millions of users.

Chapter 26 Behavioral

Most Difficult Interaction

Tell me about the most difficult interaction you had at work.

Things to Consider

- Use the DIGS Method.
- The listener must feel tension in your story. It increases appreciation and listener engagement.
- Establish a villain. It makes the story easier to follow. You, of course, should be the hero in your story.

Common Mistakes

- Blaming others.
- Answering with a shallow breath, indicating stress and tension.

Answer

CANDIDATE: Back in November, the CEO, Ines, told me that our investors weren't pleased with our progress. They wanted our company to switch from building casino games to building sports games. I was shocked. The two types were completely different. There would be almost no code reuse whatsoever. I protested, but Ines said we had no choice. The investors would withhold a $2M investment if we didn't do what they asked. Ines left the meeting saying that I had one month to figure out how I would break the news to the engineering team.

As I went back to my desk, I evaluated my options:

1. Drop the news without warning
2. Pretend that creating a sports game was no different from creating a casino game
3. Slowly have them warm up to the idea

Options one and two were equally bad; it would have either damage morale or insult the team. That left me with option three. So here's the plan I concocted:

I implemented a team bonding exercise called *Game of the Week*. *Game of the Week* would have engineers breaking up into small teams of three. Each team played and evaluated a randomly chosen sports game. As part of the evaluation, they wrote down things they liked and didn't like. Lastly, they would then present their findings with the rest of the team.

They liked *Game of the Week*. It broke the monotony of day-to-day work, fostered community and helped them keep up with new industry trends. And most importantly, after four weeks, they started to appreciate the sports game genre. I also met privately with team members one-on-one and asked how they felt about building a sports game on a trial basis. Thanks to the team exercise, several were open to building a sports game.

At the end of four weeks, I made the announcement. I explained that sports games was something our investors wanted us to pursue. Their reception went smoother than expected. They admitted that were disappointed, but they were excited to build a sports game of their own.

Helping a Customer

Walk us through a time when you helped a customer through a difficult process. What did that look like?

Things to Consider

- Did you dramatize the situation so that the process came across as difficult?
- Did you give the customer a name so the story is easier to follow?
- Did you provide an elegant and clever way of helping the customer through that process?

Common Mistakes

- Declaring that one has not had the experience of helping a customer through a difficult process.
- Responding with an example that's not perceived as difficult enough.

Answer

CANDIDATE: Three months ago, a customer, Willie, complained that he didn't receive the in-game currency he paid for, and it happened multiple times. This occurred before we got our backend completely set up, so we didn't have access to the in-game log unless we pulled from the database. That was during the New Year, so all of our developers were on vacation. However, this guy spent a lot of money. We didn't want to lose him, so we needed to move fast.

It was hard to understand the nature of his requests. Willie said that sometimes he sees the in-game currency he purchased; other times he didn't see it. Through our limited backend, I could see he did indeed pay multiple times, but I wasn't 100 percent sure.

At first, I asked him for the time of his purchases; it could help me pinpoint which transactions went wrong. Willie said he didn't remember because he had several transactions, in quick succession.

I then told him that Apple sends email receipts, and I asked him to check his email. Willie replied that he did not remember his password. I then assisted him with password recovery, using the "Forget Password" function. Willie then logged in and started digging through his inbox.

I then asked him to filter his email to just Apple's, and there were still a lot. Apparently this guy buys a lot across multiple games. I then helped Willie filter just our game, and then asked him to work patiently through all 20 transactions. He finally discerned which ones he didn't get currency for. I double checked against our backend systems and confirmed that the ones he flagged were failed transactions.

Surprisingly, he apologized for wasting my time. I told him that I was happy to get to the truth and rewarded him with in-game currency for his understanding and sympathy.

Handling a Busy Situation

Describe how you would handle a busy situation where three people are waiting for help from you.

Things to Consider

- Give at least three steps, so that your proposed process sounds substantial.
- Provide an example, if time allows, proving your ability to get a positive result.
- Do not say you would "do it all." The interviewer is evaluating your judgment on what you think is important vs. what is not.

Common Mistakes

- Claiming that you would simply to do it all.
- Sharing an example that's underwhelming.

Answer

CANDIDATE: The people that need my help: are they requesting it in-person, by email or by live chat?

INTERVIEWER: Let's go with live chat.

CANDIDATE: I would first reply with a "Hi." I want to acknowledge their presence, so they don't feel ignored. Then I would then ask them what's wrong. Based on what they say, I would prioritize requests based on:

1. Severity
2. Customer importance
3. Estimated time to resolution

If I'm time-constrained, I would see if there's anyone else on my team who can assist. If not, I would keep those that are waiting with clear visibility on when they could expect a response. I might say something like, "Give me a 30 minutes to research the issue. Can I call you when I'm ready with a fix?"

INTERVIEWER: Would you solve issues simultaneously? Or would you solve them one at a time?

CANDIDATE: I'm comfortable multitasking.

INTERVIEWER: What if a single request requires your undivided attention?

CANDIDATE: I'd tackle it one at a time, prioritizing based on the criteria I specified above. If those that are waiting get upset, I'd apologize for the situation. And if necessary, I'll provide a discount to appease them.

INTERVIEWER: Thank you.

Risk and Failure

Give me an example of when you took a risk and failed.

Things to Consider

- Did you use an example where the listener said, "Wow, that's a big career risk I wouldn't have taken?"
- After hearing your story, would someone have said, "Geez, I knew that's exactly how it would unfold, and I wouldn't have done that if I were in your shoes?"

Common Mistakes

- Selecting an underwhelming example, such as moving to a new state or taking a new job.
- Choosing an example with limited consequence. For example, sharing a time when a candidate was disappointed that he or she did not get a promotion initially but got it eventually.

Answer

CANDIDATE: In 2011, I decided to be an entrepreneur. Back then, Groupon and Living Social were popular, so I decided to build a daily deals company. After nine months, the daily deals space burst, so I decided to pivot my company into an up-and-coming trend: local meal delivery. After nine months, the local meal delivery business started to consolidate, and we went out of business. I was embarrassed. I fired more than 50 people, and the company lost five million dollars. Some of that was my own, but some belonged to investors including family and friends. Needless to say, there are some family members who still won't talk to me today.

I took a step back to analyze when went wrong. After some deep reflection, I made the following conclusions:

- **No plan**. I impulsively jumped into two business opportunities without a clear plan or research.
- **No commitment**. I didn't commit myself, often quitting after nine months in. I never fully believed in the mission of either company.
- **No customer understanding**. I didn't take time to understand customers and their needs, choosing to simply copy competitors, on the mistaken belief that I could out-execute or out-market them.

I vowed to not make the same mistakes. So I started my third entrepreneurial venture with a 30-year commitment, extensive customer research, a three-year plan and a strong commitment to the mission.

In 2014, I started my new company, a competitor to Craigslist, with an emphasis on mobile devices. It was a daunting task, fraught with competitors and lots of tough times. But I'm happy to announce that last week, we have over 10 million listings, completed over $10 billion in transactions and recently netted a $70 million in VC funding on a $1 billion valuation.

Overcoming an Obstacle

Tell me a time when you overcame an obstacle and delivered the results.

Things to Consider

- Is your dilemma clear?
- How did you approach the situation?
- Was there a happy ending?

Common Mistakes

- Using an example where you overcame an obstacle, but did not deliver tangible results.

Answer

CANDIDATE: During my time as a student, I was a part of a group of engineers who had to implement an e-commerce website using MySQL, Java, JavaScript, and HTML. We had about two weeks to do it; unfortunately, it was a project meant for four people. The problem was, two of my teammates dropped the class and the other one had multiple finals so he didn't contribute a lot.

I took it upon myself to finish the four-man project within two weeks even though I had a few finals myself. I coded about eight hours every day for two weeks straight and finished it. I even received an A for the class. My website outperformed every other team in class by 10-20% in terms of speed and stability.

Diving Deep into Data

Tell me about a time when you had to dive deep into data and the results you achieved.

Things to Consider

- Demonstrate your experience analyzing data. Experienced folks know that analyzing data is just 10% of the problem. The other 90% is getting access to the data and cleaning the data.
- Good data analysts have a hypothesis they're trying to test; they are not just looking around.
- Your story should have clear, actionable insights.

Common Mistakes

- Not going into specific details, thinking that the interviewer won't understand.
- Sharing a data analysis story that does not have clear, actionable next steps or recommend a specific decision.
- Using an example where the data set is not sufficiently complicated such as reviewing Google Analytics or AdWords data.

Answer

CANDIDATE: For one of our games, we had two hard currencies (currencies you need to purchase with real money) with 6 purchasing tiers each. We also had two purchases that only occur when you run out of money. This means we had 14 different ways to purchase and so it was very important to target our sales toward the most effective one. This is further complicated by the fact that players are different since some players like to purchase a lot, some do not, and some only purchase when they have to.

To make sure we were being effective, I began to dive deep into the data. I first extracted all the purchasing habits over the last month during our soft-launch, and then created many different views when looking at purchase. Some of these include checking purchases based on country, checking purchases based on player level, checking purchases based on player's last action, etc. By diving really deep into this data, I began to get a sense of when a certain player would be most likely to purchase what.

I started to roll out different sales to small subsets of players just to test their reaction, and wrote down what worked and what didn't. Eventually, through a month of rigorous testing, I was able to figure out what worked and didn't work, and eventually raised our revenue by about $120K.

Connected ROI

Tell me about a time when you observed two business opportunities to improve ROI, and how did you determine they were connected?

Things to Consider

- If you can't think of a good story, you might have trouble with memory recall. Take a step back and just recall what has happened in your career. Go through your resume and jot down all your experiences, good and bad. Assign a label, indicating which behavioral question can use that story. For example, "data analysis" or "data mining."
- Details are important. They convey credibility.
- Using details doesn't necessarily mean your response should be longer. For instance, "I went to a liberal arts college in New England" is longer and less precise than "I went to Harvard."

Common Mistakes

- Using corporate jargon that only your co-workers (and not lay people) can understand.
- Displaying nervous signals including: playing with your pen, stroking hair or not smiling.
- Failing to project your voice.

Answer

CANDIDATE: When we decided to launch our game in Taiwan, I realized we could either integrate a SDK of a local third-party app store, or we could integrate carrier billing. It was then I realized the two were related.

First, for the local third-party app store, it was true that while they did have their own inventory, a lot of it stems from the fact that they have their own prepaid cards that were located in local convenience stores. This was in line with the carrier billing. What I noticed was that a lot of paying users were people below the age of 18, and they did not have access to credit cards. It then became mandatory to allow them to pay through other methods, and both methods were popular alternatives.

When I found out both were related, our objective then became, "Which method do we want to integrate first?" instead. We ended up implementing both, which increased our Taiwan revenue by 60%.

Earning the Trust of a Group

Tell me a time when you earned the trust of a group.

Things to Consider

- How did you add value to the group?
- Did you rush to impose your will? Or did you assess the group's needs first?
- How did you continue to earn the group's trust going forward?

Common Mistakes

- Most interviewers do not like stories where a candidate lost the group's trust by making a mistake and earned it back by apologizing. Some may appreciate a good apology story, but most prefer that candidates not make mistakes in the first place.
- The same goes for stories where a candidate loses a group's trust by lying, gossiping or playing office politics. Most interviewers prefer that the candidate not do those things period.

Answer

CANDIDATE: When I started as PM for my current company, I inherited a project with an upset partner team in Madrid. The US team wanted to make some changes to the user experience because the product was originally successful in Spain. However, American users tend to have a different user experience when compared to Spanish users. The Madrid team didn't trust us because they never worked with us before.

To influence them to cooperate, I wrote a report for them. The report included:

- Analysis of metrics they felt were important, based on their target goals
- Suggestions for new UX improvements
- Impact estimation of those UX improvements
- Citations and inspirational sources for my UX suggestions

The report was very thorough, and the Madrid team loved it. Obviously, they weren't going to trust me based on a report alone, so I sat down with the product manager in Madrid and reviewed, line-by-line, what features and improvements we should do. In the end, we decided to soft-launch the product with minimum additions and push additional changes, as needed.

A lot of my predictions ended up being true. We started to implement changes I originally proposed to improve those areas. After 2-3 months of working together, the product radically changed for the better, and I won the Madrid team's trust, based on our success.

Creating an Innovative Product

Tell me a time when you created an innovative product.

Things to Consider

- Why did you believe the product could be improved?
- What was your innovative solution, and what other alternatives did you consider?
- What business impact did your innovation create?

Common Mistakes

- Suggesting an improvement that comes across as routine, incremental change.
- Making it hard to determine if the candidate or the team was responsible for the innovation.

Answer

CANDIDATE: Previously, I was a product manager for a global company. Since our company builds multiple apps from Finland, it was sometimes very hard to keep track of which product was using which ad network. After talking with a marketing coworker, I asked the other product managers on the team if creating a platform to organize all of this, along with all the proper permissions, would be useful. This way, both the product team and the marketing team would be able to track what's going on, and the developers we were working with in Finland would also see their own games.

After getting a few nods, I ended up working with our in-house developer to implement this product within one week. We added a lot of customizations, so marketing and the product team both could add new products and ad networks easily from their end instead of requiring us to update the portal ourselves. It took some time for everyone to get used to the product, but it ended up saving our time by 30%.

Learning Outside of Work

How do you find the time to stay inspired, acquire new knowledge and find innovation for your work?

Things to Consider

- Use the Rule of Three. E.g. "Even with my busy schedule, here are three things I do to find time to stay inspired outside of work. First, _____. Second, _____. Third, _____."
- The interviewer is expecting to "feel smarter" after hearing your response, so come up with some inspiring ideas.

Common Mistakes

- Short responses, especially ones that are less than 30 seconds. It leaves the interviewer unsatisfied.

Answer

CANDIDATE: Well, I am a huge online person, so I stay active on Reddit and Quora.

The best things about these two are that you can pick topics you are interested in and stay subscribed to those. I tend to join PM discussions, answering questions and asking my own. That tends to scratch my PM itch. I get to stay informed and use my PM skills. It's pretty great.

I also am a fan of trying out new products, both in terms of apps, websites, and physical products. It's both for my own personal interests, and I get to see what the latest trend is. That gets my creative juices following and I tend to have a habit of writing down cool things I am seeing and hope I can get inspired the next time I need something creative going.

Acknowledgments

PM Interview Questions would not have come to life without the incredible contributions from the special people below.

I owe the biggest gratitude to my co-author, **Teng Lu**. We communicated every day and as a result, forged a special bond. He showed incredibly grit, heart and tenacity as he researched questions and prepared initial drafts. I have nothing but the highest respect for Teng, and I hope I get another chance to collaborate with him. His fortitude is in the top 1% of all the people I've worked with in my career.

Joseph Watabe showed similar grit. I'm fortunate to have his assistance in whipping draft after draft into the final that we see today.

And lastly, **Elisa Yuen** contributed her keen eye for detail as she read through the voluminous drafts and asked tough questions. Without her, this book wouldn't have the polish that you see today.

Finally, there's a long list of advisors, giving input and feedback along the way. I've included them here. Any omissions are purely unintentional.

Bobby Liu

Phillip Scavulli

Daniil Lanovyi

Saurin Shah

Fahad Quraishi

Sebastian Sabouné

James Routledge

Timothy Tow

Jamie Hui

Tyler Sanchez

41968489R10178

Made in the USA
San Bernardino, CA
25 November 2016